Spirituality and Mental Health Care

Spirituality and Mental Health Care
Rediscovering a 'Forgotten' Dimension

John Swinton

Jessica Kingsley Publishers
London and Philadelphia

Table 1.1, p.25, from D.S. Martsolf and J.R. Mickley (1998) 'The concept of spirituality in nursing theories: differing world-views and extent focus' *Journal of Advanced Nursing 27*, 294–303, © 1998 Blackwell Science Ltd. Reproduced with kind permission. Table 1.4, p.32, from M.J. Donahue (1985) 'Intrinsic and extrinsic religiousness: review and meta-analysis' *Journal of Personality and Social Psychology 48*, 2, 400–19. © 1985 The American Psychological Association. Adapted with kind permission. Figures 1.2, p.36; 5.1, p.156; 5.2, p.158; 5.3, p.164; 5.4, p.166, from J. Swinton and A.M. Kettles (1997) 'Resurrecting the person: redefining mental illness – a spiritual perspective' *Psychiatric Care 4*, (3) 1–4. © 1997 Nature Publishing Group. Reproduced with kind permission. Figure 2.1, p.59, from K. Tudor (1996) *Mental Health Promotion: Paradigms and Practices*. London: Routledge. © 1996 Routledge. Reproduced with kind permission. Figure 3.1, pp.65–6, from B. Roe (1993) 'Undertaking a critical review of the literature' *Nurse Researcher 1*, 31–42. © 1993 RCN Publishing Company Ltd. Adapted with kind permission. Table 4.1, p.98, from Y.S. Lincoln and E.G. Guba (1985) *Naturalistic Enquiry*. London: Sage. © 1985 Sage Publications Inc.; Corwin Press Inc.; Pine Forge Press. Reproduced with kind permission. Table 5.1, p.137, from L. Eisenberg and A. Kleinman (eds) (1981) *The Relevance of Social Science for Medicine*. Dordrecht: Reidal Publishing Co. © 1981 Reidal Publishing Co. Adapted with kind permission. Reproduced with kind permission of Kluwer Academic Publishers.

First published in the United Kingdom in 2001 by
Jessica Kingsley Publishers Ltd
116 Pentonville Road
London N1 9JB, England
and
325 Chestnut Street
Philadelphia, PA 19106, USA

www.jkp.com

Library of Congress Cataloging in Publication Data
A CIP catalogue record for this book is available from the Library of Congress

British Library Cataloguing in Publication Data
A CIP catalogue record for this book is available from the British Library

ISBN 1 85302 804 5

Printed and Bound in Great Britain by
Athenaeum Press, Gateshead, Tyne and Wear

Contents

Acknowledgements

There are many people who deserve thanks for their advice and contribution to the process of putting together this book; it is not possible to mention them all here. However, there are some for whom extra thanks is due: many thanks to all of those people with mental health problems with whom I have worked over the years. It is they who have taught me what spirituality is and how it relates to mental health. I am grateful to all of them for the changes they have brought about in my life and for the ways in which they have enabled me to see the world very differently from the way I saw it before. Special thanks to the participants of the research project presented in Chapter 4. Without their honesty and openness, this book would never have come into existence.

I would like to acknowledge with special thanks my friend and colleague Alyson Kettles, for her contribution to the literature review, and also for her advice in modifying the diagrams that we put together for our paper 'Resurrecting the person' (Swinton and Kettles 1997) and which are replicated in Chapter 5 in a more fully developed form. I am very grateful to her for her friendship and encouragement to push on and finish this book in the face of a multitude of barriers.

I would also like to thank Andy Mckie of Robert Gordon's University for spending time reading through portions of the text and commenting helpfully and critically. Thanks to John Boyd of the Royal Cornhill hospital for his comments on the nature of psychopathology and the intricacies of discerning spirituality and pathology.

Most thanks must go to my wife Alison and my long-suffering children, Paul, Ryan, Kerri and Micha. Without their support and persistent loving presence, the long hours of research and writing that lie behind this text would not have been possible. Thanks for putting up with me. Maybe now we can get our lives back!

Introduction

One might be tempted to ask why, in a 'post-Christian', materialistic and technologically oriented society, mental health professionals should take seriously the therapeutic implications of something as apparently ethereal and 'unscientific' as spirituality. Surely, one might argue, in an age of science, reason, pharmacology and therapy such an intangible human quality as spirituality cannot hold a central place within the therapeutic complexities of contemporary mental health care practices.

On the surface, the idea of spirituality does appear to belong to a previous era and a way of looking at the world which is outdated and outmoded. It does not fit easily with our understandings of science and what constitutes the scientific truth and authentic knowledge that can be used to develop evidence-based caring practices. Likewise, the falling interest in established religion within Western societies and the concomitant decline in church attendance might lead us to assume that even if there is such a thing as a spiritual dimension to human experience, no one is really interested in it anyway. This being so, a focus on spirituality would, at first glance, appear to be irrelevant.

However, if one scratches the surface of such negative assumptions about spirituality, one discovers a different picture underneath the sceptical veneer. While it may *appear* that interest in the spiritual dimension has been superseded by humanity's technological prowess, in fact within Western cultures there is a significant *rise* in interest in spirituality. Institutionalized religions may be toiling, but the human quest for the transcendent remains as strong as ever.

When, later in this book, we look at the empirical evidence, it will become clear that this general cultural quest for the spiritual dimension is reflected in the lives of many if not all of those people with mental health problems to whom we seek to offer care. While spirituality remains a peripheral issue for many mental health professionals, it is in fact of central importance to many people who are struggling with the pain and confusion of mental health problems.

In the light of the significant body of research, some of which is reviewed in Chapter 3, that points towards a positive correlation between spirituality and mental health and the growing focus on the spiritual dimension of human experience within society, one would assume that there would be significant implications for the way in which we understand and practise mental health care. However, as will become clear in Chapter 2, spirituality remains a 'forgotten' dimension within the contemporary practice of mental health care. There is evidence that while the official documentation of the mental health professions emphasizes spirituality and holism (National Association of Health Authorities and Trusts 1995), in practice, spirituality is frequently excluded, in terms of both research and practice.

As will become clear, the reasons for the exclusion of spirituality from the process of mental health care are complex. However, at the heart of the difficulty lies the problem of what type of knowledge and evidence are deemed acceptable by the professions. In an 'age of science', spiritual care has come to be regarded as a form of 'soft knowledge' which is perceived as lying primarily within the domain of the religious professional, and as such, outwith the remit of the caring professions who prefer to derive their theory and practice from 'hard', empirical knowledge. The assumption seems to be that spirituality is a purely 'religious' concept (religion being assumed to represent unverifiable values and beliefs), that sits outside the realms of science and as such cannot provide a firm foundation for the development of mental health care practices.

The mental health professions have been deeply affected by the influence of the medical model and the pathology-oriented worldview that accompanies it. Consequently, it is often difficult to focus on issues of mental *health* that may not fit neatly within such an empiricist worldview. Issues of growth, value, hope, meaning and purpose are frequently excluded from the vision of carers who, often with the best of intentions, look towards science as the 'new god' who can bring hope and temporal salvation in the midst of psychological storms. Such things are recognized as existing, but only as a backdrop to the *real* task of caring which finds its foundation in a certain form of evidence, based on a particular understanding of science and empiricism.

However, human beings do not live by reason alone! The dimensions of emotion, feeling, intuition and a sense of something beyond what there is are not illogical irrelevancies to the process of care. They are in fact the very fabric of meaningful human existence. If we exclude issues of hope, meaning, purpose and transcendence from the heart of our caring practices, what type of care are we going to offer?

This book calls for mental health carers to begin to look at their caring practices not simply through the eyes of science, but also through the eyes of the real people they are privileged to offer care to: unique individuals whose spiritual desires are often quenched by the insensitivity and spiritual blindness of contemporary mental health care practices. If we take the time to step back from our normal stance of objectivity and distance, to move beyond the limitations of our current worldview and begin to listen to the actual experience of people with mental health problems, it becomes clear that spirituality can be central in the enabling of mental health, even in the midst of deeply disturbing forms of mental health problems. Chapter 4 picks up on the significance of human experience and the need to respect the uniqueness of individuals within the research and practice of mental health care and presents an alternative approach to researching spirituality and mental health which focuses on the lived experience of mental health problems. By listening intently to the voices of people with mental health problems, the chapter draws out the role of spirituality in developing and sustaining meaning, purpose and hope in the midst of situations that are frequently stripped of such things. The perspective presented challenges the presumptions of the medical model and opens up a fresh way of looking at the relationship between spirituality and mental health which is empirically sound, but radically different from many of our normal assumptions about empirical research.

The practical implications of such an approach form the basis for the understanding of spiritual care that is presented in Chapter 5. Here the book explores ways in which carers can 'cross over' and meaningfully enter into the experience of people with mental health problems. When we enter into the experience of others and look around 'with their eyes', many of our commonly held assumptions about both spirituality and mental health problems come under challenge, and our caring responses are changed and modified. In this way carers can be enabled to work with the spiritual dimension of clients in a way that is truly person-centred and genuinely therapeutic.

The chapters of this book present a systematic exploration of the spiritual dimension of mental health care and draw out the implications of this for the practice of mental health care within a multidisciplinary context. This book is *not* a theological text that seeks to explore questions of spirituality in terms of whose perspective or religion is right and whose is wrong. As will be argued in Chapter 1, a basic premise of the book is that spirituality is a common human phenomenon that is encountered in various ways in *all* human beings. Consequently, it is an inevitable aspect of genuinely holistic care. Within a mental health care context, the need is not for dogmatic, exclusivistic debate, but for sound practical reasoning that will justify and enable the inclusion of the spiritual dimension within current caring practices. Mental health carers are expected to deal with the spiritual needs of clients of varying persuasions, spiritualities and religions. The object of the book is not to propagate any one form of spirituality, but to raise the consciousness of carers to the importance of the spiritual dimension and to provide them with knowledge, understanding, practical models and approaches that will enable them to carry out their caring task effectively. The book is not a 'how to' book in the traditional style of textbooks on spiritual care. It does not provide an ABC of spiritual care. Rather, it aims to provide a framework of insights, concepts, ideas and fresh understandings that will enable carers to identify and meet the diverse spiritual needs that they encounter on a daily basis in a way that is sensitive and appropriate to their specific context.

The intention is therefore to provide an open, 'non-denominational' framework within which people of varying spiritual persuasions can find direction and assistance in fulfilling what is a vital health care task. It is hoped that, irrespective of the carer's particular spiritual perspective, the information supplied within this text will be usable and effective in enabling genuinely person-centred spiritual care.

CHAPTER 1

What is Spirituality?

The Rise of Spirituality in Contemporary Western Cultures

Contrary to what might often appear to be the case, the latter part of the twentieth century has seen a major upsurge of interest in spirituality within the Western world. As Davie and Cobb observe (in Cobb and Robshaw 1998, p.89),

> Despite a commonly held assumption – strongly bolstered by unrepresentative voices in the media – that secular attitudes prevail in modern Britain, the sociological evidence reveals that relatively few people in the population have opted out of religion altogether or out of some sort of belief; in other words, experiences of the sacred or spiritual remain widespread, notwithstanding a recognized and much talked about decline in religious practice.

It is true that institutionalized religion is becoming less popular. All of the major Christian denominations have seen a sharp decline in the post-war period, and this decline has carried on into the new millennium. However, whilst people may be becoming less *religious*, it would be a mistake to assume from that that they are necessarily becoming less *spiritual*, or that they are no longer searching for a sense of transcendence and spiritual fulfilment. What seems to have happened is that the spiritual beliefs and desires that were once located primarily within institutionalized religions have migrated across to other forms of spirituality. The spiritual quest continues, but in very different and much more diverse forms than those traditionally assumed to be normal.

This migration of spirituality from the 'religious' to the 'secular' has led to a change in the meaning of spirituality, as popularly conceived. Rather than being viewed as a specifically religious concept, spirituality has broadened in meaning into a more diffuse human need that can be met quite apart from institutionalized religious structures. This changing meaning of spirituality is reflected in the variety and diversity of definitions and understandings that are found in the literature on spirituality and mental health. The concept of spirituality is no longer confined to religion, nor is the practice of spiritual care necessarily located within any formal religious or spiritual tradition. Spirituality has become a wide and multi-vocal concept (i.e. it has many different meanings and interpretations), which is understood and interpreted in numerous different ways, from Christianity to Buddhism, to Islam, humanism and the New Age (Barnum 1998).

A slippery concept

Spirituality has therefore become a slippery concept within Western culture. As one works through the literature that explores the relationship between spirituality and mental health, it very soon becomes clear that whilst there may be a number of common themes such as God, meaning, purpose, value and hope, there does not appear to be a common definition that can fully encapsulate what spirituality is.

Positively, the disparate understandings of spirituality present within culture alert us to the need for thoughtfulness, imagination, creativity and flexibility when we are seeking to address the spiritual needs of people with mental health problems. A view of spirituality that does not look beyond institutional religion risks missing out on some of the very significant spiritual needs that are experienced by people with no formal religious interest, on a daily basis. Negatively, the very diffuseness of definitions and understandings makes it difficult to tie down precisely what spirituality is, and what its implications are for the process of caring. When spirituality is defined primarily in terms of a particular religious tradition or denomination, it is relatively straightforward to identify and meet spiritual needs through such avenues as prayer, scripture reading, meditation and so forth. However, when spirituality appears to mean all things to all people, it is more difficult to tie down specific strategies to deal with people's spiritual needs. One of the tasks of this book will be to explore ways in which spirituality, in all of its divergent forms, can be identified, understood and worked with. For now the significant thing to bear in mind is that spirituality may well be highly significant to many people with mental health problems, even though they may not express an interest in or adherence to an established religious tradition.

Spirituality: a usable concept?

This does not mean however that spirituality is so diffuse as to be meaningless as a working concept. Irrespective of the diversity of its manifestations, it does contain identifiable components and experiences that can be understood, nurtured and cared for. However, in order to understand spirituality it will be necessary to let go of our positivistic desire for absolute certainty, neat definitions and universally applicable categories, in order that we can enter into an aspect of human experience which, in many respects, transcends final categorization. Alongside the cultural changes highlighted above, one of the main reasons for the lack of conceptual clarity surrounding spirituality relates to the difficulties of capturing, in words, dimensions of human experience that are essentially inexpressible. Experiences and feelings such as spirituality, love, meaning and hope are not easy to analyse and conceptualize in the language of science. Consequently writers find themselves stretching their language and concepts beyond the boundaries of the normal scientific discourse, as they attempt to express something of the inner depths of human experience. If we are to develop a therapeutic understanding of spirituality it will be necessary to learn to be comfortable with uncertainty and mystery. This is not to say that we need to become 'unscientific' in the sense that we refuse to seek empirical evidence for our claims. To adopt such an approach would be to exclude spirituality from participating in what is undoubtedly the dominant epistemological discourse within contemporary Western culture, and one which has been deeply influential on the development of mental health care practices. As we shall see, spirituality can in fact be studied scientifically, although our understandings of science may have to alter to accommodate for the new perspectives that spirituality brings to it.

What we *do* need to do, however, is to begin to expand our understandings of science and empirical evidence to include methods and ways of looking at the world which will not overlook the spiritual dimension of the person. This chapter will seek to wrestle with the tension between the inherent inexpressibility of the spiritual dimension, and the need to find ways of identifying and working with this important dimension of human experience. In working through these issues it will be possible to develop a working understanding of spirituality that will guide and inform the remainder of the book.

What is the Human Spirit?

In developing an understanding of spirituality, it is necessary to begin by reflecting on the nature of the human spirit. This starting point is not in itself uncontroversial. Within a cultural milieu that has come uncritically to accept the assumptions of science, empiricism and positivism, there might appear to be no justification for drawing upon such an ethereal and apparently unverifiable concept as 'spirituality'. However, one of the continuing arguments of this book is that the way in which we currently view the world is only one possible construction of it. Certainly a narrowly conceived scientific perspective will not recognize or acknowledge the reality of the human spirit. Nevertheless, this study will aim to expand our view of science to include aspects of human experience that may be excluded from the present paradigm of ideas and worldview.

It is important to begin by noting that while the terms 'spirit' and 'spirituality' are closely connected, they are not synonymous. The human spirit is the essential life-force that undergirds, motivates and vitalizes human existence. *Spirituality* is the specific way in which individuals and communities respond to the experience of the spirit. This distinction is quite subtle, but very important.

The word 'spirit' is derived from the Latin *spiritus* meaning 'breath'. An analogy would be human respiration, by which oxygen is taken in to sustain and maintain the existence of the person. The spirit provides a similar sustaining and maintaining role on a more ontological level. The spirit is the fundamental breath of life that is instilled into human beings and which animates them and brings them into life. An example drawn from the Judaeo-Christian tradition will help clarify this point.

> The word [spirit] is etymologically related, in Hebrew (*ruach*) and Greek (*pneuma*), to the concept and picture of the stirring of air, breeze, *breath* and *wind*. In Hebrew anthropology, *ruach* was the enlivening force of a person – the breath of God which turned the prepared clay into a living soul. In the second creation story in the book of Genesis, Yahweh breathes into the prepared earth and the clay becomes a living nephesh. Thus the very being of the person is permeated by the *ruach* [spirit/spiritus] of God. (Lartey 1997, p.114)

The spirit energizes human existence and fills it with meaning and purpose. The source of the spirit is open to a number of understandings. It is variously described as God, Brahma or energy, and can be understood as an internal or interpersonal force of interconnectivity, or an external force that is given to people by some form of higher power. However it is perceived, it is 'usually considered to be untouchable, indescribable and untestable by any physical science,' (Pullen, Tuck and Mix 1996). Although ultimately mysterious and, to an extent, indefinable, the effects of the spirit *can* be described and understood.

Spirit as personal force

In contrast to the assumptions that the use of words such as 'life-force' and 'energy' might conjure up, the human spirit is not an impersonal, distant power that is unaffected by the experiences of the individual. As van Kaam in Goddard (1995, p.809) puts it, the human spirit is 'the dynamic force that keeps a person growing and changing continuously involved in a process of emerging, becoming and transcending of self; it is through this gestalt process that life is imbued with meaning and a sense of purpose for existence.' One of the dangers in using metaphors such as 'energy' to help us understand and describe the human spirit is that there is a temptation to forget about the metaphorical nature of our language, and to assume that spirituality *is* energy, rather than *is like* energy. The spirit is a unique force that has a quality of its own. We may be able to reach towards it using analogy and metaphor, but we must be careful to acknowledge these explanatory concepts for what they are.

A good example of this type of confusion between metaphor and reality is found in Goddard's (1995) use of the term 'integrative energy' to describe the human spirit. She argues that 'spirituality pervades, unites and directs all human dimensions and, therefore, constitutes the internal locus of natural health. Consequently, a definition of spirituality as integrative energy is hereby proposed' (p.813).

However, as Dawson (1997, p.283) correctly observes, there is a

world of difference between agreeing to consider spirituality, for discursive purposes, *as* an integrative energy, and stating that spirituality *is* integrative energy. The first statement is metaphorical. As all metaphors do, it attempts to explain the unfamiliar (spirituality) by the familiar (energy). The second statement asserts an isomorphic relationship between spirituality and integrative energy; the two are deemed equivalent in every respect. In any context one can then replace the term spirituality with integrative energy and the meaning will be retained.

In order to understand any new thing it is necessary to begin by drawing it into our current frame of reference and exploring and describing it using that which is familiar to us. In this way we build up concepts and understandings that enable us to make sense of that which is alien. Terms such as 'force' and 'energy' are familiar concepts drawn from physics that enable us to approximate an understanding of some aspects of the way in which the spirit functions. These analogies and metaphors are helpful in enabling understanding. However, though the spirit may be *like* force and energy, that is not what it *is*. Energy is an impersonal force that functions according to fixed laws and principles. As such it is predictable and unchanging. The spirit is a personal force that responds to the life experience of human beings. Common expressions such as: 'her spirits are high'; 'his spirits are at a very low ebb'; 'her spirit has been quenched'; 'I feel inspired (inspirited)'; 'he is feeling rather dispirited'; 'she has lost her spirit'; point towards the ways in which the spirit can be nurtured or quenched in response to human experience. The human spirit is therefore seen to be more of a continuing *process* than a fixed form of energy. The important point to bear in mind as we move on is that the spirit is a unique aspect of the human being that can be *illustrated* by drawing on language from other areas, but cannot be *translated* into that language. As such it challenges narrowly scientific language, and may well require the introduction of a broader, more appropriate range of vocabulary that captures this dimension of the human person.

Spirit and wholeness

Ellison describes the essence of the spirit thus:

> It is the *spirit* of human beings which enables and motivates us to search for meaning and purpose in life, to seek the supernatural or some meaning which transcends us, to wonder about our origins and our identities, to require mortality and equity. It is the spirit which synthesizes the total personality and provides some sense of energizing direction and order. The spiritual dimensions does not exist in isolation from the psyche and the soma, but provides an integrative force. It affects and is affected by our physical state, feelings, thoughts and relationships. If we are spiritually healthy we will feel generally alive, purposeful and fulfilled, but only to the extent that we are psychologically healthy as well. The relationship is bi-directional because of the intricate intertwining of these two parts of the person. (Ellison 1983, pp.331–2)

Ellison's reflections on the spirit are helpful. First, he emphasizes the important point that the human spirit is not simply a *component* of the person, which can be treated apart from the whole. Rather, the human spirit is seen as an integrative presence that permeates and vitalizes *every* aspect and *every* dimension of the human person. In other words, while we might legitimately separate body, mind and spirit for the purposes of exploration and clarification, it is crucial to bear in mind that 'we are totally present in every cell of our body. You cannot have a 'soul – or whatever you call it – without a body' (Ashbrook 1991). The human spirit is therefore not measurable as an independent variable in and of itself, any more than 'would be such concepts as physicality, emotionality or wholeness' (Reed 1992). The human person

> 'is an animated body, and not an incarnated soul.' ...Man [sic] does not have a body, he is a body. He is flesh-animated-by-soul, the whole conceived as a psychospiritual unity: 'The body is the soul in its outward form. There is no suggestion that the soul is the essential personality, or that the soul (nephesh) is immortal, while flesh (basar) is mortal...' (Robinson 1957, p.14)

Such a suggestion regarding the unity of persons is fully in line with the findings emerging from a number of health care disciplines. For example, contemporary developments within the field of psychoneuroimmunology have made it increasingly apparent that the relationship between a person's body, soul/spirit and mind can no longer be understood in dualistic terms (Althouse 1985; Birney 1991; Gatchel, Bawn and Krantz. 1989; Hillhouse and Adler 1991; Houldin *et al.* 1985). Psychoneuroimmunology is the scientific investigation of the ways in which the brain affects the body's immune cells and how the immune system can be affected by emotions, feelings and behaviour. It concentrates on the ways in which personality, behaviour, emotion and cognition can all change the body's immune response, and thereby increase or decrease the risk of a person suffering from particular immune-related diseases. Psychoneuroimmunology emphasizes the wholeness of persons and the interconnectedness of emotions, experiences and somatic processes. Although the majority of the research does not concentrate on the human spirit, some of the therapies that have emerged from this field have recognized and sought to work with the spiritual dimension (Hill and Mullen 1996).

Within neurobiology and psychology the connection between the mind and the brain is becoming more and more apparent (Jeeves 1997; Kitwood 1997a). Similarly, within psychiatry, the lines between the biological, psychological and sociological etiology and treatment of mental health problems are no longer as clear as they once appeared to be (Kendell and Zealley 1993). More and more it is being recognized that human beings are *whole* persons whose physical, emotional, social and spiritual needs are inextricably interlinked.

This suggestion concerning the wholeness and interconnectivity of persons has important implications in terms of mental health care. Mental health problems are not entities that simply affect one dimension of the person: the mind. They are whole-person experiences that affect a person in every dimension of their existence. What goes on in the psychological and spiritual realms can have a profound influence on what goes on in the physical realms, and vice versa (Kendell and Zealley 1993). Malfunctioning in one aspect of the person, be that their psychological, social or biological processes, can have an impact upon the person's spirit. This can manifest itself for example, in the deep dispiritedness of depression or the delusional religious identities and spiritual experiences of people living with psychotic disorders, both of which may have a biological root, but which at the same time, are deeply spiritual in their consequences. Again, disturbance in a person's spirit may have a significant impact upon their illness experience. For example, the loneliness, exclusion and lack of value experienced by many people with highly stigmatized forms of mental health problems such as schizophrenia are a profoundly spiritual problem that can significantly impact upon the recovery and stability of the person (Swinton 2000b).

Because of this deep interconnectivity within human persons, it is a mistake to assume that forms of spirituality that appear to be distorted by pathological experiences are *nothing but* an aspect of their pathology (although of course they may be profoundly influenced by it). A person's spirit may well be affected by their mental health problem. However, even distorted spirituality can reflect a genuine response to the types of spiritual longings and responses highlighted by Ellison in the previous quotation. The task of the spiritual carer is to acknowledge the implications of human interconnectedness and to develop the ability to discern between forms of spirituality that may be negatively affected by the person's mental health problems, and the more helpful and constructive responses of individuals to the longings of their spirits. One of the tasks of this book will be to explore ways of enabling carers effectively to achieve such a task of discernment and develop effective forms of care and intervention in the face of confusing forms of spiritual expression.

Second, Ellison's exploration of the nature of the human spirit shows clearly that it is this aspect of the person that provides the drive and the desire to find meaning, purpose and value in our lives. Again this reinforces the difference between impersonal energy and the purposeful process of the spirit. The human spirit is an essential, dynamic life-force which vitalizes human beings and provides the motivation to discover God, value, meaning, purpose and hope. A useful analogy for understanding this aspect of the spirit is the difference between *reflexive* and *meaningful* action. *Reflexes* are actions that have no meaning or purpose beyond their immediate function. Reflexive actions are actions that are nothing more than automatic responses to electronic stimuli. They have a technical/functional meaning in the sense that biologists and anatomists can identify their source and highlight their function within the overall bodily processes, but they do not have any *personal* meaning or independent sense of purpose beyond their specific function. It is a person's *spirit* that makes the difference between *reflexive* human existence in which human actions and experiences are viewed simply as the effect of an unending stream of meaningless causes, and *meaningful* human existence in which actions and experiences are understood as containing meaning, hope, purpose, direction and possibilities beyond themselves.

Take, for example, a person who is depressed. What we find here is that a person's spirit has been inhibited, crushed or flattened by biological, social or psychological events. Often they feel as if they are simply going through the motions. Their actions and experiences appear to have no meaning beyond themselves. They are living *reflexively*, rather than *meaningfully*. Within such a situation, the task of the spiritual carer is not simply to locate the locus of *pathology*, but also to locate the locus of *meaning* within the person's life and in so doing begin to explore ways in which the person's spirit can be revitalized and the movement from reflexive existence to meaningful living can be initiated and followed through.

It would of course be possible simply to translate this process into psychological terms that exclude the spiritual dimension as a valid interpretative framework. However, the empirical evidence presented later in this book would suggest that such a process of translation may not be as easy to justify as previously assumed. Translation may be the easiest option, but it may well not be the most authentic.

The necessity for a multidisciplinary approach to care

The suggestion that human beings have spirits presents an important corrective to understandings that see them simply as a conglomerate of parts reacting blindly to an unending series of environmental stimuli. To suggest that human beings have a spirit presupposes that they are creatures who require more than basic needs to achieve health and well-being, and that issues of meaning, hope, purpose and transcendence are not secondary to the caring task, but are in fact a fundamental part of it (Frankl 1964; Moltmann 1985). An approach that accepts the reality and significance of the human spirit is also a corrective for the fragmented forms of 'specialist' care that have become the norm within contemporary health care practices. If human beings are whole persons and if mental health problems affect every aspect of the person, then spiritual care on its own will not be enough. Nor will pharmacological or psychotherapeutic intervention be sufficient to meet the needs of the whole person. What will be required is a multidisciplinary approach that seeks through constructive dialogue between the disciplines to develop ways of caring that acknowledge and reach out to the whole person, including those more mysterious and less tangible aspects that emerge from reflection on the human spirit. One of the aims of this book is to provide a foundation from which such a multidisciplinary approach might be built.

What is Spirituality?

A particular understanding of spirituality flows directly from this understanding of the human spirit. *Spirituality is the outward expression of the inner workings of the human spirit.* It is a personal and social process that refers to the ideas, concepts, attitudes and behaviours that derive from a person's, or a community's interpretation of their experiences of the spirit.

> Spirituality...is a way of being and experiencing that comes through awareness of a transcendental dimension and that is characterized by certain identifiable values in regard to self, others, nature, life and whatever one considers to be ultimate. (Elkins *et al.* 1988)

Spirituality is an intra, inter and transpersonal experience that is shaped and directed by the experiences of individuals and of the communities within which they live out their lives. It is *intrapersonal* in that it refers to the quest for inner connectivity highlighted in the previous discussion on the spirit. It is *interpersonal* in that it relates to the relationships between people and within communities. It is *transpersonal* in so far as it reaches beyond self and others into the transcendent realms of experience that move beyond that which is available at a mundane level.

While the human *spirit* may be deeply mysterious, pointing as it does towards aspects of reality that are deep, unfathomable and transcendent, *spirituality* is a human activity that attempts to express these profound experiences and inner longings in terms that are meaningful for the individual. The form and content of spirituality is therefore diverse, contextual and to greater or lesser extent defined by its prefix: Christian, Buddhist, Jewish, humanistic, agnostic and so forth. Each of these prefixes indicates specific ways in which human beings have chosen to respond to the inner experience of their spirits.

The universal and the particular

Emmanuel Lartey (1997) offers a useful model that will enable us to understand clearly what is being said here. In reflecting on how care and counselling can effectively cross cultural boundaries, Lartey develops a model of what he describes as 'intercultural care'. Rather than assuming that cultures are monolithic wholes within which all people believe the same things and act in a similar, predictable manner, Lartey highlights the critical tension between the uniqueness of individuals and the uniformity of cultural systems. In order to avoid stereotyping, negative and at times racist assumptions, Lartey, drawing on the cross-cultural thinking of David Augsberger (1986), argues that every human person is in certain respects:

Like all other people (the Universal Human Dimension)

Like some other people (the Historical, Cultural, Social and Political Dimensions)

Like no other people (the Intrapersonal Dimension)

This framework captures something of the universal and unique aspects of being human. Understood from this perspective, it is not possible to assume that simply because a person comes from a particular country or culture they will necessarily behave or believe in the same way as everyone else within that culture or country. In order to understand and to care for them appropriately, it is necessary to enter into their cultural life-worlds and look around for the meaning structures that enable them to make sense of the world.

When translated into the realm of spirituality, Lartey's model is illuminating. At one level, spirituality is a universal human experience. At this level we might safely approach everyone whom we encounter with the expectation that the spiritual dimension will be present either implicitly or explicitly.

At a second level, spirituality manifests itself in different ways according to culture, context, experience, cognitive set, personality factors and so forth. Spirituality is inevitably expressed through the particular concepts of context, culture and personality, as well as via the particular spiritual assumptions and religious traditions that exist within different cultures. A person will therefore express their spirituality in ways that may be similar to those of certain others. This is particularly so with regard to formal religious systems.

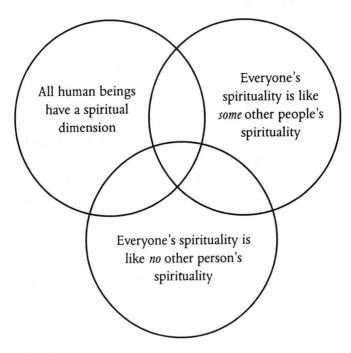

Figure 1.1. The universal and the particular dimensions of spirituality (adapted with permission from Lartey 1997)

At a third level, spirituality is a unique and deeply personal thing that people express in their own specific ways. Even people who appear to share the same religious tradition may well express it very differently and have a diversity of beliefs. The knowledge that a person is Christian, Muslim, Jewish, Buddhist or whatever is not particularly helpful, apart from providing a general field of reference in itself. It is only when we are enabled to enter into the person's life experiences that the meaning of their faith commitment becomes clear. In order to discern the meaning of a person's spirituality for their lives and their illness experiences, it is necessary to hold in tension all three dimensions of human spirituality: the *universal*, the *cultural* and the *intrapersonal*. Figure 1.1 illustrates what is being said here.

Spirituality as a common human experience

For current purposes, spirituality can be categorized into two types: non-religious and religious. Both forms of spirituality have implications for mental health care. Although traditionally spirituality has been understood primarily in religious terms, as has been suggested, a good deal of the literature looking at the relationship between spirituality and health works with a wider understanding of spirituality which may include, but is not defined by, institutional religion. While human spirituality is institutionalized and ritualized within particular religious traditions, it is not defined as a specifically religious concept. Formal, organized religion is viewed as one of a number of vehicles for the expression of human spirituality. This broader understanding views spirituality as a common human experience that forms an integral part of every person's striving to make sense of the world and their life within it. Such understanding incorporates humanistic, existential and philosophical perspectives as well as religious ones. Larson, Swyers and McCullough (1997, p. 21) define the criterion for such a wider understanding of spirituality thus:

(A) The feelings, thoughts, experiences, and behaviours that arise from a search for the sacred. The term 'search' refers to attempts to identify, articulate, maintain, or transform. The term 'sacred' refers to a divine being or Ultimate Reality or Ultimate Truth as perceived by the individual...

(B) A search for non-sacred goals (such as identity, belongingness, meaning, health, or wellness) in a context that has as its primary goal the facilitation of (A)...

(C) The means and methods (e.g. rituals or prescribed behaviours) of the search that receive validation and support from within an identifiable group of people.

Like religion, spirituality strives to answer deep existential questions pertaining to the meaning of life, suffering, illness and so forth, as well as recognizing the need for human interconnectivity and the desire to transcend the self in meaningful ways. However, unlike religion, this wider understanding of spirituality does not necessarily find its primary focus in any kind of transcendent being or force. Nor does it require affiliation with a specific community. 'God' is conceptualized as whatever a person takes to be their highest value in life. 'The key element in this broader definition is that whatever the "god" may be, it provides a force which activates the individual or is an essential principle influencing him/her' (Oldnall 1996, p.139). Meaning is assumed to be found in a person's relationship with their god, with others and with their inner selves (Dyson, Cobb and Foreman 1997). Oldnall (1996) points out that within this wider model of spirituality:

> [t]he concept of god does not constitute a transcendent being or a set of religious beliefs. Instead, the person has consciously or unconsciously chosen a set of values which become the supreme focus of life, and/or around which life is organized… From this perspective it may be argued that the perceived values embraced by the individual have the ability to motivate the individual's life style towards fulfillment of their individual needs, goals and aspirations. Leading to the ultimate achievement of self-actualization. (Oldnall 1996, p.139)

This expanded understanding of spirituality manifests itself in various forms and includes perspectives drawn *inter alia* from religious, humanistic, atheistic and agnostic conceptions of spirituality. Table 1.1 draws together some of the central features of this expanded definition of spirituality. Here, spiritual care pertains to identifying and working with that which gives the person their source of meaning, value and a sense of inner and outward connectedness. Some of these spiritual needs are outlined in Table 1.2. In order to fulfil such needs, carers need to learn skills that will enable them to identify spiritual needs without reducing them to *nothing but* psychological phenomena. This will mean learning skills of spiritual exploration that will allow both carer and cared for to enter into the spiritual experience and feel comfortable sitting in those realms that are not part of our normal therapeutic world.

Table 1.1. The central features of spirituality	
Meaning	the ontological significance of life; making sense of life situations; deriving purpose in existence.
Value	beliefs and standards that are cherished; having to do with the truth, beauty, worth of a thought, object or behaviour; often discussed as 'ultimate values'.
Transcendence	experience and appreciation of a dimension beyond the self; expanding self-boundaries.
Connecting	relationships with self, others, God/higher power, and the environment.
Becoming	an unfolding of life that demands reflection and experience; includes a sense of who one is and how one knows.

Data extrapolated from Martsolf and Mickley 1998.

Why call this spirituality?

It could of course be argued that the 'spiritual needs' identified above can be explained equally as well in psychological terms without having to draw upon the rather ethereal and 'unscientific' idea of spirituality. However, on deeper reflection it becomes clear that such words as 'hope', 'faith' and 'purpose', and ideas such as 'the search for meaning' and 'the need for forgiveness', are not adequately captured in language that assumes they are *nothing* but thought processes or survival needs. Although it may not fit neatly into the current scientific paradigm, as one encounters such language, one experiences a deep, intuitive sense of affirmation that these desires refer to dimensions that include, yet at the same time transcend psychological explanation. Of course the idea of intuition and intuitive knowledge is not popular in an atmosphere that thrives on evidence-based practice, with evidence tending to be understood in narrow, positivistic terms. However, intuition and feeling form a significant aspect of the ways in which human beings make sense of large parts of their experiences. This book will argue that this dimension of human experience should be taken seriously.

Table 1.2. Non-religious spiritual needs

Values/structures of meaning
Hope
Faith
Search for meaning/purpose to life
Dealing with guilt and initiating forgiveness

Relationships
Therapeutic presence
The possibility of intimacy

Transcendence
The need to explore dimensions beyond the Self
The possibility of reaching God without the use of formal religious structures

Affective feeling
Reassurance
Comfort
Peace
Happiness

Communication
Talking and telling stories
Listening and being listened to

Adapted from Swinton 1999a and Emblen and Halstead 1993.

A second reason why we should be wary of translating spiritual experiences into the language of psychology, or any other discipline, relates to issues of *reductionism*. Simply to baptize experiences such as those mentioned above into the psychological worldview is to engage in a form of reductionism that reflects a Western milieu that has come to assume that everything can be explained in either material or psychological terms. Psychology, science and medicine have become very powerful interpretative frameworks within which we assume that all knowledge can be captured and understood. The language of these disciplines is so ingrained in our cultural worldview that it is difficult to imagine a world that could not be explained in such terms. Consequently, when we encounter something that is different (such as the suggestion that there may be a spiritual dimension to human beings), and which in some senses falls out with this interpretative perspective, the temptation is simply to draw it within the accepted plausibility structures

(Newbigin 1989) and to explain it using the categories that we are most familiar with. It is true that it is easier to avoid spiritual language and engage with these needs at a level and within a structure with which we are comfortable. However, before we do so, we must ask ourselves *why* we would want to do that. The questioning of the reality of the spiritual dimension is a relatively new innovation for Western cultures, and is in fact, as we have seen, unrepresentative of the views of a good deal of the population. This being so, the psychologizing of spiritual experience may simply be a product of the limitations of our cultural worldview and the ways in which we have constructed society's understanding of what are considered legitimate forms of knowledge in general, and the knowledge used to underpin mental health care in particular.

Spirituality as a Religious Concept

The expanded understanding of spirituality is a growing strand within the literature on spirituality and mental health. However, a high percentage of the research literature refers to spirituality that manifests itself in religious forms. Despite the decline of interest in institutionalized religion within the Western world, on a worldwide scale, as Table 1.3 indicates, religion remains a highly significant aspect in the lives of billions of people.

Table 1.3. The major world religions
Christianity: 2 billion
Islam: 1.2 billion
Hinduism: 900 million
Secular/Non-religious/Agnostic/Atheist: 900 million
Buddhism: 350 million
Chinese Traditional Religion: 225 million
Sikhism: 19 million
Judaism: 15 million

Data extrapolated from Adherents.com.

If one places these figures alongside the fact that the United Kingdom, Europe and the United States are very much multicultural and religiously plural societies, it becomes clear that the religious aspects of spirituality require to be taken seriously as a potentially significant factor in the lives of people with mental health problems. It will therefore be useful to spend some time looking at religion and exploring some of its implications for mental health care.

Defining religion

Religion refers to a formal system of beliefs, usually centring on some conception of God and expressing the views of a particular religious group or community. The word 'religion' originates semantically from the Latin word *religio. Religio* 'implies that "foundation wall" to which one is "bound" for one's survival, the basis of one's being' (Sims 1996, p.444) More specifically it 'signifies a bond between humanity and some greater-than-human power.' (Larson *et al.* 1997, p.15). A person's religion, at least in its purest form, is something that is foundational to the way in which they experience themselves and make sense of the world they inhabit.

Peter Cotterell (1990, p.16) suggests that religion essentially seeks to answer three foundational existential questions:

Who am I, Where did I come from, Where am I going to, Why?

Who are you, Where did you come from, Where are you going, Why?

What is this world, Where did it come from, Where is it going, Why?

Thus religion asks deep questions about the nature of human beings, their identity and place within the world, the purpose and meaning of human life, and the destiny of humankind. Organized religions are rooted within a particular tradition or traditions, which engender their own narratives, symbols and doctrines that are used by adherents to interpret and explain their experiences of the world. As such, religion provides a powerful worldview and a specific epistemological and hermeneutical framework within which people seek to understand and interpret and make sense of themselves, their lives and their daily experiences.

Religions also have access to symbolic avenues of expression, such as rituals, prayers and worship, which can be used as powerful tools within the process of mental health development and care (Taggart 1994). While some theorists argue that religion can be detrimental to mental health (Ellis 1986; Freud 1959, 1966) there is also strong evidence, some of which will be reviewed later, to suggest that religion can be beneficial to the development and maintenance of mental health (Ellison and Smith 1991; Gartner, Larson and Allen 1991; L. B. Brown 1994). As such it is a form of spirituality which needs to be taken seriously and its potential importance for the process of mental health care acknowledged fully within mental health care strategies.

Intrinsic and extrinsic religion

Religion can be a powerful force in a person's life. However, its effect is mediated by a number of intervening factors. One important mediating factor is the form that it takes, and the specific meaning it has for individuals. This meaning dimension has been explored in some depth within the psychology of religion, through the investigation of *religious orientation*. In its original form religion was argued to be present in two primary forms or orientations: *intrinsic and extrinsic*. Kirkpatrick and Hood (1990) note that the conception that religion manifests itself in two forms, intrinsic and extrinsic, currently represents the backbone of empirical research in the psychology of religion. Paloutzian (1996) suggests that 'the development of the intrinsic and extrinsic concepts constitutes a turning point in the psychological study of religion' (p.205). Likewise Donahue (1985) in his meta-analysis of the concepts of intrinsic and extrinsic religiousness concludes that, 'no approach to religiousness has had greater impact on the empirical psychology of religion than Gordon W. Allport's concepts of intrinsic (I) and extrinsic (E) religiousness.'

This dichotomy between intrinsic and extrinsic forms of religiosity refers to the *nature, quality* and *function* of a person's religious commitment. The idea that religiousness manifests itself in two forms, intrinsic and extrinsic, and that the nature of these manifestations has significant implications for behaviour and mental health, was proposed in its original form by the psychologists Gordon Allport and Michael Ross in their 1967 paper entitled 'Personal Religious Orientation and Prejudice'. Allport and Ross observed that on average, church attenders tended to be *more* prejudiced than non-attenders. This struck them as strangely paradoxical in the light of the Judaeo-Christian tradition and its emphasis on equality, acceptance, forgiveness and loving one's neighbour. However, they also noted that, whilst it was true that most attenders were more prejudiced than non-attenders, a significant minority of them were less prejudiced. The paper set out to solve this dilemma. On analysing their results further, they discovered that:

It was the casual, irregular fringe members who are high in prejudice; their religious motivation is of the extrinsic order. It is the constant, devout, internalized members who are low in prejudice; their religious motivation is of the intrinsic order. (Allport and Ross 1967, p.434)

In order to understand the significance of this piece of research, and its relevance for this book, it is necessary to clarify what Allport and Ross, and those who have followed them, actually mean by the terms *extrinsic* and *intrinsic*.

Intrinsic religion

Put simply, *intrinsic* religiousness is religion perceived as a meaning-endowing framework in terms of which one's self and one's life experiences are interpreted and understood. The reasons for intrinsically motivated faith lie within rather than outside the person. Paloutzian (1996, p.201) uses the analogy of biological digestion to illuminate the psychological concept of intrinsic religiosity.

When you consume food, it is digested and becomes part of your body, part of the same biological system that took it in in the first place. It becomes internalized, intrinsic to your system, part of the very fabric of it. In a similar way, a religious faith may be internalized and thus become part of the fabric of your personality.

The intrinsically religious person extends their religion beyond the boundaries of a specific service of worship into every aspect of their life. In their working life, economic activities, sexual encounters, in every aspect of their lives, their religion provides the guiding motive and determines the boundaries of behaviour.

Persons with this orientation find their master motive in religion. Other needs, strong as they may be, are regarded as of less ultimate significance, and they are, so far as possible, brought into harmony with the religious beliefs and prescriptions. Having embraced a creed the individual endeavours to internalize it and follow it fully. It is in this sense that he lives his religion. (Allport and Ross 1967, p.434)

A person with an intrinsic religious orientation is able to draw upon the resources of a religious tradition and a religious community, and incorporate them fully within their lives and their understanding of the world. In this way, the meaning of their lives is inextricably connected to and defined by their religious beliefs. Their religious orientation is thus seen to be foundational to their concept of self. A person's religious beliefs provide them with their primary role, around which they can organize and make sense of the other roles that constitute their life experiences. The interpretative framework of their religion determines who and what they understand themselves to be.

Extrinsic religion

In contrast, *extrinsic* religiousness is the religion of comfort and social convention, a self-serving, instrumental approach shaped to suit oneself (Donahue 1985). This form of religion finds its motivation primarily outside, rather than within the person.

> Persons with this orientation are disposed to use religion for their own ends…[religion is understood as] an interest that is held because it serves other, more ultimate interests. Extrinsic values are always instrumental and utilitarian. Persons with this orientation may find religion useful in a variety of ways – to provide security and solace, sociability and distraction, status and self-justification. The embraced creed is lightly held or else selectively shaped to fit more primary needs. In theological terms the extrinsic type turns to God, but without turning away from self. (Allport and Ross, 1967 p.434)

Religion for such persons is simply one role amongst many, and as such detachable from their essential sense of self. A person with an extrinsic religious orientation uses their religion to provide security, comfort, status, self-esteem, significance and/or to gain social support for themselves. An extreme example of extrinsic religiosity would be an insurance salesman who only attends church to make contacts and to sell his wares (Paloutzian 1996, p.202).

Extrinsic religiousness is very similar to a *neurosis* in the sense that it is a defence against anxiety, whereas intrinsicness makes for positive mental health. As Donahue (1985, p.416) puts it,

> Extrinsic religiousness…does a good job of measuring the sort of religion that gives religion a bad name. It is positively correlated with prejudice, dogmatism…trait anxiety…and fear of death…and is apparently un-correlated with altruism.

In contrast an intrinsically motivated person *lives* their religion. Consequently, they tend to be more tolerant, accepting and altruistic, having a stronger sense of identity, self-respect and sense of meaning and purpose to their lives. Table 1.4 highlights the main differences between these two forms of religiosity orientation.

Table 1.4. Intrinsic and extrinsic religion	
Intrinsic	**Extrinsic**
Relates to all of life	Compartmentalized
Unprejudiced; tolerance	Prejudiced; exclusionary
Mature	Immature; dependent; comfort; security
Integrative; unifying; meaning-endowing	Instrumental; utilitarian; self-serving
Regular church attendance	Irregular church attendance
Makes for mental health	Defence or escape mechanism

Donahue 1985.

Religion as a quest

Since its original formulation, some researchers have expressed concerns over the certain imitations surrounding the intrinsic–extrinsic dynamic of religious behaviour. Allport's original formulation appears to omit a significant aspect of religious experience, namely the *quest* dimension, i.e. the existential challenge of moving towards spiritual understanding. Whereas intrinsic and extrinsic orientations are more static, the quest dimension has a sense of process and movement which, it is argued, better represents the religious experience and orientation of some individuals. In *Religion and the Individual* (1993), Batson, Schoenrade, and Ventis highlight certain methodological problems in Allport's original research. They argue that the ideas Allport attempted to deal with were not adequately measured by his questionnaire. Allport's original tool 'the religious orientation scale' certainly measured religious commitment and personal dedication to one's belief system. However, they felt that it did not measure the characteristics outlined by Allport in his definition of the religiously mature person: integrative thought and the ability to face complexity; doubt and self-critical thinking; and incompleteness and tentativeness in the construction of personal concepts of truth. Batson *et al.* suggest that a third dimension be included within the understanding of religious orientation in order better to address Allport's concept of mature religiosity. This dimension they named the *quest* dimension. The quest dimension of personal religion is quite independent of either the extrinsic or the intrinsic orientation (Batson and Schoenrade 1991).

Religious orientation and mental health

There is some evidence to suggest a positive relationship between intrinsic and quest-oriented forms of religion and mental health. Fagan (1996) notes that the intrinsic and extrinsic orientations lead to two very different sets of psychological effects.

> For instance, 'intrinsics' have a greater sense of responsibility and greater internal control, are more self-motivated, and do better in their studies. By contrast, 'extrinsics' are more likely to be dogmatic, authoritarian, and less responsible, to have less internal control, to be less self-directed, and to do less well in their studies (Kahoe 1974). Intrinsics are more concerned with moral standards, conscientiousness, discipline, responsibility, and consistency than are extrinsically religious people (Wiebe and Fleck 1980). They also are more sensitive to others and more open to their own emotions. By contrast, extrinsics are more self-indulgent, indolent, and likely to lack dependability. For example, the most racially prejudiced people turn out to be those who go to church occasionally (Donahue 1985) and those who are extrinsic in their practice of religion (Donahue 1980). These findings have been replicated (Bergin, Masters and Richards 1987) in a number of different forms (Baker and Gorsuch 1982).

A number of studies have shown that people with an intrinsic religious perspective are more mentally healthy than those whose religiosity is extrinsic. Mickley, Carson and Soecken (1995) note in their review of the literature on religion and mental health that:

> A wide range of studies has shown that individuals who demonstrate high levels of intrinsic religiousness tend to have less depression, anxiety and dysfunctional attention seeking, and high levels of ego strength, empathy, and integrated social behaviour. People with high extrinsic religiousness tend to have high anxiety, feelings of powerlessness and maladjustment, low ego strength, and less integrated social behaviour. (Mickley *et al.* 1995, p.347)

Baker and Gorsuch (1982) in their study of anxiety and its relationship to intrinsic and extrinsic religiousness make some similar observations concerning the positive correlation between intrinsic religiousness and mental health. They note that anxiety has correlated both positively and negatively with religion in previous research. They also propose that one of the reasons for this is that the intrinsic/extrinsic dynamic has not been adequately taken into research equations. Their results of their own research shows that extrinsicness is positively correlated with anxiety, and intrinsicness negatively correlated with it. The results concur with those of Mickley *et al.* (1995) in confirming that intrinsicness is associated with greater ego strength, more integrated social behaviour, less paranoia or insecurity and less anxiety (Baker and Gorsuch 1982). Extrinsic religiousness appears to act in an opposite manner. Intrinsic religiousness is also associated with the ability to integrate anxiety into everyday life in an adaptive manner, while extrinsicness is associated with the inability to do so. Baker and Gorsuch (1982) conclude that, '[t]hese general findings are consistent with the thesis that being committed intrinsically to a religion does in fact bring peace.'

Mental health and the spiritual quest

The evidence for the benefits of the quest dimension is less well researched, but nonetheless significant. Ventis (in Paloutzian 1996, p. 253) placed the three orientations within a framework of seven definitions of mental health (see Table 1.5). Within this framework, extrinsic religion was found to be negatively associated with all seven conceptions of mental health. Intrinsic religion was 'positively, but not uniformly, associated with the seven definitions.' It did not tend to be associated with self-acceptance and self-actualization and open-mindedness and flexibility. The quest orientation 'showed neutral associations with the definitions, except for one: quest was positively associated with open-mindedness and flexibility.'

Table 1.5. Seven definitions of mental health
1. The absence of illness
2. Appropriate social behaviour
3. Freedom from worry and guilt
4. Personal competence and control
5. Self-acceptance and self-actualization
6. Unification and organization of personality
7. Open-mindedness and flexibility

Data extrapolated from Paloutzian 1996.

The significance of meaning

This discussion of religious orientation has opened up a very important aspect of mental health and mental health care: the significance of *meaning*. The intrinsic–extrinsic–quest dimensions make it clear that in order to comprehend the relationship between a person's religion and their mental health, it is not enough simply to know the bare facts that a person is religious/spiritual, or that they are church attenders. In order to assess the therapeutic potential of religion it is necessary to discern precisely what it *means* to the individual. One of the difficulties with quantitative studies which seek to explore the relationship between religion and mental health is that they frequently only measure single variables such as church attendance, belief in God, an afterlife and so forth. While they may be able to measure the frequency of an action or the commonality of proclaimed beliefs, they fail to take cognizance of the *meaning* that such things have for people. A similar difficulty is encountered by practitioners as they attempt to assess the needs of clients. As HRH the Prince of Wales (1991) correctly observed in his address to the Royal College of Psychiatrists: 'We ask patients to which religion they ascribe, but we neglect the much more important question of "what does your religion and your faith mean to you?"' To understand the possible benefits or otherwise of religion for a person's mental health, it is necessary to know what their religion *means* to them as individuals, how this is worked out in their lives and the ways they use it to understand and come to terms with their life experiences. How this might be done in practice is the subject of the later chapters of this book.

This being so, one must be wary of any form of statistical analysis which does not control for the intrinsic, extrinsic or quest dimensions of the sample's religious beliefs. This point will be developed more fully later. For now the thing to bear in mind is that understanding the spiritual needs of clients requires more than simply technical excellence. It requires an ability to enter into the lived experience of those to whom we seek to offer care to, in order that together, we can discover how their needs can best be met.

Summary

It has become clear that from the perspective developed within this chapter, spirituality and spiritual care is not simply something that pertains only to the religious client. Spirituality is a dimension in the lives of *all* of those to

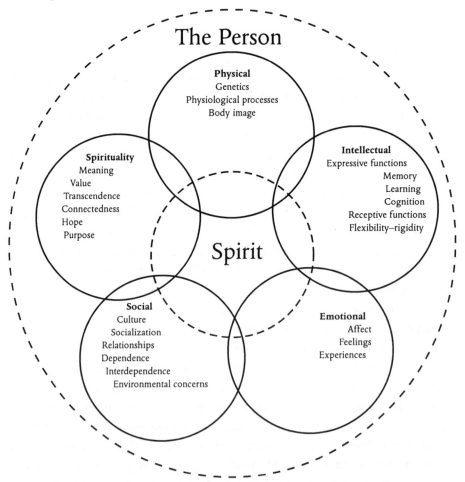

Figure 1.2. The five dimensions of the person (adapted from Swinton and Kettles 1997)

whom we seek to offer care. As such, being prepared to care for this aspect is not a *choice* but a *necessity* for mental health carers who seeks to care for persons in all of their fullness. Figure 1.2 draws together and helps conceptualize the developing understanding of spirituality and the human person presented within this chapter. This model is developed from Hildegard Peplau's interpersonal model of care (Peplau 1952; Swinton and Kettles 1997). It is based on Peplau's suggestion that there are five dimensions to the human person, each of which demands equal attention within the caring process. The central, broken circle indicates the movement of the spirit as it permeates the various dimensions of the human person. In this diagram, spirituality is viewed as one of the five vital dimensions of the human person that derives its purpose from this movement of the spirit, and its meaning and content from the particular context and spiritual tradition of the individual. Within this model, spirituality is seen as the outward manifestation of the longings inspired by their experiences of their spirit: the search for transcendence, meaning, value, hope and so forth. The spirit cannot be observed directly. However, a person's spirituality is accessible in that it manifests itself in thoughts, behaviours and language that can, to some degree, be observed, understood and nurtured. The diagram shows clearly that there can be no separation between the spiritual and the physical, nor between the spiritual and the emotional/psychological aspects of human beings. The person is an indivisible whole with the person's spirit both integrated within the other realms and also manifesting itself through them. The various dimensions can be isolated and examined for the purpose of analysis. However, it is not possible to understand one without taking full cognizance of the others. Thus, the human person is seen to be an inextricable continuum of body, mind and spirit. It is important to observe that the outer circle that indicates the boundaries of the self is also broken. Spirituality is not simply a personal possession; an internal structure that can be built up quite apart from relationships and context. The broken outer boundary signifies the necessary permeability of human persons, and highlights the outward dynamic of spiritual need as the spirit reaches beyond the boundaries of the self and connects with others and with God.

The division between religious and non-religious spirituality might be conceptualized in terms of two circles, each representing a different aspect of spirituality (Figure 1.3). (The circles are not intended to be proportional.) The outer circle represents the wider dimensions of spirituality that have been discussed previously. The inner circle represents forms of spirituality that are specifically religious. The two circles are intimately interconnected, that are specifically religious. The two circles are intimately interconnected, and reflect genuine attempts to express the experiences of the spirit. Understood in this way, spirituality is seen to be of relevance to all people, and spiritual care is something that extends beyond the remit of the religious professional and into the working life of the whole multidisciplinary team. While the two models are wholly compatible, they differ in their focus and consequently in the types of care they engender. Within the religious model of spirituality, spiritual care will have to do with the meeting of specifically religious needs such as nurturing the person's connection with God, prayer, confession, scripture reading and so forth. Spiritual care in its widest sense pertains to strategies designed to endow meaning, value, hope and purpose to people's lives. Interventions here would include the development of meaningful personal relationships, meditation, enabling access to sources of value and so forth.

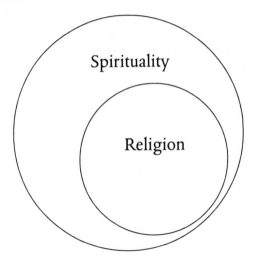

Figure 1.3. Religious and Non-Religious Spirituality

Conclusion

Spirituality has been shown to be a significant aspect of the human condition that requires specific forms of understanding and care in order that people can flourish and find wholeness in a real and meaningful sense. Such a suggestion is not simply the product of abstract theorizing or theological wish-fulfilment. As we shall see in Chapters 3 and 4, there is strong evidence to support the suggestion of the importance of spirituality within the context of mental health care.

It is possible of course simply to dismiss the idea of the spiritual as unscientific and therefore unworthy of serious consideration with regard to the therapeutic process. However, before doing this one would be wise to consider the evidence for the benefit of including the spiritual dimension within caring strategies. One would also be wise to reflect on precisely why one might wish to reject or downgrade the idea of spirituality and its significance to the process of mental health care. It *may* be that, in our quest for verifiable evidence and scientific/professional credibility, we have allowed ourselves to become blind to some vital aspects of the people we work with and some critical dimensions of the process of mental health care. The literature review in Chapter 3 deals with the former point and presents an empirical basis for the development of spiritual care within a mental health context. However, before we get to the point where such evidence can be taken seriously by carers, it is necessary to reflect on the latter point regarding the reasons why mental health carers in general, and mental health care professionals in particular find it so difficult to take seriously spirituality and the spiritual dimensions of mental health care. This will be the subject of the following chapter.

CHAPTER 2

The Neglect of the Spiritual

In Chapter 1 we noted that, despite the decline of institutional religion, spirituality continues to play an important part in the lives of many people within Western societies. There is also a growing body of evidence, some of which will be examined in Chapter 3, which suggests that spirituality plays a significant role in the lives of many people experiencing psychiatric problems (Kroll and Sheehan, 1989; Mental Health Foundation 1998; Neeleman and Lewis 1994). Given the types of empirical evidence that will be reviewed in Chapter 3, one might assume that spirituality and the development of effective strategies for spiritual care would be considered a priority by the mental health professions. However, while it may be clear that this is an area of care that in many ways should be addressed by mental health carers, as one turns to the evidence surrounding this area, it very soon becomes apparent that this is not the case.

Psychiatry and religion

Lukoff, Turner and Lu (1992, p.25) point to the fact that historically,

> mental health professionals have tended to either ignore or pathologize the religious and spiritual dimensions of life... [As a result] individuals who bring religious and spiritual problems into their treatment are often viewed as showing signs of mental illness.

This tendency for psychiatry to adopt a stance that excludes the significance of spirituality, other than as a form of pathology or pathological response has also been noted by other writers (Hall 1996; Horsfall 1997). While some do take issues of spirituality seriously (Bergin and Jensen 1990; Sims 1997), on the whole psychiatrists have tended not to acknowledge that spirituality may have a positive contribution to make to the process of mental health care. This is a strange situation, bearing in mind the specific task of psychiatry. As King and Dein (1998) correctly point out,

> Psychiatrists concern themselves with human mental suffering. Behind the consulting room door they reflect with their patients on questions of

meaning and existence, issues that concern philosophy and religion as much as psychiatry. It is striking, therefore, that psychiatrists regard spirituality and religion as, at best, cultural noise to be respected but not addressed directly, or at worst pathological thinking that requires modification. (King and Dein 1998)

Spirituality may be accepted as 'background noise' which is inevitably present within all therapeutic encounters but it is assumed not to bear any real relationship to the central therapeutic task.

In a recent systematic review of research on religion in four major psychiatric journals from 1991 to 1995. (Weaver *et al.* 1998), the researchers discovered that only 1.2 per cent of the 2766 quantitative articles reviewed contained a religious/spiritual variable. This figure is about half that found in the same four journals of psychiatry over the period between 1978 and 1982 (2.5 per cent) (Larson *et al.* 1986). Andrew Sims (1994) makes a similar observation, noting that the *British Journal of Psychiatry* published *no* articles with a central focus on spirituality and religion between 1988 and 1992. The reasons for such wariness and scepticism within psychiatry are diverse and complex.

The impact of psychoanalysis and other therapeutic theories

Historically, the assumed association between religion and psychopathology has not always been a positive one. In a 'post-Freudian' culture there remains a deep suspicion amongst many psychiatrists and psychotherapists about the potential that religion and spirituality have for damage and increased disturbance. As Crossley (1995, p.285) points out,

> Ignorance among psychiatrists concerning behavioral and attitudinal aspects of religious belief is a recognized educational issue within the Royal College of Psychiatrists. Furthermore, theoretical opposition to metaphysical beliefs has been both influential and orthodox in the development of psychoanalytic and in some cognitive therapies. The risks of a prejudicial analysis of religious phenomena – for example by failing to distinguish psychopathological forms from their religious content – are therefore potentially high.

Religion has always had its staunch supporters (Bergin 1980; Jung 1933; Koenig, 1997; Larson *et al.* 1997; Maslow 1968, 1985). However, as Larson *et al.* (1997) point out, others have been more critical. Religion has been referred to as a universal obsessional neurosis (Freud 1959), distorted and irrational thinking (D. Ellis 1980), a regression (Group for Advancement of Psychiatry 1976), a psychotic episode (Horton 1974), and even temporal lobe dysfunction (Mandel 1980)! Irrespective of the truth (or otherwise) of such claims, taken together they have injected a degree of scepticism and wariness amongst psychiatrists regarding the role of spirituality for mental health care.

The under-representation of spiritually aware psychiatrists

Religiously inclined professionals are underrepresented in psychiatry (Crossley 1995). Neeleman and Persaud (1995) discovered that somewhere in the region of 67 per cent of British psychiatrists do not believe in God. Bergin and Jensen (1990) in a national survey found that a similarly high proportion of American psychiatrists had little or no spiritual affiliation. They asked members of the public to respond to the statement, 'My whole approach to life is based on my religion'; 72 per cent agreed with the statement. However, when psychiatrists and psychologists were asked to respond to the same statement, 39 per cent and 33 per cent, respectively, agreed. This indicates a lower rate of spiritual interest amongst these groups than among the general public. Other studies have shown a similar lack of interest in the spiritual dimension amongst psychiatrists (Neeleman and King 1993; Neeleman and Persaud 1995; Toone et al. 1979).

Professional pride and research credibility

There is evidence that psychiatry can be prejudiced against spirituality, owing to assumptions that it is not an area which is deemed credible in terms of research. King refers to this phenomenon as the 'repression' of religion in psychiatric practice:

> While general psychiatrists look the other way at the mention of religion, their academic colleagues take flight. Researchers who try to address the issue risk being branded as fanatically religious or as purveyors of soft science in which each variable correlates in some vague way with every other… Young researchers avoid the area for fear of negative repercussions on their career advancement. (King and Dein 1998, p.1260; Sherrill and Larson 1994, pp.149–177)

American psychiatrists have described this phenomenon as the 'anti-tenure factor' of religious research.

Spirituality and nursing

This bias is not only confined to psychiatrists. Fry (1998, p.28) writing from the perspective of nursing points out, that:

> The attitude prevails among mental health professionals that religion and spirituality are generally marginal issues bordering on the psychotic or, at least, 'misguided normal' and should be ignored in order to focus on reality based issues.

Even when care appears to be fulfilling current mandatory objectives of holism and person-centredness (DOH 1993b), a deeper investigation reveals that ideas of holism and holistic care become fragmented when it comes to the actual practice of nursing. Holistic care, which includes spirituality as a basic component, is often acknowledged as of significance to the caring process (DOH 1993b and c). However, in practice it is frequently omitted from the caring equation, with carers tending to focus primarily on the body and the mind to the exclusion of the spirit. Instead of holistic care, what tends to be practised is a fragmented or incomplete holism that omits the spiritual dimension (Oldnall 1996). Commenting on the omission of spirituality from nursing theories and models, Oldnall (1995, p.141) states that:

> On reflection, if the human being consists of four essential domains (i.e. biological, psychological, sociological and spiritual) instead of the usually acknowledged three (i.e. biopsychosocial), then practitioners, guided by the academics, have been operating under the delusion that they have been delivering truly holistic care when in reality the spiritual domain is generally ignored.

Oldnall goes on to suggest that there is a serious educational gap in both the initial and post-registration education of nurses. This fragmentation in nurses' understanding of holistic care has serious implications for the practice of nursing. If the spiritual dimension is omitted,

> then it is arguable whether or not practitioners are correctly assessing, planning, implementing and evaluating the individual's care correctly. What may be diagnosed as anxiety by the practitioner may in fact arise from spiritual distress, and although care may be given, from a psychological perspective that may be totally inappropriate to that individual if it does not address his/her spiritual needs at that time. Thus, the patient may be made to fit into an easily defined category imposed by the educationalists and theorists, and reinforced by the practitioners, owing to lack of guidance and

education in determining and meeting the spiritual needs of patients. (Oldnall 1995, p.417)

Taylor, Amenta and Highfield (1995) suggest some reasons for this failure within nursing:

Narrow conceptions of spirituality

Spirituality is frequently assumed to be a specifically religious concept. When this happens, it is presumed that spiritual care is something which falls primarily within the remit of 'religious professionals' such as chaplains, ministers or other religious agents. There is some evidence that when this happens, nurses assume that spirituality does not lie within the domain of nursing (Carson 1989).

Fear of incompetence

Nurses are aware that patients have spiritual needs but they are unable to give spiritual care because their education does not adequately prepare them to provide it. Granstrom (1995) suggests that such fear of incompetence, coupled with uneasiness with the circumstances which bring spiritual needs to the surface, is a significant underlying factor in the development of negative attitudes towards spirituality and a major barrier to the carrying-out of effective spiritual care.

Uncertainty regarding personal spiritual and religious beliefs and values

Nurses are frequently unaware of their own spirituality and spiritual needs. Consequently they are often unprepared to recognize and care for the spiritual needs of others. It is very difficult to give what one does not have oneself. It has been suggested that health carers need to clarify what they believe to be important and what brings meaning to their lives before they can effectively enable others to do the same (Harrington 1995).

Lack of time and low nurse/patient staffing ratios

Lack of time, a focus on physical needs and low nurse/patient ratios also interfere with the provision of spiritual care (Boutell and Bozett 1987; Highfield 1992; Piles 1990; Sodestrom and Martinson 1987). Spiritual care can be time-consuming and stands in sharp contrast to the spirit of activism that tends to guide a good deal of health care practices. As such it is not deemed to be cost efficient or open to the types of time management and constraints that mark contemporary mental health practices.

To this list of barriers to spiritual/holistic care, we might add three more:

Fear of imposing personal beliefs on the client

Some carers avoid spiritual issues for fear of imposing their own views on a person, and/or intruding on their privacy (Pullen, Tuck and Mix 1996). They therefore steer clear of questions that might lead to them negatively influencing those whom they seek to offer care to.

Fear of intruding on a patient's privacy

Spiritual issues are avoided for fear of intruding on the patient's privacy. This inhibition provides an interesting contrast 'with intrusions into matters like client's elimination, menstrual and sexual habits that are allowable because they fall comfortably within the biomedical model' (Harrington 1995, p.11).

Problems of patient assessment

Mental health carers may diagnose their client's difficulties as *nothing but* psychological distress, without considering the possibility that what they are experiencing may have a spiritual dimension. As a result, the strategies which are implemented and the models of care utilized will be determined by the psychological or biomedical paradigms with no necessary reference to the spiritual. In other words, spiritual needs are drawn within the psychological model that the carer has been trained to recognize and feels most comfortable in using.

All of these factors and more combine to exclude the spiritual dimension from the process of nursing.

Education and professional prejudice

In education, the area of spirituality is not one that ranks highly on the curricula of any of the mental health disciplines. Some colleges and universities may put on courses or occasional classes for students, but few give the area of spiritual care a high profile. This omission is significant. It was noted above that one of the reasons why psychiatrists tend not to conduct research into spirituality and mental health is the lack of professional credibility that surrounds this area. Oldnall (1996) notes a similar strain of professional prejudice within nursing. Commenting on the general lack of education given to nurses on the spiritual dimensions of care he suggests:

> Nurses do not receive adequate education about the fourth domain of holistic care *due to the narrow outlook imposed on them by the nurse theorists, educationalists and society...* Educationalists may feel *embarrassed* to acknowledge such a phenomenon that cannot be quantified easily, and feel that they are possibly betraying the profession's quest to be classified as an academic discipline. (Oldnall 1996, p.141, italics added)

It appears that within a milieu that has come to associate 'hard science' with 'ultimate therapeutic truth', and the basis of 'good care' with narrow definitions of 'technical excellence', spiritual knowledge has fallen out of favour as a credible professional pursuit. The intangible qualities of spirituality mean that it sits uneasily as a legitimate form of professional and therapeutic knowledge upon which the credibility of the health care professions can be built. Consequently, when it comes to the academic education of health care professionals and the development of research strategies within the professions, spirituality is not treated as a significant aspect that should be included in the therapeutic portfolio of the mental health professionals. Bearing in mind the weight of evidence that would suggest a positive correlation between spirituality and health, this is an unusual situation. In order to understand the dynamics of the present situation, it is necessary to spend some time reflecting on the cultural milieu within which the mental health professions currently function.

As one explores the literature surrounding the area of mental health care, one is immediately struck by the current emphasis across the disciplines on 'evidence-based practice' (DOH 1972, 1991, 1993a, 1996, 1997, 1998). Evidence-based practice has been described as: 'the conscientious, explicit and judicious use of current best evidence when making decisions about individual patients' (Muir Gray 1997). Evidence-based practice is of course an important development for all of the health care professions. It is quite correct that in order to try to avoid unsubstantiated forms of practice based on outmoded tradition or blind pragmatism, it is necessary and therapeutically vital that mental health care practitioners strive to base their theory and practice on appropriate and well-researched evidence. The question is: *what actually constitutes acceptable evidence, who decides, and why?* On the whole it seems to be evidence which is deemed scientifically credible according to quite specific standards and criteria that are most attractive to the health professions. At first glance, such assumptions appear sensible and reasonably straightforward. However, on a deeper reflection they are found to be highly problematic.

Positivism, Empiricism and the Power of the Medical Model

One of the main difficulties with trying to find spirituality a valid and valued place within current caring practices is that it doesn't really fit the mould that has been carved out by Western culture's deep affiliation with positivism and the scientific model. The scientific/rationalist paradigm has exerted a powerful influence on the development of Western culture, and has been deeply influential in the development of health care practices since the time of the Enlightenment (Capra 1983; McSherry and Draper 1998). Its twin assumptions of positivism and a narrowly defined empiricism form a powerful worldview within which the spiritual dimensions of existence are frequently excluded. Within the mental health professions and the body of research that underpin and support them, there is a tendency to assume that hard science and the scientific method provide the most legitimate and useful forms of evidence upon which practices should be based (compare, e.g., Gournay 1996). So-called 'soft' forms of knowledge such as spirituality may have their place, but they are only allowed to eat at the table after the hard sciences have finished their meal.

Positivism

Underpinning this approach are the philosophical assumptions of *positivism*. Positivism limits knowledge to observable facts and their interrelations. This view is associated with classical (or naive) realism, in that it assumes that there is a world outside the observer that can be objectively explored using particular research techniques and methods. In other words, if you cannot see it or sense it, it cannot exist in any kind of meaningful sense. It assumes that there is a direct, unadulterated correlation between the concepts, thoughts and perceptions of the observer and the reality of what is observed in the world. Assuming a position of objectivity is maintained by the observer, it is possible to stand back from the world and observe it 'as it is'.

Thus, positivists believe that it is possible for scientists to be objective, value-free observers and that through empirical observation the verification of scientific facts and theories will provide a complete understanding of reality. (Richards and Bergin 1997, p.26)

In this way the world can be understood and eventually mastered through the increase in human knowledge and the effective utilization of the scientific method.

Empiricism

Closely linked to the perspective of positivism is *empiricism*. Empiricism refers to the epistemological belief that sense experiences such as touch, smell and taste provide us with reliable and accurate knowledge about the world. Empiricism in its narrow sense, assumes that 'knowledge has its source and derives all its content from experience. Nothing is regarded as true save what is given by sense experience or by inductive reasoning from sense experience' (Honer and Hunt 1987, p. 220). Empirical research in its wider sense is of course not a bad thing. An empirical explanation seeks to ground itself in and explain things from the perspective of the observable, experiential world. Such an approach makes perfect sense as *one* way of gaining useful and verifiable knowledge. However, when disciplines assume that this is the *only* way in which truth and knowledge can be gained, that is when they become *empiricistic*, problems arise. An empiricistic view assumes that:

> Its reading of the observable corresponds to an independent reality of which the assumptions of modernism are accurate descriptions... Empiricistic denotes reliance on necessity and simple causality in scientific explanation. (Williams and Faulconer 1994, p.336)

When an empirical approach assumes that it can discern a direct, uninterpreted relationship between what is seen and what is recorded, and that there is no other reality apart from its own that can be accessed via its own methodologies and understandings, it becomes empiricistic. The twin perspectives of positivism and an empiricistic form of empiricism lie at the heart of the scientific method, which claims to provide a way of obtaining knowledge that is objective and value-free. The objectivity of scientific theories means that they are verifiable and as such, legitimate sources of truth. Science, in this view, is considered to be the primary, and often the only valid source of knowledge and truth, with the scientific method viewed as the primary conduit through which such knowledge can be accessed.

Within the worldview that springs from these assumptions, spirituality, if it is considered at all, is viewed as a weak, or 'soft' form of knowledge, which cannot be tested or objectively verified. As such, it is often relegated from the public arena of verifiable facts, to the realm of 'private values' that individuals can pick and choose at their leisure, but which do not directly impinge upon professional practices.

This positivistic attitude (i.e. a view within which positivism appropriates to itself an exclusive claim on truth) is reflected within the mental health research literature where, as Swinton and Kettles (1997, p.118) have observed,

> Relatively few researchers, focus on the unpredictability and unquantifiable aspects of the person and how their *experience* of illness might affect the outcome of that illness. In general, a good deal of contemporary thinking and theorizing within mental health research and practice tends to find its primary focus in the diagnostic complexities of *illness* rather than the ways in which a person suffering from an illness might experience it, and the impact that experience might have on the illness process.

The medical model

The emergence of the medical model as a powerful ideology is a direct response to the worldview created by the assumptions underlying positivism and empiricism. Within this model the focus falls on overcoming disease through the development and utilization of universally applicable diagnostic criteria and specialized technical interventions. It draws on empirical research that is designed to develop *universal* methods and treatments that will deal with the symptoms of the *typical* illness within the *average* patient. Empirical/scientific knowledge is considered to be objective, value-free, and therefore a legitimate form of *public* truth (Newbigin 1989). Within such a framework, as has been noted, spirituality and spiritual knowledge are dismissed from the realm of public knowledge that is considered to have relevance for *all* human beings, to the realm of 'private values', which *may* be of use to *some* people but which bears no direct relevance to the therapeutic process. The focus here is on disease, with the primary emphasis falling on identifying and solving particular problems and developing cures for specific diseases. Within this worldview there is no necessity for health carers to consider spiritual issues such as love, hope, meaning, transformation and growth. The person's pathology takes centre stage with specialized techniques, therapies and pharmacological interventions assumed to be the primary conduits through which health can be attained and maintained.

The psychiatric medical model

When applied more specifically to the realm of mental health, the medical model takes on similar dimensions. Here the assumption is that mental health problems are like diseases which primarily require accurate diagnosis and treatment carried out using 'published standardized diagnostic categories agreed on by the medical community' (Hall 1996). It is assumed that mental health problems have specific causes which, when identified, can be dealt with through the use of particular psychological, physical or pharmacological techniques and interventions. It is taken for granted that, to a greater or lesser extent, all people who fall within a particular diagnostic category will have similar experiences and will respond in a similar manner to treatment interventions. The underlying assumption is that 'for each diagnostic category, there is now, or will be in the future, an associated medical cure' (Hall 1996). Diagnosis therefore dictates understanding, treatment and research aimed at developing and testing treatment. Although 'causality in psychopathology is often assumed to be substantially more complex and much more difficult to discover, seldom do mental health carers question the assumption that psychological causality is at least analogous to medical causality' (Williams and Faulconer 1994, p.336).

Losing the soul: the rise of techno-medicine

The danger for mental health carers who uncritically place their faith in this perspective is that they develop a mindset not dissimilar to what Thomas Moore (1992, p.206) has described as *psychological modernism*: an uncritical acceptance of the values and understandings which make up the worldview of the modern world. Such a view restricts the parameters within which decisions are made, situations are assessed and understood and persons are treated to the idea that the practice of mental health care can progress towards freedom from psychiatric distress through the increase in human knowledge using positivistic methodologies, standardization and statistical quantifiability as the primary sources of legitimization underlying the development of identity and professional credibility. In this modernist syndrome there is no room for those less quantifiable aspects of care such as the quest for hope, the search for meaning and the possibility of a loving relationship with a transcendent God. Instead *technology* rather than *theology* becomes the root metaphor for dealing with psychological problems (Moore 1993).

Wig (1995, in Nolan and Crawford 1997) describes such an approach to health and illness as *techno-medicine*: 'In techno-medicine, the questions related to the moral and spiritual side of the individual are considered merely as frills of culture and have no place in an economically driven scientific regime.' Within such a context, the deeper existential questions which seek to explore the nature of human being and human living are not even on the agenda.

> The dominance of techno-medicine has resulted in a redefinition of the issues which once preoccupied philosophers: What is human nature? How is happiness achieved? What is a good life? These questions have been restated as: What is normal? How can it be measured? What conclusions are generalizable? (Wig 1995, p.291)

Significant as the second set of questions may well be within the overall process of mental health care, the reality of human experience would suggest that authentic and meaningful living demands that the first set of questions be given equal and perhaps, at times, greater priority. The complexity and uniqueness of human existence cannot be captured by statistical norms and universal generalities. Human beings exist in a meaningful, relational world that is filled with a richness which transcends the limits of human language and stretches beyond the boundaries of narrow scientific explanation. The approach of techno-medicine may be useful in *explaining* certain aspects of mental health and illness, and in developing techniques and forms of intervention that bring significant relief to people who are deeply wounded. However, its tendency towards materialism, reductionism and a mechanistic view of persons means that it is lacking in significant ways. It is *materialist* in that it presumes that matter is the fundamental reality in the world, and whatever else exists is dependent upon matter. Such a view necessarily downgrades and often excludes immaterial aspects such as the human spirit, aspects which may in fact be of fundamental importance to the therapeutic process. It therefore takes no meaningful cognizance of the rich wealth of religious and spiritual experience which has been and continues to be a vital and continuing aspect of all human cultures. This is a serious omission. As Turner *et al.* (1995, p.435) correctly point out, the 'religious and spiritual dimensions of culture are among the most important factors that structure human experience, beliefs, values, behaviour, and illness patterns.' If this is so, then to omit this dimension from one's conceptualization of mental health and ill-health is to overlook a vital aspect of the experience of people with mental health problems.

The techno-medical approach is also deeply *reductionistic* and *mechanistic*. It is reductionistic in that it assumes that mental health problems can be understood and dealt with by focusing on a single aspect of the person, be it their genetics, their psyche or whatever. It assumes that

> diagnosis can be arrived at from a simple and narrow understanding of patients' lives. In determining a diagnosis, it is only necessary to take into account the symptoms listed for that disease. Surrounding elements of culture, social status, or personal, and familial beliefs about illness are not part of the algorithm. (Hall 1996, p.17)

Such an approach tends to reduce the person to their *disease*, focusing on issues of cure and control rather than on exploring ways of restoring *wholeness*. The person is compartmentalized, with their illness viewed in isolation from other aspects of their life experience, the assumption being that it can be understood and treated without any necessary reference to the person as a whole.

> The result is a contrived and sanctioned dehumanization of the person during the diagnostic process. Prognosis arises from diagnostic categories that do not take into account personal differences and contextual factors, forcing competing social, economic, [spiritual] and cultural factors that might be considered as foreground to recede into a very obscure background. (Hall 1996, p.17)

Here one finds an image of the human person as a machine that malfunctions or is badly made. In order to fix it, the problem needs to be located and the particular malfunctioning part repaired in order that the machine can function effectively again. The context of the person or their particular belief structures are not deemed important to the process of care.

While the treatment of pathological conditions is obviously important, the problems with the approach of the medical model is that in its quest for universally applicable forms of *cure, control* and *explanation*, it overlooks the positive aspects and strengths of individuals, and what their illness *means* to them. Issues of meaning and value are not secondary to the therapeutic process. Rather they are central to coping with and recovering from mental health problems. Taken on its own, the approach of the medical model tells us nothing about the meaning of mental health and illness, and the significance of the hopes, expectations and personal experience of those who experience them. It assumes such things to be of little relevance to the *real* task of eradicating pathology. It takes little cognizance of the fundamental and crucial fact that mental health problems do not exist apart from the unique individuals who experience them, unique individuals whose life experience can have a profound influence on the shape, form, trajectory and progress of their illness.

From fragmentation to wholeness

To ignore issues of spirituality and side-step questions of meaning, purpose happiness and what it means to be human, is to risk developing understandings and forms of practice that ignore the essence of what it means to be human and to live humanly. The view of the universe presented by the view of techno-medicine is only *one* way of looking at the world, albeit a culturally powerful one. As William James (1936, in Richards and Bergin 1997, p.21) astutely observes,

> Many worlds of consciousness exist...which have a meaning for our life...the total expression of human experience...invincibly urges me beyond the narrow 'scientific' bounds. Assuredly, the real world is of different temperament – more intricately built than physical science allows.

James's words offer a powerful reminder of the tremendous breadth and depth of human experience. Statistics, averages and universal norms may be useful for certain purposes, but they cannot capture the intricacies and richness of the experience of being human. Reflection on what it means to live as a human being draws us beyond the confines of empiricism and a mechanical view of persons, towards an understanding of human existence that is multifaceted, mysterious and frequently deeply spiritual. People live their lives in a constant process of exploration, mystery and wonder, within which issues of love, hope, meaning and transcendence are of fundamental importance. Issues of spirituality may not be on the agenda of many mental health carers. However, they are often central to the lived experience of people with mental health problems. If we are going to offer mental health care that respects the fullness of human experience, then it will be necessary to expand the scientific worldview to include forms of evidence that may be different from that which we assume to be the scientific norm. We need to consider the possibility of developing what Abraham Maslow (1985) has neatly defined as an 'expanded science'; a form of science which does not insist on a single reading of reality and takes seriously issues of value, hope, meaning and the unpredictable nature of lived experience. This will involve realigning our thinking and caring practices to the possibility of wholeness as well as brokenness. It will mean opening our perspectives to include the experience of clients and allowing their experiences, expectations, hopes and desires to guide professional practice. It will mean recognizing that part of the task of mental health care has to do with exploring those dimensions that are hidden from the scientific gaze of contemporary mental health care practitioners, but yet which contain the very meaning of life.

Spiritual Healing: A New Role for Mental Health Carers

This is not to suggest that we reject science or the positive benefits that have been gained through the use of the medical model's approach to mental health care. The purpose of this book is not to develop an alternative model of mental health care, but rather to develop a complementary understanding of care that will help overcome some to the inadequacies within current caring practices. The argument here is that current caring practices need to be supplemented by other perspectives which take seriously issues of *meaning*, *care* and *understanding* alongside the current emphasis on *explanation* and the quest for *cure*. A focus on spirituality provides precisely that dimension. In practice this will mean mental health carers learning what it means to seek to bring *healing* to people with mental health problems as well as the possibility of cure and control of symptoms. This is an important point and a significant conceptual distinction. In closing this chapter it will be helpful to spend some time exploring the difference between 'healing' and 'curing' before beginning to engage more directly with issues of spirituality and mental health. If spirituality is to be given a significant place within contemporary mental health care practices, it is important that carers understand and learn to work constructively with the critical tension between the two concepts of 'cure' and 'healing'.

Mental health care as spiritual healing

When the word 'heal' is used, it is frequently associated with the idea of 'cure', that is, with the eradication of disease or distress. Within medical circles, the word 'heal' infers ideas of recovery or remission from particular forms of physical or psychological distress and trauma. In the sphere of religion and spirituality, the idea of healing often has similar curative assumptions, being associated with, for example, the healing miracles of Jesus, the miraculous signs and wonders of the Charismatic movement, or

New Age innovations that utilize crystals, energy fields and so forth to rebalance inner energies and forces in an attempt to bring about health, understood in terms of an equilibrium of energetic forces. The assumption is that healing refers to the freeing of individuals from their particular problems. To be a healer is to have the power to liberate persons from disease and distress.

The influence of the medical model with its assumptions of cause and effect, specific etiology, diagnosis and appropriate treatment of the 'bad spot' is apparent in such understandings of healing. This understanding leads to a very particular understanding of mental health: *the absence of mental illness*. Trent (1999, p.19) notes that

> while most people no longer define mental health *as* the absence of mental illness, it continues to frequently be defined by the absence of illness. The assumption is that if people are not ill, they must *by default*, be healthy. Therefore the less ill they are, the healthier they are.

There is of course an apparent 'natural logic' to such a position. Few would argue that mental health problems are desirable things for people to have. Strategies and understandings that seek to cure mental health problems are obviously valid, and should be encouraged. However, the reality for a significant number of people is that certain forms of mental illness are interminable, i.e. the person will never be completely free of them. This being so, those experiencing interminable forms of mental health problems (those that will not ever be rid of their ailment), will, according to this understanding, always be mentally unhealthy (Swinton 2000a and b). The only question is the degree of their unhealthiness. Mental health care strategies based on this understanding will find their primary focus on controlling the worst manifestations of the person's illness, without any necessary reference to or concentration on that which might in fact be indicative of mental health. Viewed from this perspective, healing will reflect similar ideological assumptions, finding its primary focus on ridding the person of whatever ailment they may be experiencing.

Healing as a quest for meaning and value

However, an understanding of healing and the healing task based on the assumptions of the medical model is only one way in which the concept of healing can be interpreted. While it *may* involve a movement towards cure, this is not the primary task of healing or healers. If we change the frame slightly, it is possible to develop a different understanding of what healing is and what the priorities of the healer are. In order to clarify what is being said here, it will be useful to draw on some insights from the field of medical anthropology. Medical anthropologists make a distinction between the concepts of *disease, illness, cure* and *healing*. In common parlance we tend to merge these concepts, assuming that the dyads of healing–cure and illness–disease are synonymous. However, within medical anthropology, these concepts are separated into four discrete categories, indicating four different aspects of a person's condition. When this is done, the meaning of healing is transformed.

Disease

From the perspective of medical anthropology, diseases are organic, viral, or some other physical basis of a condition (Kleinman 1988, p.3). Cancer, influenza, and measles would constitute diseases and disease processes, as would neurological, genetic or biological factors relating to mental health problems. Current explorations into the biological basis of mental health problems assume a disease model as an explanatory framework within which an understanding of mental health problems can be developed.

Illness

A person's illness is the social aspect or social consequences of disease processes. Illness pertains to:

> the human perception, experience, and interpretation of certain socially disvalued states including but not limited to disease. Illness is both a personal and a social reality and therefore in large part a cultural construct. Culture dictates what to perceive, value, and express, and then how to live with illness. (Pilch 2000, p.25)

Diseases are always experienced within some sort of context. That context, to a greater or lesser extent, shapes the response of the individual, their family and the wider society to the person's experience. The interaction between the person's psychological condition and their social context forms the illness experience of a person with mental health problems. Thus, for example, such things as stigma, rejection and alienation which are not directly caused by biological deficiency or damage are central to the illness experience of people with conditions such as schizophrenia and bipolar disorder (Swinton 2000b).

Curing

Curing has to do with the eradication of disease processes. It is the 'anticipated outcome relative to *disease*, that is, the attempt to take effective control of disordered biological and/or psychological processes' (Pilch 2000, p.25). The search for cure and the eradication of disease forms a significant aspect of many people's understanding of mental health, mental health care and what the priorities of the research agenda should be.

Healing

If we accept these distinctions, we are led to a particular understanding of healing. Healing directs itself towards illness and attempts to 'provide personal and social meaning for the life problems created by the illness' (Pilch 2000, p.25). Healing is much more than simply ridding a person of particular difficulties. Healing relates to that aspect of care which attends to the deep inner structures of meaning, value and purpose that form the infrastructure to all human experience, irrespective of the presence or absence of distress and illness. Healing is a deeply spiritual task that stretches beyond the boundaries of disease and cure and into the realms of transcendence, purpose, hope and meaning that form the very fabric of human experience and desire. The aims and objectives of healers are to enable a person to find enough meaning in their present struggles to sustain them even in the midst of the most unimaginable storms. The quest for cure of course continues, but the process of enabling healing is a vital and immediate aspect of the daily task of caring.

The problem with approaches that focus primarily on biology, genetics and chemistry, is that while they may be effective in *curing* and *controlling* mental health problems, they do not necessarily bring *healing*. Healing does not come simply through 'fixing' abnormal biological processes. Healing relates to a person's continuing life journey within which they seek ways of being enabled to find enough meaning to allow them to maintain their sense of self, purpose, transcendence and direction even in the midst of severe difficulties. Psychological technologies such as pharmacology and therapy have a useful role to play within this process, in terms of helping to alleviate suffering, raising a person's mood, or assisting to change unhelpful ways of thinking and working through experiences that may be distressing or unwanted. However, on their own, they cannot bring about healing. This becomes particularly apparent when a person discovers that their mental health problem is not going to go away, and that their lives may well never be quite the way they hoped. David Karp (1996) in his research into the experience of depression discovered that when people came to accept the fact that they were going to have to live with depression in some form for the rest of their lives, their personal quest moved from searching for cures, to exploring new, specifically spiritual possibilities.

> Despite their physicians' best efforts, most of those I have talked with come to realize that their therapists will not clear away their confusions about depression. In a more fundamentally existential way, many conclude that their depression is likely never to be fixed once and for all. Such a consciousness, in turn, requires a shift in thinking about coping with depression. The new thinking is typically less mechanistic and more spiritual in nature. As the reality of pain's permanence sinks in, the good shifts from dedicating depression to living with it. (Karp 1996, p. 123)

For people in this situation, the hope of cure may be distant and perhaps unattainable. However, the possibility of healing remains despite the continuing presence of depression. A similar movement from cure to healing has been noted within the context of other forms of enduring forms of mental health problems (Barham and Hayward 1995; Kirkpatrick *et al.* 1995; Swinton 2000b).

In order to be mentally healthy a person does not need to be freed from their particular mental health problem (although there remains the hope and the desire that this may happen). In order to develop mental health they must be able to find enough meaning in their life to carry them through their trials and their joys and retain their humanity in the midst of both. It is the meaning and purpose that a person has discovered within their life which gives them the strength to find meaning and purpose within their sufferings. If this is so, then mental *health* care will have as much to do with providing a relational and spiritual context that will enable a person to live with their problems and find meaning and hope in the midst of them, as it will have with overcoming difficulties and curing illnesses. Healing understood in this way is intricately connected with spirituality and the spiritual quest.

Health within Illness?

In terms of understanding mental health and ill-health, we might draw on Trent's (1999) suggestion that we conceptualize mental health in terms of two continua, one a mental health continuum and the other a mental disorder continuum. The mental disorder–curing continuum focuses on pathology and explores where the person is in terms of the severity of their illness. This continuum runs from maximum mental disorder at one extreme, to minimum mental disorder at the other. It is along this continuum that the medical model works itself out and establishes a legitimate role within the process of mental health care. This continuum is of course an important *aspect* of mental health. It is not however the whole of mental health. The second continuum is the mental health continuum. This runs from minimum mental health through to optimum mental health. Along this continuum *healing* provides the central locus of concern. Here the focus is on issues of personhood, relationships, spirituality, meaning and so forth, that is, those aspects of the experience of being human that are omitted from the medical gaze. As I have written elsewhere (Swinton 2000a), rather than mental health being judged according to the level of a person's illness, it can now be understood in terms of growth and personhood, which, whilst obviously affected by the person's illness experience, is not necessarily defined by it. In this way it is possible to define mental health in terms of the whole person, rather than simply as one aspect of them or their experience. Mental health care can thus be viewed in terms of persons being provided with adequate resources to enable them to grow as unique individuals and to live their lives humanly as persons-in-relationship. The aspects of spirituality outlined in Chapter 1 provide vital resources for this process of healing. As such, mental health inevitably incorporates such spiritual aspects as relationships, growth, meaning, hope, love and so forth. As one reflects on this, it becomes

Range of diagnosis from
severe to mild

| Maximal mental disorder/illness | _____ | Minimal mental disorder/illness |

| Minimal mental health | _____ | Optimal mental health |

including, for example

subjective distress
impaired or
underdevelopment of
abilities

subjective well-being
optimal development

Figure 2.1. The two continua of mental health and mental illness (Tudor 1996)

clear that a person's spirituality, far from being epiphenomenal to issues of mental health and disorder, is in fact intricately bound into the nature and development of mental health.

By holding Trent's two continua in critical tension, it is possible to develop a holistic understanding of mental health that includes, but is not defined by the absence of illness. In terms of the practice of mental health care, this understanding has significant implications. For example, a person with a chronic mental health problem may have few signs of pathology at certain times, yet be mentally unhealthy in that their relationships are fragmented, their sense of the transcendent is lost, and their self-esteem and confidence are undermined by the stigma of their illness. Likewise, a person may suffer from the long-term effects of mental health problems, and remain relatively mentally healthy along the health continuum, in that they may have stable relationships, strong sources of value, purpose and spiritual foundations that override the limitations of their illness experiences. This revised understanding of mental health allows for fresh possibilities in terms of healing and spiritual development.

Changing paradigms

The task then for mental health carers is to develop a new role as *spiritual healers*. Such a role will involve the development of modes of being and methods of care that can inject meaning, hope, value and a sense of transcendence into the lives of people with mental health problems even in the midst of conditions that frequently seem to strip them of even the possibility of such things. Becoming spiritual healers will demand the development, not only of new skills, but more importantly of new ways of seeing the world and being in it. It will require looking beyond the cultural, historical and professional boundaries and worldview that prevent us from seeing human beings in all of their fullness. It will involve developing an attitude of humility and openness to the possibility that the ways in which we have seen things in the past may not be the only way in which they can be viewed. It will involve opening ourselves to the possibility of a new spiritual paradigm that sits alongside, yet challenges, the scientific paradigm that has been so influential in shaping the ways in which we see the world. Becoming spiritual healers will require us to participate in a *paradigm shift* in understanding that moves carers beyond the confines of a narrowly scientific worldview towards an expanded scientific position. Such a position will allow scope to explore the issues and dimensions of the human person that have been highlighted thus far, and in so doing, may alter at least some aspects of the way in which we see the world and the caring practices we choose to utilize to offer hope and new possibilities to people with mental health problems.

Paradigms

The idea of paradigms and paradigm shifts is important and needs some clarification. At its simplest a paradigm is a framework of ideas through which people view and come to understand the world. A paradigm contains the thoughts, concepts, methodologies and assumptions that form the worldview of individuals and cultures and determine the boundaries of reality and plausibility at particular moments in history (Kuhn 1970; Newbigin 1989). It is a set of beliefs that acts as a model for one's sense of reality. Consequently a paradigm will ultimately shape the thought and actions of those who accept its reality. It has been suggested that the particular paradigm that has greatly impacted upon the research and practice of mental health care professionals draws its root concepts from a narrowly scientific view of the world represented paradigmatically in the development of the medical model.

Paradigm shifts

Paradigm shifts involve a significant change in worldview in response to new data that suggests a different way of viewing a particular phenomenon. As evidence for an alternative way of viewing the world or an aspect of the world emerges, and as more people begin to adhere to this new perspective, so a movement begins, from one way of viewing the world to another which is sometimes radically different. The ideas of the old paradigm are not necessarily discarded, but they are relativized and understood within a different conceptual framework. For example, the shift from Newtonian physics based on the principle of cause and effect to quantum physics with its inherent indeterminism and chaos is a good example of a contemporary paradigm shift within science. Newtonian physics remains valid in certain circumstances, but it no longer fully explains the way the universe functions.

In a sense paradigm shifts are similar to the experience of religious conversion, wherein a person discovers a new understanding of the world and everything in it. This in turn forces them to rethink and restructure the ways in which they see the world in the light of the new knowledge they have acquired. The difference with paradigm shifts is that they not only affect individuals. They also affect and change groups of people such as cultures, professional and scientific communities and so forth.

There is of course always resistance to an emerging paradigm. Some will want to cling onto the old paradigm and the way in which reality has been perceived previously. Periods of paradigm shift can therefore be very tense and filled with conflict as some accept the discoveries of the new paradigm, whilst others remain sceptical. Paradigms take a long time to establish themselves and demand that certain individuals take a 'leap of faith' and move from one paradigm to the other irrespective of the ridicule and lack of credibility that this might mean in the short term.

A spiritual paradigm?

A number of commentators (Capra 1983; Davie and Cobb 1998; Davie 1994) have suggested that Western culture is currently undergoing a significant paradigm shift. The certainties promised by the Enlightenment's prioritization of human knowledge, reason and technology as the mediators of both truth and 'salvation' have been shaken by the stark fact that the past hundred years has seen more human beings kill other human beings than at any other point in history. Two world wars, the holocaust and the challenge of AIDS to the supremacy of medicine has led to a loss of faith in humanity's own abilities. All of this has contributed to a general dissatisfaction with the types of all-embracing frameworks – science, religion, Marxist materialism – within which human beings sought to explain life, the universe and everything! Western culture is beginning to become more attentive to experience, personal stories and those aspects of experience that cannot be explained by wide narratives that seek to provide a common explanatory framework within which all human beings can make sense of reality.

This shift is moving our understanding of the world from a materialist view based on the assumptions of dualism, rationalism and empiricism, towards an understanding which acknowledges the significance of such things as personal stories, emotions and experiences that cannot be explained purely in the terms of science. The shifting paradigm is moving culture away from self-centred individualism towards a recognition of the fundamental wholeness and interconnectedness of human beings, and indeed of the whole of creation. Fritjof Capra (1998) sums up these emerging changes in Western culture thus:

> [T]he old culture, which was basically the scientific culture of the seventeenth century, of the Enlightenment and Newtonian physics and the

Copernican revolution...this way of seeing the world, in mechanistic terms, in reductionist terms, has come to a close and is now declining. And what is rising is a more holistic or more ecological way of seeing things.

This changing worldview appears much more conducive to accepting the possibility of the reality of a spiritual dimension.

By providing data that challenges the medical paradigm to consider shifting itself into a wider framework which can incorporate spirituality in a way that is therapeutically beneficial and constructively challenging to current practices, the insights provided by this book contribute to this shifting paradigm as it works itself out within the specific area of mental health care.

The suggestion that we should add a spiritual dimension to the research and practice of mental health care does not invalidate the scientific approach or the medical model. Indeed, a good deal of the methodologies that lie behind the research presented in the following chapter fits quite well within the present positivistic paradigm. Introducing the spiritual dimension *does* however challenge and relativize aspects of narrowly conceived scientific approaches, and in so doing, it moves mental health care into another dimension within which new concepts, ideas and assumptions merge creatively with the old to form a new paradigm of care that includes but is not defined by the positivistic paradigm.

Not everyone will accept this as a valid direction for mental health care to move in. There will be inevitable dissonance and criticism from those who feel that the incorporation of this dimension is inappropriate or therapeutically irrelevant. Worldviews do not shift overnight. Nevertheless, those who catch the vision of the new paradigm will be enabled to move on to explore new and exciting dimensions of care that include, but are not defined by, the ways of the old paradigm.

The remainder of this book will seek to present evidence, insights and ways of caring that can contribute to the development of a new paradigm of mental health care that takes seriously the contribution of the scientific paradigm, yet strives creatively to move it on by introducing spiritual insights and perspectives that can help to expand and fully humanize the scientific model in a way that is creative, life-enhancing and conducive to the development of forms of care that are truly spiritual and holistic.

CHAPTER 3

Spirituality and Mental Health Care

Exploring the Literature
(With Alyson Kettles)

Reviewing the Literature

In order to develop a new paradigm of care that includes the spiritual dimension as a significant aspect, it is necessary to lay down a firm empirical (as opposed to empiricistic) foundation that can inform us of the role of spirituality within the process of mental health care. This chapter consists of an overview of some of the literature exploring the area of spirituality and mental health care. In working through this data, it will be possible to highlight some of the pros and cons of spirituality for the process of mental health care, as well as some of the important methodological difficulties that arise as we seek to understand the relationship between spirituality and mental health care. We will begin by examining something of the methodology that lies behind the following review of the literature.

Methodological issues

The *Report of the Taskforce on the Strategy for Research in Nursing, Midwifery and Health Visiting* (DOH 1993c) defines research as 'rigorous and systematic enquiry, conducted on a scale and using methods commensurate with the issue to be investigated and designed to lead to generalizable contribution to knowledge'. The emphasis in research is on systematic inquiry. Similarly, the approach to reviewing the literature in any particular field of research is that of a systematic and thorough inquiry. If a literature review is to work, a number of questions need to be asked of the works under review. For example, is the literature comprehensive, up to date, logical? Does it critically evaluate the literature? Is there a research problem and is that problem important? Are hypotheses, aims and objectives clear and relevant, are ethics considered and is the research design the best for the question under study? An outline of standard review questions is given in Table 3.1.

Table 3.1 Critical review of research

1. **Introduction**
   - Is there a research problem and does it inform you of why this problem is important?
   - Is the research problem concisely and clearly stated? Can it be answered with evidence?

2. **Literature review**
   - Is it comprehensive and up to date?
   - Is it logical?
   - Does it evaluate critically?

3. **Hypotheses**
   - Are there clear hypotheses, aims and/or objectives?
   - Are they relevant?

4. **Research design**
   - Is it the best design for the question?
   - Is the design appropriately/adequately described?
   - Is it valid?
   - Has the Local Research Ethics Committee or the Multi-Centre Research Ethics Committee been consulted for approval or advice? Are there any ethical considerations postulated?

5. **Sample**
   - Size – are there power calculations if they are necessary?
   - How was the sample chosen?
   - Is there any bias to the sample?
   - What demographic characteristics are there?
   - Are inclusion/exclusion criteria applied?

6. **Research methodology**
   - Are the methods used appropriate to the question being asked?
   - How were they developed? Was there a feasibility study?
   - Was there a pilot study? If there was, is there a description of it included?
   - Was the reliability of the method/data collection addressed?
   - How was the data handled?

7. Analysis

- Was the analysis appropriate to the sample and the research design?
- Is it clear, relatively easy to understand and complete?
- Is it comprehensively reported in relation to the methods described?

8. Discussion

- Does the discussion interpret the findings in relation to the methods used?
- Does the discussion relate the findings to research questions/objectives/hypotheses?
- Can the findings be generalized to other populations?
- Are the implications for practice discussed?

9. Conclusions

- Are recommendations clear, concise and do they relate to the findings and/or research aims and objectives?
- What are the recommendations or action plans for clinical practice or clinical management?
- Are recommendations for further research identified or made?

10. References

- Are the references accurate, comprehensive and correctly written?

11. Other items to take into consideration

- Is the title clear and indicative of what was studied?
- Does the abstract clearly restate the research problem/s and restate the important findings?
- Is the overall paper/report – clear? detailed? well written and without jargon? pleasant to read?

Adapted from Roe (1993).

If each piece of work is asked the same sorts of questions, an overall picture will build up. In a rigorous systematic review, criteria for inclusion or exclusion would be laid down and adhered to. For example, all studies that have a sample size above a certain number and are selected through specific sampling procedures would be included and those works which do not meet these criteria would not be included for review.

Reviewing the literature on spirituality and mental health

Spirituality does not readily lend itself to randomized controlled trials, although, as we shall see, some researchers have used this as an approach to explore certain dimensions of spirituality. However, while this method may be popular within current health-care research communities, it may in fact be inappropriate to the specific subject matter of spirituality, which may well demand a much more subjective approach if understanding and effective intervention are to be achieved. The importance of matching tools and validation criterion to the specific object of research is an area of continuing debate amongst those striving to validate both qualitative and quantitative research, and one which will be discussed in more detail in Chapter 4. Limiting such a review to randomized controlled trials in spirituality research would not capture the essence of the body of literature that explores the interface between spirituality and mental health.

Most research into the relationship between spirituality and mental health comes in the form of quasi-experimental designs, qualitative approaches or survey research. This being so, rather than attempting to produce a truly systematic review of the literature, the overview presented here will try to encapsulate the essence of the body of knowledge in a way that can enable the development of practical understanding and clarity of thought. Where possible, rigorous studies, which use quantitative data as their source, will be referred to, as well as those which provide a rich and meaningful qualitative treatise on the subject of spirituality.

The relationship between spirituality and mental health

Literature reviews can be divided into the types of literature being produced in any given field of study. In the field of spirituality related to health care there are particular aspects under study including religious commitment; conceptual analysis; meaning, attitude and belief; hope; measuring and facilitating well-being; religious practices; distress; care; and spiritual interventions and healing related to particular disease conditions such as cancer, HIV/AIDS and mental health. In this chapter the primary focus will be specifically on the relationship between spirituality and mental health, the object being to lay down the beginnings of an empirical foundation that will support the continuing argument of the book.

Spirituality and Mental Health

Systematic reviews of the research literature have consistently reported that aspects of religious and spiritual involvement are associated with desirable mental health outcomes. (Bergin 1988; Dyson *et al.* 1997; Gartner *et al.* 1991; Larson, Swyers and McCullough 1997; Martsolf and Mickley 1998; Mickley *et al.* 1995). Spirituality has been shown to be positively correlated with depression (Karp 1996; Morris 1996), anxiety (Baker and Gorsuch 1982; Gibbs and Achterberg-Lawlis 1978), addictions (Koski-Jaennes and Turner 1999; Miller 1998), suicide prevention (Gartner *et al.* 1991), anorexia (Garrett 1998) and schizophrenia (Chu and Klein 1985). There is therefore evidence to support the suggestion that spirituality is relevant to mental health care practices and that it has the potential to benefit people's experiences of a variety of mental health problems.

However, despite the body of literature that suggests that spirituality can be an important aspect of mental health care and development, there remains a degree of ambiguity surrounding some of the research. This ambiguity is addressed in a widely cited paper by Gartner *et al.* (1991). In their study on the relationship between religion and mental health, they reviewed over 200 studies and searched for patterns depending upon what aspects of mental health were studied and how they were measured. They noted that the 'methodological complexities', which have supposedly contributed to the inconsistencies in pinpointing a relationship between religious commitment and psychopathology, have yet to be ascertained. Despite this, several factors were clearly identified as having a relationship between religious commitment and mental health (e.g. suicide, depression, physical health) or religious commitment and psychopathology (e.g. authoritarianism, suggestibility, dependence). There were also some factors which were ambiguous, such as psychosis and sexual disorders. What does come out of this review is that the research on the relationship between religious commitment and psychopathology has produced mixed findings but the team identified some additional trends, including:

1. Behavioural measures of religious participation are more powerfully associated with mental health than attitudinal measures.

2. Disorders characterized by under-control of impulses are related to low levels of religiosity, whereas high levels of religiosity are most often associated with disorders of over-control.

3. The studies which showed a link between religious commitment and psychopathology tended to employ 'soft variable' measures, that is, personality-type tests which attempt to measure theoretical constructs. Most of the research which links religion to positive mental health uses real-life behavioural events or 'hard variables' which can be reliably observed or measured. In other words, although people may well answer a researcher's questions in an interview situation in a way which suggests a negative correlation between spirituality and mental health, when one examines people's actual life-behaviours and the ways in which they use and relate to spirituality, one tends to find a positive correlation between religion, spirituality and mental health. These authors call for more of an emphasis on *real-life* behaviour, rather than on questionnaire behaviour in research into the psychology of religion.

Despite the ambiguity of some of the findings related to religious commitment and mental health (30 per cent) the other findings are clearly unambiguous (70 per cent) in that there is a relationship which is either with mental health or with psychopathology.

Point 3 above, regarding the observations of Gartner *et al.* on the methodological difficulties of exploring the relationship between religion and mental health, is interesting. It may be that the tests using hard variables reflect the assumptions and biases of the researchers who construct them on the basis of their own ideas of mental health. For example, if a researcher who did not share the belief structures of a fundamentalist Christian was to judge the state of their mental health according to their negative response to such questions as, 'does your religion make you feel you are a good person?' or 'do you feel yourself to be a person worthy of God's love?' they would get a false impression regarding the self-esteem and mental health of the individual and the relationship of their religion to their mental health. In reality, the person may well be extremely mentally healthy and very comfortable within a worldview that emphasizes human sinfulness and the need for salvation. However, tests using hard variables could easily misinterpret their mental state because of the way they expressed their situation in the language of their faith. This being so, it may be that there is in fact a bias against spirituality in studies that link it to negative mental health outcomes.

Well-being

The ability of spirituality to bring about well-being is a significant theme in the literature. Relatedness and connectedness of self to others and to God are part of this theme. Several writers have observed that spiritual well-being enhances inner resources (Burkhardt 1989; Hay 1989; Moberg 1984). Ellison and Levin (1998) present a systematic review of the research conducted using the Spiritual Well-Being Scale, from 1982 to 1990. The 'Spiritual Well-Being Scale' (SWB) is a questionnaire in which participants are asked to answer twenty questions such as whether they find much satisfaction in prayer; whether they feel they know who they are, where they have come from and where they are going; whether they believe God loves and cares for them; whether God is involved in the mundane aspects of their lives; whether they have a personal meaningful relationship with God; whether they believe God is concerned about their problems; whether life has meaning and purpose; whether their relationship with God contributes to their sense of well-being; and so forth.

This tool is well established and has become one of the most widely used instruments for assessing spiritual well-being, 'second only to Allport and Ross's Intrinsic-Extrinsic Religious Orientation Scale in the number of research articles it has generated (Lukoff, Turner and Lu 1993). Nevertheless, there are significant difficulties with it. For example, the questions are rather vague and open to various and differing possible interpretations. There is also no qualitative follow-up that might allow for clarification of understandings and the analysis of the meanings that emerge from responses to the questions. These criticisms do not invalidate this spiritual assessment scale, but they do highlight some significant limitations.

The studies reviewed by Ellison and Levin examined the relationship between spirituality and physical well-being, adjustment to physical illness, health care, psychological well-being, relational well-being as well as a number of religious variables. Amongst their findings was the observation that people who are motivated by an inner guiding force have higher spiritual well-being, and that depression in response to life change is mediated by a person's sense of spiritual well-being. They also found that a state of spiritual well-being was positively related to self-esteem and hope, and inversely related to stress, aggressiveness and conflict avoidance. Spiritual well-being was also:

> positively correlated with general assertiveness, self-confidence, initiating assertiveness, giving of praise, and asking for help, whereas it has been

negatively correlated with physical and passive forms of aggression, dependency, and orientation towards passivity or avoidance of conflict. (Ellison and Levin 1998, p.38)

There is thus seen to be a good deal of evidence to suggest a positive correlation between spirituality and well-being in a variety of different contexts.

Spiritual and Social Support

The elements of social support and cognitive realignment form a common theme within the literature exploring spirituality and mental health. The research of Brown, Prudo and Harris (1981) into depression amongst women living on the island of Harris showed that women with some sort of religious connection (assessed by their level of church attendance) were considerably less likely to become depressed than women without a church connection. One of the main reasons they put forward to account for this was that crofting and churchgoing were external indicators of the state of the women's integration within the community. The less integrated a woman was, the higher the chances were of her becoming depressed. The religious community therefore acted as a protective agent, buffering these women against the isolation and hopelessness which often bears the fruit of depression. The religious community appears to have functioned in at least four ways:

1. by protecting women from the effects of social isolation;

2. by providing and strengthening family and social networks;

3. by providing individuals with a sense of belonging and self-esteem;

4. by offering spiritual support in times of adversity. (Loewenthal 1995, p.47)

The supportive role of religious communities is evident also in the research of Diane Brown *et al.* into religiosity and psychological distress among woman within a black church community. This research similarly points towards the importance of religious involvement as a form of social participation, and a force which enables a person, in this case marginalized black women, to become integrated into a community, with a concurrent prophylactic effect against depression (Brown *et al.* 1990). It would appear that the very fact of belonging to, participating in and feeling a part of a religious community can be beneficial in terms of reducing psychological distress and preventing mental health problems.

Other researchers have come to similar conclusions about the significance of the spiritual and social support of religious communities and its relationship to mental health (L. B. Brown 1994). A particularly helpful study was carried out by Shams and Jackson into the role of religion in predicting well-being and moderating the psychological impact of unemployment. This study suggests that the findings highlighted above concerning the significance of spiritual and social support in women may have similar implications for men.

Shams and Jackson sought to examine the relationship between the employment status of British Asian men and their psychological well-being. They interviewed 68 employed and 71 unemployed male British Asians. Their findings showed the unemployed group to have poorer psychological well-being. This was particularly so for men who were middle-aged, an observation that replicated the findings of similar studies into groups of white men. The study confirmed the hypothesis that religiosity acted as a buffer against the impact of unemployment. It is proposed that stress lies at the heart of many of the mental health problems which are caused by unemployment. Shams and Jackson define stress as 'a relationship between person and environment, such that demands made of the person exceed his or her resources. Stress therefore is not solely a property of the environment apart from the person' (Shams and Jackson 1993, p.342).

Jacobson (1986) refers to this model of stress as a *transactions model of stress* whereby stress occurs when

> perceived demands exceed perceived resource, with ensuing negative consequences for the individual's well-being… In the transactional view, any demand which exceeds the individual's resources may cause stress… It is not the nature of the event that matters (whether it is major, or minor, acute or chronic), but rather its significance as a demand which exceeds the individual's response capacity.

Thus, the level of stress a person experiences is dependent on the ongoing interplay between personal resources, and the resources which are available to them within their particular social context. Within such a model, high levels of demands on their own are not enough to bring about pathological stress. Stress is not something that is imposed on an individual apart from their ability to act upon it. It is only when a person does not have the material, relational, psychological or spiritual resources to cope with the demands made on them by their environment that pathological stress will arise.

Within this definition of stress Shams and Jackson argue that involvement within a religious community is beneficial to mental health in three main ways.

1. The religious community offers *emotion-focused coping*. A person's religious belief system offers an interpretative framework within which they can reappraise and redefine threatening or disturbing situations, and manage distressing affective emotions.

2. The religious community offers *problem-focused coping*. Belief systems can also provide a means of construing a threatening environment in such a way that the individual can take positive action to alter the source of stress.

3. The religious community provides *social support*. Religious beliefs are corporate beliefs, stemming from and binding a person to a particular community and social network. They are thus an important source of social support.

The research concludes that men who are religiously active and involved with a religious community are protected from the potentially detrimental psychological effects of unemployment.

A slightly more problematic study was carried out by Lindgren and Coursey (1995). They conducted research with people who regularly attended psychosocial rehabilitation centres. Despite certain methodological difficulties with this study (outlined below), the overall results include a balanced reporting of the ways in which spirituality can provide *emotional support* and *support networks* as well as dealing effectively with some of the problems associated with negative emotions. The problems with the methodology of the research are worth reflecting on. One of the central difficulties is that multivariate statistics have been used with a biased sample. The authors state that 'all denominations and members of all faiths were encouraged to join [the study]' but 'that only individuals who were interested in spirituality are represented in this study'. This implies that a normal distribution was not obtained and therefore multivariate statistics were inappropriate. Also, there are several different scales and inventories used but no reporting of an appropriate Bonferroni or Scheffe post hoc test to determine which means differ from one another. These post hoc tests should always be used after finding a significant main effect for a multilevel factor and they help to determine which conditions are significantly different from one another. The sample size in the final analysis was only 30 participants who took part in the interviews, and only 28 of the 30 completed the five questionnaires. This small sample adds to the difficulty with conducting multivariate analysis in this particular study. The results included a balanced reporting of the ways in which spirituality can provide emotional support and support networks as well the problems associated with negative emotions. It is therefore necessary to approach these results with some caution, accepting that they are *indicative* rather than definitive. This study has been included here because it illustrates some of the methodological difficulties encountered in this type of research, and the need for rigour and care when exploring this area.

Cognitive Realignment

The importance of the cognitive, attributional influence of spirituality on mental health is present in a number of studies. Sullivan (1993) described the results of a qualitative study of 40 respondents. Despite the obvious methodological questions which arise from the way the study has been reported, the results clearly indicate that a proportion of the respondents (48 per cent) utilize spirituality as a coping or problem-solving device and that spiritual social support is very important for their general well-being. Additionally, Sullivan found that there was a need to have mental health problems explained and that spirituality was helpful to individuals in providing a view of themselves that enabled each person to take responsibility for themselves.

Sullivan suggests that spirituality encourages mental health benefits through three main pathways. It provides:

1. a framework within which life events can be explained and understood;

2. a significant source of social support. This support involves others, a higher power, and the sense of being in community;

3. a coping mechanism. The meaning of events can be evaluated and interpreted in the light of the individual's spiritual belief system with consequent enhanced coping.

Sullivan found that 48 per cent of his sample felt that spirituality was important in dealing with serious mental illness.

Examples of the methodological questions arising from the reporting of this piece of research include the statement that 47 subjects had been interviewed, of whom 40 met the criteria for inclusion in the study. There is no report of the inclusion criteria; in addition to this there is a selection bias towards those patients who were viewed as successfully surmounting their illness.

Sullivan's findings are similar to those of Maton (1989) in his research into the stress-buffering role of spiritual support. Maton examined the relationship between spiritual support and the well-being of two high- and two lower-stress groups of people (spiritual support was defined as 'the perceived, personally supportive components of an individual's relationship with God'). The two groups comprised of:

1. recently bereaved parents, who were considered to be under a great deal of stress, and parents whose bereavement had occurred some time previously and who were less stressed;

2. college students who had encountered three or more uncontrollable life events which were deemed to be highly stressful, and another group who had experienced two or fewer such events over the past six months and who were considered to be less stressed.

Maton concludes that the stress-buffering role provided by spiritual support is provided through two avenues:

• *cognitive mediation*, which refers to the ways we interpret and give meaning to events because of our spiritual beliefs

• *emotional support*, which refers to the feeling of being valued and cared for.

Maton concludes that spiritual support encouraged positive cognitive mediation and emotional support in the high-stress group of recently bereaved parents. It was also inversely related to depression and positively related to self-esteem within this group. For the college students, spiritual support positively correlated with personal-emotional adjustment for the high-stress group of students, although it did not appear to be significant to the lower-stress group. The key finding was that spiritual support was positively related to personal and emotional adjustment.

Similarly, Peterson and Roy (1985) focus on the significance of meaning and the cognitive realignment that spirituality can bring about. While acknowledging the potential for religion to produce a negative effect on mental health they note that spiritual well-being is positively correlated with the importance of religion in a person's life (i.e. what it means to them), belief in God as a causal agent (that life has meaning beyond themselves), and attributions to supernatural intervention (constructing meaning using a spiritual belief system as a lense through which the world is looked upon).

Divine Relations

Melvin Pollner (1989) drew upon data from the 1983 and 1984 General Social Survey conducted by the National Research Center to throw light on another aspect of social and spiritual support that is often overlooked or misunderstood. Pollner used regression analysis to explore the ways in which relationships with 'divine others' impact upon psychological health and well-being. The relationships of respondents to divine others were assessed by asking three questions:

1. How close do you feel to God most of the time?

2. How often do you pray?

3. How often have you felt as though you were very close to a powerful spiritual force that seemed to lift you out of yourself?

He observes that the majority of research has focused on what one might call *real* relationships, that is, relationships with real people. However, Pollner points to the fact that alongside a person's real social network, there exists a network of imagined others which overlaps and interacts with the person's actual social network and significantly affects their relational encounters. These imaginary others include contemporary figures such as film stars, pop stars, media personalities and religious and divine figures such as Jesus, Buddha, Mohammed and so forth. Individuals construct elaborate forms of imaginary interaction with these people, and often use them as imaginary dialogue partners when deciding on particular courses of action. For example, when confronted with a particular situation, a fan of Elvis Presley might ask 'what would Elvis do?' and act according to their perception of the singer. Likewise a Christian might ask how Jesus would act in a particular situation; a Muslim what Mohammed would do; a Buddhist what Buddha would do, and so forth. The way in which the person perceives the imaginary character and the type of relationship they develop with them will determine the nature and efficacy of the resultant action. These imaginary figures can become central to the cognitive and interpretative mindset of individuals, who draw upon their identification with them, and ascribe meaning to situations according to the nature of their imaginary dialogue with them. In this way, these imaginary figures can have a major impact on a person's self-esteem and coping abilities, and are often an important source of advice and support.

> Religious texts and symbolism provide many resources for personifying the divine as an other who can be engaged interactionally for support, guidance and solace... Identification with textual figures allows individuals to define their problematic situation in terms of a biblical figure's plight and to perceive their own situation from the point of view of the 'God-role'. (Pollner 1989, p.93)

Pollner found that participation in divine relationships was 'the strongest correlate in three of four measures of well-being, surpassing in strength such usually potent predictors as race, sex, income, age, marital status, and church attendance.'

Collaborative style

Pollner's observations regarding the nature of divine–human relationships is further expanded by reflecting on the observations of Pargament *et al.* (1988) on styles of religious coping. They suggest that religious coping manifests itself in three different styles: *collaborative, deferring, self-directing.* When a person encounters a problem, they enter into a constructive collaboration with God in an attempt to solve it. God is seen as a partner in the process of coping with the individual sharing their burdens with God in a way that is constructive and health-bringing.

Deferring style

The person hands over all responsibility for their problems to God. When a situation becomes difficult or anxiety-provoking, the person does not act themselves, but waits for God to act in a protective fashion. Thus, responsibility for dealing with difficulties is shifted from the individual to the Divine.

Self-directing style

Here the person assumes full responsibility for their actions and considers him- or herself capable of solving them with no necessary reference to God.

These researchers found that within the intrinsic religious orientation, collaborative religious problem solving improved competence whereas deferring religious problem solving was not conducive to the development of competence. The deferring style could also be unhelpful if people developed particularly negative images of God, or felt that their illness was the result of being punished by God.

Religion is thus seen to have the ability to shape people's cognitive appraisal of stressful situations in very specific ways, as well as contributing significantly to the appraisal of the personal resources available to respond to stress. It can therefore significantly influence a person's attributional processes as these are activated by situations that threaten a sense of meaning, control, and self-esteem.

Negative Divine Relationships

Spirituality and a person's relationships with divine others is not without its dangers. Mickley *et al.* (1995) in their review of the literature surrounding religion and mental health, while recognizing its beneficial effects, also acknowledge the dangers inherent within certain forms of religion. Relationships with a divine other are not always construed as positive. Some argue that the manner in which divine relations are addressed may be detrimental to mental health, as in the case of certain forms of 'fundamentalism'.

Fundamentalism might be defined as 'a dogmatic and highly centralized cognitive system in which a few absolute beliefs about authority are central and other beliefs are based on or emanate from these' (Kirkpatrick, Hood and Hartz 1991, p.157). Here there may be a possible correlation between religion and psychopathology. However, a causal link between fundamentalist beliefs and psychopathology has not yet been established, primarily because there has been little empirical work done on the subject (Hartz and Everett 1989). However, there is some evidence to suggest that religion in this form can be problematic (Gartner *et al.* 1991).

Is Religion Pathological?

Albert Ellis (1980, 1986) suggests that all religion is nothing more than irrational thinking:

> Human disturbance is largely (though not entirely) associated with and springs from absolutist thinking – from dogmatism, inflexibility, and

devout shoulds, oughts and musts – and that extreme religiosity or...true believerism, is essentially emotional disturbance. (Ellis 1980, p.635)

Ellis proposes that:

Devout, orthodox, or dogmatic religion (or what might be called religiosity) is significantly correlated with emotional disturbance. People largely disturb themselves by believing strongly in absolutistic shoulds, oughts and musts, and most people who dogmatically believe in some religion believe in these health-sabotaging absolutes. The emotionally healthy individual is flexible, open, tolerant, and changing, and the devoutly religious person tends to be inflexible, closed, intolerant and unchanging. Religiosity therefore, is in many respects equivalent to irrational thinking and emotional disturbance... The elegant therapeutic solution to emotional problems is to be quite unreligious and have no degree of dogmatic faith that is unfounded or unfoundable in fact. (Ellis 1980, p.637)

For Ellis, religion is directly correlated with the development of emotional disturbance. In essence, people disturb themselves by adopting absolutist belief systems which trap them in a maze of 'absolutistic shoulds, oughts and musts', which inevitably inhibit their emotional development and sabotage their mental health.

Ellis's perspective, whilst challenging, and perhaps applicable to certain forms of religion, is open to criticism. In a systematic review of the literature from 1951 to 1979, Bergin (1983) found that religious spirituality had a positive association with mental health in nearly half of the 24 studies examined. He found that only 23 per cent manifested the negative relationships with mental health assumed by Ellis. Forty-seven per cent indicated a positive relationship and 30 per cent a zero relationship. He found little relationship between religiousness and psychopathology, with 77 per cent of the results examined running contrary to the suggestion that religion is detrimental to a person's emotional health. Rather than being a negative form of cognition, it would appear that spirituality has a good deal of potential for developing positive cognitions and reframing that enable coping and the development of mental health.

While Ellis's view may arguably apply to a particular type of fundamentalist or cultic religion, it is not necessarily or, in the light of the research reviewed here, empirically valid to generalize it to include *all* forms of religion. The fact that one particular form of spirituality or religion may be detrimental to mental health need not lead one necessarily to conclude that the same can be said for all forms of religion. It is correct to be wary of forms of spirituality and religion that might affect individuals in an unhelpful way. Spiritual perceptions which involve oppressive images of God, or which engender inappropriate guilt and increase anxiety may well be detrimental to mental health. However, while we may wish to maintain an ability to assess critically spiritual experiences, to suggest that spirituality is *always* pathological is to move beyond the available evidence. As Laurence Brown correctly observes: 'Any assumption that religion is necessarily a "danger" to health or closely related to mental illness is not supported by the evidence from carefully controlled studies that follow a social science perspective (L. B. Brown 1994, p.1).

Comfort, hope, value and meaning

From the perspective of people experiencing mental health problems, spirituality has been found to be of concern to many people. Kroll and Sheehan (1989) found that religious beliefs and practices assumed an important and often central place in the lives of many patients. Ninety-five per cent of their sample (52 psychiatric inpatients) professed a belief in God, and 75 per cent believed that the Bible referred directly to their daily lives. They found that patients with depressive and anxiety disorders tended to score lower than those with other diagnoses on a wide variety of indexes of religion. Depressed patients were found to be the least religiously oriented diagnostic group, implying that this group of people have lost their sense of meaning and purpose for life, at least temporarily. This point regarding depression and the loss of meaning is highlighted here, and will be developed more fully in Chapter 4. The authors conclude that 'belief in God, and in the teachings of the Bible, the sense of an afterlife, and involvement with a church community are relevant dimensions of our patients' lives that certainly deserve more consideration than the psychiatric profession has currently provided.

Fitchett *et al.* (1997) in their research into the religious needs and resources of psychiatric inpatients came to similar conclusions. They surveyed 51 adult psychiatric patients and, for comparison, 50 general medical/surgical patients. They discovered that 88 per cent of the psychiatric patients reported three or more current religious needs. The most frequently reported needs were:

- expression of caring and support from another person
- knowledge of God's presence

- prayer
- purpose and meaning in life
- a chaplain to visit and pray.

Psychiatric patients were found to have lower spiritual well-being scores and were less likely to have talked with religious specialists. Importantly, the researchers found that religion was an important source of comfort and support for a significant majority (72 per cent) of the psychiatric patients who participated in their study. This compares favourably with Lindgren and Coursey's (1995) findings indicating that 83 per cent of their sample believed that spirituality helped them through their illness, with half of these people indicating that it helped mostly through the comfort it provided, feelings of being cared for, and feelings that they were not alone.

Significantly, Fitchett *et al.* conclude that 'religion is important for psychiatric patients, but they may need assistance in finding resources to address their religious needs.' The need for spirituality to be affirmed and enabled also comes through in the research of Lindgren and Coursey, who found that some individuals reported guilty feelings about the times they thought they had neglected their beliefs. This would indicate a need to provide a context within which people can be enabled to express and develop those aspects of their spirituality that are of most significance to them.

Both of the above studies were carried out within an American context. This may well be significant. Koenig (1997) observes that within the United States, 90 per cent of people express a belief in God to be a significant factor in their lives, and somewhere in the region of four out of ten Americans attend a place of worship at least once a week. Bearing this in mind, the religious preference discovered amongst mental health patients may well be a reflection of the wider cultural context that cannot necessarily be generalized beyond the USA.

However, there is evidence to suggest that findings such as these may apply within a British context. Charters (1999) surveyed the religious and spiritual needs of mental health clients in inpatient and acute elderly wards and residents in elderly residential settings. His findings indicated that 69 per cent of those involved with the project (n = 89) stated that religion was important to them and that they regularly or intermittently engaged in some form of religious behaviour, i.e. prayer, meditation, scripture reading or attending a religious meeting. Twenty per cent 'said that their admission to hospital had in some way affected their religious or spiritual life, while 31 per cent (28 responses) felt that their religious and spiritual needs had not been taken into consideration in their care planning.'

The sample size within this study is small, and any results can at best be considered indicative rather than conclusive. Nevertheless, it does suggest the proposition that mental health clients do have significant spiritual needs which are either not recognized or not considered relevant to mental health carers. Recent research produced by the Mental Health Foundation (Currey 1997; Mental Health Foundation 1998) which has strongly suggested that spirituality is an important part of the lives of many people who are experiencing mental health problems would add weight to such a suggestion.

Summary

It is clear from the literature that has been reviewed thus far that spirituality and adherence to religious communities can be beneficial for the development and maintenance of mental health. Taken as a whole, the evidence presented provides a case for taking seriously the suggestion that spirituality may have a positive contribution to make to the process of mental health care. The main themes that have arisen with regard to the benefits of spirituality are presented in Table 3.2.

Table 3.2. Primary ways in which spirituality contributes to the enhancement of mental health

Well-being

Relatedness and connectedness of self to others and to God

Self-esteem

Hope

Spiritual support

Knowledge of God's presence

Access to the symbols and rituals of spiritual communities

Perceived relationship with religious and divine figures

The reading of scriptures

Prayer

Social support through religious communities

Providing and strengthening family and support netw

Emotional support

Protection from social isolation

Providing individuals with a sense of belonging and self-est

Spiritual support in times of adversity

Coping and positive cognitive mediation

A framework within which life events can be explained, understood and interpreted according to particular beliefs.

Emotion-focused coping – an interpretative framework within which a person can reappraise and redefine threatening or disturbing situations, and manage distressing affective emotions

Problem-focused coping – belief systems can also provide a means of construing a threatening environment in such a way that the individual can take positive action to alter the source of stress

Comfort, hope, value and meaning

The feeling of being valued and cared for

Purpose and meaning in life

Comfort during times of distress

Feelings that one is not alone

Hope in the midst of apparent hopelessness

Despite these positive findings, there remains some degree of ambiguity with regard to the relationship between spirituality and mental health. This ambiguity does not only pertain to the methodological difficulties high-lighted previously. While the evidence does appear to point towards a positive correlation between spirituality and mental health, acknowledge-ment of these positive aspects must be held in tension with the potentially negative impact that certain beliefs and belief systems can have on mental health. However, a degree of ambiguity is present within many if not most therapeutic understandings and interventions. Medication can bring about unpleasant side-effects in certain individuals; psychotherapy can cause damage and confusion to some and health and healing to others; electro-convulsive therapy can bring release to some and devastating memory loss to others. It is therefore necessary to approach the area of spirituality with the same kind of critical discernment that one would use in assessing and

understand and work within any area of care. The task of the
ual carer will be to develop appropriate forms of insight, understanding and empathy to enable them to discern between healthy and
unhealthy forms of religion and to utilize that which will be beneficial to the
overall therapeutic process. There is no obvious reason why the ambiguities
surrounding spirituality and mental health should not act as a stimulus
towards better research, understanding and practice, rather than as a barrier
to further critical exploration of the spiritual dimension.

The Question of the 'Superempirical'

Alongside the type of mainstream empirically based literature that has been
reviewed thus far is another emerging body of research that utilizes similar
methods, but from a distinctively different starting point: the possibility that
the transcendent referent of human spirituality is *real* rather than simply
functionally present. Research findings such as those reviewed above show
that commitment to a religious or spiritual system, belief in an interventionist God and deference to the existence of a particular metaphysical
system, far from being a sign of emotional immaturity or disturbance, can in
fact be psychologically health-bringing. Nonetheless, a criticism of the
approach outlined thus far might be that it could be interpreted as revealing
a purely *functional* understanding of spirituality that could just as easily be
explained by psychology without any necessary reference to God or the
existence of a spiritual dimension. A functional view of spirituality

> encompasses an individual's or society's ultimate commitment, most
> comprehensive principle of order, or final value, that is, the most passionate
> and powerful arguments offered for choices that are made. In this view the
> spiritual dimension is a human phenomenon, 'an apparently generic
> consequence of the universal human burden of finding or making meaning.'
> (Fitchett *et al.* 1989, p.187 quoting Fowler)

In this view it is the beliefs themselves that are significant in terms of mental
health development, rather than the objective reality of any divine or
transcendent referent. This of course may be an appropriate understanding if
one assumes the validity of understandings of spirituality that adopt a
secular/humanistic position. However, a purely functionalist understanding
of spirituality is much less attractive to those with a theistic understanding.
Depending on one's starting position and personal presuppositions, the
findings presented above are indeed open to various interpretations with

regard to the reality or otherwise of God. Nevertheless, whilst not proving the existence of the divine, they in no way preclude the adoption of more substantive understandings which might accept the objective reality of a person's spiritual beliefs. 'A substantive definition of spirituality is based on the belief that there is an ultimate or transcendent being, power, or force in the universe' (Fitchett *et al.* 1989, p.187). Such substantive understandings of spirituality underpin the approach and assumptions of the billions of adherents to the world's theistically oriented religions. As such they cannot easily be ignored. This is an important point. The assumption of this chapter is *not* that God, spirituality, religion, or 'imaginary' biblical/spiritual figures are *nothing but* the product of human imagination, or that religious communities are nothing *more than* relational 'safe spaces' that can function in a health-bringing way irrespective of the truth or otherwise of their belief systems. While it may be true that spirituality manifests itself through social and psychological processes, there is no evidence to support the assumption that that is *all* it is. The model of personhood developed in Chapter 1 clearly showed that the human spirit is not separate from the other elements of the person. It permeates all of the dimensions of the person, with the relational dynamic reaching beyond the boundaries of the individual to seek relationships with others and with God. The fact that this spiritual movement involves and is affected by psychological processes is fully in line with this understanding of human beings. Nothing that has been presented in this chapter would preclude the reality of God or the possibility of experiences that reach beyond the psychological into hidden realms and new dimensions.

Research into such hidden and apparently 'non-empirical' dimensions is, by definition problematic, particularly if we insist on trying to measure it with tools that are designed to explore areas that are qualitatively different from our normal assumptive worlds. Nevertheless, there are a number of researchers committed to working at this interface between what is assumed to be normal and the 'supernormal' dimensions of spirituality and spiritual experiences. Some of the research that has emerged from this approach is interesting and worthy of further reflection.

Pargament (in Larson *et al.* 1997, p.61) identified a theoretical perspective that assumes spirituality *actually* connects an individual with the divine: 'The motivation to find God through religion is a central element of being religious, an element that may have unique effects on mental health and well being.' Levin (1996b) develops a similar perspective which he refers to as the 'superempirical'. The superempirical dimension influences the religion–mental health dynamic in ways that cannot be explained by reducing religiousness and spirituality into purely psychological or social phenomena:

> The motivation to find God through religion is a central element of being religious, an element that may have unique effects on mental health and well-being…religiousness also may influence health status through 'superempirical' routes, which cannot be explained by simply reducing religiousness and spirituality into purely psychological phenomena. (Levin 1996b, p.66)

Levin urges researchers and practitioners to retain an openness to new possibilities that might transcend current understandings and move beyond the boundaries of our present paradigms:

> The concept of the supernatural is by definition, outside of or beyond nature. Herein may reside an either wholly or partly transcendent Creator-God who is believed by many to heal through means that transcend the laws of the created universe, both its local and non-local elements, and that are thus inherently inaccessible to and unknowable by science. Such an explanation for the effects of prayer [for example] merits consideration and, despite its inability to be proved by medical science, should not be dismissed out of hand. (Levin 1996b)

Quantum physics and the healing power of prayer?

One aspect of the superempirical dimension of spirituality that has generated a large amount of interest and research data is the area of prayer, and its ability to bring about healing. Recent research into the healing power of prayer has suggested that there may well be another dimension to the spirituality–health debate that cannot be encapsulated using standard scientific methodologies. A good example of this approach is found in the work of the medical doctor Larry Dossey (1993). Dossey, drawing on the theories from the new physics, proposes that prayer may heal through non-local means. The expression 'non-local' is a term drawn from quantum physics and used by Dossey to account for some of the ways in which consciousness manifests itself. The suggestion is that consciousness is not completely confined or localized to specific points in space or time. It is therefore possible for conscious events initiated within one location to affect events in another location. Dossey draws on the thinking of Nobel physicist Erwin Schrodinger, a prominent proponent of quantum physics.

Schrodinger believed that mind by its very nature was singular and one. Consciousness is not confined to separate, individual brains, but is ultimately a unified field. The suggestion is that consciousness is not derived from, nor reducible to, anything. Rather it is fundamental in the universe, similar to matter and energy. Non-local events which are known to occur at the subatomic level, can be amplified and may emerge in everyday experience. Dossey (1999) suggests that:

> Prayer is a genuinely nonlocal event – that is, it is not confined to a specific place in space or to a specific moment in time. Prayer reaches outside the here-and-now; it operates at a distance and outside the present moment. Since prayer is initiated by a mental action, this implies that there is some aspect of our psyche that also is genuinely nonlocal. If so, then something of ourselves is infinite in space and time – thus omnipresent, eternal, and immortal. 'Nonlocal,' after all, does not mean 'really big' or 'a very long time.' It implies *infinitude* in space and time, because a limited non locality is a contradiction in terms. In the West this infinite aspect of the psyche has been referred to as the soul. Empirical evidence for prayer's power, then, is indirect evidence for the soul. It is also evidence for shared qualities with the Divine – the Divine within – since infinitude, omnipresence, and eternality are qualities that we have attributed also to the Absolute.

Dossey's well-documented research can be interpreted in a number of different ways. At one level, he may be tapping into a truly transcendent force, and revealing from the perspective of neo-science new possibilities for the existence of an interventionist God. Alternatively, he might be entering into the world of telepathy, and throwing some light on the idea of a universal conscience/energy that individuals can tap into and utilize for the benefit of themselves or others. Dossey's ready acceptance by New Age healers would suggest that this interpretation may contain at least a grain of truth. However, his perspective may also be explained in terms of the types of discoveries emerging from the field of quantum mechanics (Barbour 1990) wherein we are discovering new physical laws that may be unbelievable or unfamiliar, but which may end up simply providing a revision of our understanding of the laws of the natural universe. Quantum physics might be described as a micro-physics that seeks to explore the incredibly small. Quantum physics tells us that the common laws of Newtonian physics begin to deteriorate when we get to the subatomic levels of matter. Although Newtonian mechanics of cause and effect are still applicable at the macro-level, many of our commonly held assumptions disappear at these lower levels. For example, Heisenburg's uncertainty principle suggests that, at a subatomic level, the objectivity and neutrality of the observer that is so vital to the scientific method is actually impossible to achieve. The process of observation itself may alter the nature and properties of the object being observed, and the ability to perceive or observe reality accurately may be fundamentally limited (Richards and Bergin 1997. p.36). For example, the light particles used by an observer to illuminate an object of research actually interferes with and changes that object. In contrast to the assumed certainties of *realism* and *positivism*, and the idea of a mechanical, deterministic universe, the findings of modern-day physics suggest that scientific theories and observations are only 'partial representations of limited aspects of the world as it interacts with us' (Barbour 1990, p.99). Thus, rather than a deterministic universe, 'there is a complex combination of law and chance... Nature is characterized by both structure and openness. The future cannot be predicted in detail from the past' (Barbour 1990, p.220).

Quantum theory forces us to reconsider some of our deepest convictions about reality. It tells us that the world is unpredictable; not just that we do not have enough information to understand what is going on but that there are aspects of the world that are fundamentally unknowable. At the quantum level, any measurement of a phenomenon affects it, and relationships between elements are more important in understanding a system than the elements themselves. In quantum physics, the image of the universe as a machine is superseded by a view of the universe as an indivisible, dynamic whole whose parts are interrelated in vital and fundamental ways.

Bearing such discoveries in mind, it is clear that Dossey's work is challenging and may *well* open up some interesting new perspectives on God, prayer and human consciousness. Nevertheless, it is far from conclusive. The question of whether or not there truly is a personal referent for human spirituality remains unanswered by science.

Researching Prayer

The area of research into the healing power of prayer is very much in its infancy, and Dossey's approach is only one, if a particularly interesting, way of exploring aspects of spirituality such as prayer. There are some interesting findings emerging from the work of other researchers working within the mainstream scientific paradigm. A number of randomized control trials have highlighted the possibility that intercessory prayer (i.e. prayer for others) can be beneficial for health in general and mental health in particular. Byrd (1988), in a seminal study of the effect of intercessory prayer on people with cardiac problems, applied a prospective, randomized double-blind protocol to patients attending a coronary care unit. Over a ten-month period he randomly assigned 393 patients admitted to the coronary care unit to either an intercessory prayer group (192 patients) or a control group (201 patients). Between three and seven intercessors prayed daily for each patient in the prayed-for group. Intercessors prayed for three specific outcomes for all patients and added other requests perceived beneficial to particular patients. Byrd's positive results are widely cited. The prayed-for group had a number of significantly better outcomes:

- reduced incidences of congestive heart failure ($p < 0.03$)
- reduced incidences of cardiopulmonary arrest ($p < 0.02$)
- reduced incidences of pneumonia($p < 0.03$)
- reduced use of intubation ($p < 0.002$)
- reduced use of diuretics ($p < 0.05$) and antibiotics ($p < 0.005$).

The prayed-for group had a significantly better outcome overall ($p < 0.01$).

In a similar study, Harris *et al.* (1999) carried out a randomized, double-blind study on a group of 990 consecutive patients who were admitted to the coronary care unit of the Mid-America Heart Institute in Kansas City, Missouri. This study was designed to replicate Byrd's findings by testing the hypothesis that 'patients who are unknowingly and remotely prayed for by blinded intercessors will experience fewer complications and have a shorter hospital stay than patients not receiving such prayer.' At the time of admission, patients were randomized with some receiving remote, intercessory prayer and others receiving basic care that did not include this element. The intercessors, who had no contact with the patients, were drawn from various denominations within the local community. The first names of patients in the prayer group were given to the team who prayed for them daily for four weeks. They were asked to pray for 28 days for 'a speedy recovery with no complications'. Patients were unaware that they were being prayed for.

Harris and colleagues concluded that those who were prayed for by an intercessory group fared 11 per cent better than those who weren't prayed for. In other words, 'the supplementary, remote, blinded, intercessory prayer produced a measurable improvement in the medical outcomes of critically ill patients.' The authors conclude that the results of these this randomized control trial taken in conjunction with Byrd's original study suggest the possible benefits of intercessory prayer and indicate the need for further studies to develop and further validate their conclusions.

Interesting as studies such as these undoubtedly are, it nevertheless remains difficult to assess precisely how valid their results are. There are a plethora of uncontrollable variables involved in such projects. Gauging the usefulness of the research product is inevitably very problematic. For example, neither of the studies highlighted above indicates anything about the psychological status and spiritual beliefs and practices of the groups who are prayed for or not prayed for. In the light of the complexities of religious orientation highlighted in Chapter 1, combined with the insights relating to the mind–body connection provided by current developments in psychoneuroimmunology, the lack of such information is potentially problematic. Reflecting critically on Byrd's study, Matthews (1999, p.200) observes that,

> Since patients were randomly assigned to the groups, one may reasonably assume that the groups were similar after the randomization process with regard to these characteristics. But a confirmation of their similarity on these points would have been helpful in ensuring that the results did not simply reflect that the prayed-for group may have had greater belief in the power of prayer or greater devotion in their personal prayers for their own health.

As well as such technical criticisms, there are other important uncontrollable variables. For example, how does the fact that a person may decide to pray for themselves affect the possible outcome? What if members of the health care team decide to pray for the patients in the non-intercessory group? What if religious communities are in fact interceding on behalf of the 'non-prayed for' group? There are also difficulties with assuming that prayer works according to the laws of cause and effect. Such an understanding reflects the mechanism of Newtonian physics and ignores the changing views of physics as well as the inherent mystery and uncertainty surrounding prayer which is present within the understandings of the major world religions. The idea of prayer being offered 'for 15 minutes daily for 12 weeks' (O'Laoire 1997) as part of a randomized control trial provides a very good illustration of the power of the medical model in shaping our approaches to research into spirituality and our expectations of research outcomes. That which might be new and radically different is simply drawn within the existing paradigm and presumed to function in the same way as current forms of intervention.

Quite apart from criticisms such as these, taken as a whole, the evidence relating to the healing power of prayer is not as convincing as the two major studies highlighted above might suggest. While there is some evidence that would support the conclusions of Byrd and Harris *et al.* (O'Laoire 1997; Rees 1995; Sicher *et al.* 1998; Wirth and Cram 1994), other studies are less conclusive. Walker *et al.* conducted a randomized, double-blind study designed to explore the relationship between prayer and alcohol abuse. They found no difference between those groups that had been prayed for and those who had not in terms of alcohol consumption. While there was a degree of controlled drinking associated with those participants who prayed themselves, the report concluded that 'intercessory prayer did not demonstrate clinical benefit in the treatment of alcohol abuse and dependence under these study conditions. Prayer may be a complex phenomenon with many interacting variables.'

Roberts, Ahmed and Hall (2000) also throw some doubt on the general state of research within this area. In the Cochrane database of systematic reviews they present an extensive literature review of randomized and quasi-randomized trials done to explore the relationship between intercessory prayer and the alleviation of ill health. They conclude that the link between prayer and the alleviation of ill health was non-conclusive, owing to the fact that there are so few completed trials exploring the value or otherwise of prayer. However, they do suggest that the evidence presented thus far is interesting enough to warrant further investigation. Perhaps most significant is their concluding observation that:

> If prayer is seen as a human endeavor it may or may not be beneficial, and further trials could uncover this. It could be the case that any effects are due to elements beyond present scientific understanding that will, in time, be understood. If any benefit derives from God's response to prayer it may be beyond any such trials to prove or disprove. (Roberts, Ahmed and Hall 2000)

Whether or not the depths of the divine can truly be plumbed using scientific methods is open to question. We certainly require continuing and rigorous research within the area of spirituality and mental health. However, we also must recognize that some elements of the faith experience may transcend scientific investigation (Larson *et al.* 1992). This is not to suggest that we abandon scientific exploration of the relationship between spirituality and health. Rather, if we are to come to an understanding of the spiritual dimensions, we may need to expand our horizons in order to incorporate aspects and understandings that may lie beyond the boundaries and methodologies of our current narrow scientific assumptions.

Conclusion

This chapter has presented an overview of some of the key areas of research within the area of spirituality and mental health. As the chapter has progressed through the data, it has become clear that while there are aspects of spirituality that are immeasurable, it is possible, given the appropriate tools and understandings, to identify and to an extent measure the impact of spirituality on the development and maintenance of mental health. The key areas of benefit were highlighted in Table 3.1 above. Viewed in this way, it is clear that spirituality is potentially of relevance to the process of mental health care. A minimal claim would be that the evidence presented within this chapter suggests that spirituality is an important dimension of human experience which can significantly affect the process of mental health care. The actual mechanisms through which the benefits of spirituality are acquired are diverse and complex. Continuing research within this area is required in order to sharpen our understanding of this dimension of care and to provide ways of caring that can effectively incorporate this aspect of human experience.

The discussion on the superempirical raised some important questions concerning the possible reality of the transcendent and how one might access, measure and understand this dimension; it also highlighted some of the difficulties that occur if researchers do not recognize that their tools may be inappropriate for exploring certain dimensions of the world and the experiences of human beings within it.

Taken together, the research findings presented within this chapter provide a useful foundation for models of informed spiritual care.

CHAPTER 4

Living with Meaningle...

The Lived Experience of Spirituality
in the Context of Depression

The research presented in the previous chapter utilized the standard methods of science to explore the area of spirituality, spiritual care and their relationship to mental health. At a number of points it was suggested that, while there was much to be learned from utilizing such methodological approaches in developing an understanding of spirituality and its relationship to mental health, the very nature of spirituality makes such methodologies useful but problematic. Spirituality cannot be captured within the parameters of wide generalizations. It is not statistically quantifiable in the ways that traditional scientific methods might desire it to be. Spirituality relates to such things as love, hope, meaning, purpose – things which cannot be fully captured by the traditional methodologies of science. Thus, whilst such ways of exploring human beings remain valid within certain parameters, there is a need to develop complementary methodologies and ways of exploring the spiritual dimension that can dig into the hidden depths of human emotion and experience and reveal aspects and perspectives that are unavailable to other ways of doing research. The development and acceptance of alternative ways of researching and understanding spirituality within the context of mental health problems is an important aspect of the emerging paradigm, and an important part of the process of mental health carers becoming spiritual healers in the ways that have been outlined previously.

If spiritual healing is to be achieved, and the beginnings of a new paradigm initiated, mental health carers need to discover new ways of approaching the task of caring and researching which adequately include them and enable them to understand the spiritual dimension of those to whom they seek to offer care. This will involve developing forms of research and practice that will allow them to access those regions of people's experience that may well be overlooked by current forms of practice and rd research methodologies. While the type of empirical research nted earlier is useful in providing insights into what spirituality is and w it might function in developing and maintaining mental health, ithout the complementary perspective of the real life-experience of people, our knowledge of spirituality and mental health will inevitably be limited and quite possibly deceiving. If we confine our research into spirituality and mental health simply to one method and listen only to the voices of one group of people – mental health professionals – then we risk accepting constructions of mental health and ill-health that are biased and possibly even oppressive.

One way in which this dimension of the caring process can be developed and enhanced is through the use of research methodologies and approaches to care which will enable the development of spiritually aware understandings of the lived experiences of people with mental health problems, that is, what spirituality *feels* like within the context of a mental health problem. This chapter presents an account of a research project carried out by the author into the lived experience of people with enduring forms of depression. In working through the method and reflecting on the findings it will be possible to present an understanding of depression and its relationship to spiritual issues that will provide insights and which will inform the model of care that will be worked out in the final chapter of the book. It will also provide a good example of an alternative way of researching spirituality and mental health which is equally as rigorous in its approach as traditional scientific methods, but which adopts a very different epistemological standpoint and approaches the research process from a significantly different angle.

Silent Voices

As one searches the literature surrounding the area of spirituality and mental health, one finds oneself asking the question, *where are the voices of people with mental health problems?* A great deal of the research that has been carried out into the relationship between spirituality and mental health has relied on objective methodologies that draw their assumptions and practices from the positivist paradigm. Few studies have sought to explore the inner experiences of people with mental health problems and the ways in which spirituality functions within their lived experience. Those that do, tend to touch on the spiritual dimension as part of a wider study of some other aspect of mental health, rather than having spirituality as a central focus

(Smith 1996, 1998; Karp 1996). The research that seeks to explain the relationship between spirituality and mental health tends to approach people with mental health problems as *objects* of research, rather than as spiritually oriented *subjects* who need to be listened to, understood and related to. Over all there is a paucity of rigorous research that seeks to understand the relationship between spirituality and mental health from the perspective of people experiencing mental health problems.

This study seeks to contribute to filling this gap within the literature. The purpose of the research described below was to explore the lived experience of depression and to examine some of the ways in which a person's spirituality might function in living with this particular form of mental health problem. By listening to the voices of sufferers, it was hoped that therapeutic forms of understanding could be developed that would enable carers to gain a deeper insight into what depression is like as a human experience. In so doing, carers would be enabled to care more insightfully and empathetically for the spiritual needs of clients.

Spirituality and Depression

Depression is one of the most prevalent forms of mental health problems within both the United States and Great Britain. It is often referred to as the 'common cold' of mental health problems. This is an unfortunate analogy, as such assumptions can underplay the devastating effect that this condition has on individuals and their families. Depression manifests itself in various forms and to varying degrees.

> People with mild depressive episodes find it difficult to continue with their work and social lives, but usually continue to function, albeit less well than normal. Moderate depressive episodes have a wider range of symptoms, which are present usually to a greater degree. Sufferers find it very difficult to function normally at work or home. Severe depressive episodes typically may also include features such as: great distress and agitation, slowed thought and movement (psychomotor retardation), ideas of guilt, suicidal fantasies or plans which may be acted upon, pronounced somatic symptoms, psychotic symptoms. (Gilbert 1992, p.22)

As one reflects upon the nature of depression it becomes clear that it is a profoundly spiritual experience that cannot be understood and dealt with through drugs and therapy alone. Its central features of profound hopelessness, loss of meaning in life, perceived loss of relationship with God or higher power, low self-esteem and general sense of purposelessness, all indicate a level of spiritual distress. Commonly expressed feelings such as *why me? what is the point? why can't I find a point in living?* in a real sense express the depths of meaningless which are the hallmarks of clinical depression. There is thus seen to be a sense of spiritual crisis inherent within depression that will not necessarily be alleviated by psychotherapy or pharmacology, particularly if the true nature of the crisis goes unnoticed (Karp 1996). Describing precisely what that element of crisis consists of and how it finds its resolution within the overall experience of depression, was one of the primary objects of the research presented below.

The Research Approach

Epistemological assumptions

The research method outlined below assumes a particular view of the world and the nature of truth and knowledge. As such, it belongs to the emerging holistic paradigm that was discussed in Chapter 2. In order to understand the approach and to reflect critically on its validity, it is necessary to be very clear as to the epistemological perspective that underlies the research perspective.

CONSTRUCTIVISM

The underlying philosophical assumption that underpins the way of doing research outlined below is the perspective of *constructivism* (Lincoln and Guba 1985). It offers a perspective on truth and knowledge and the ways in which they are perceived by human beings and human communities. In line with Kuhn's observations concerning the contextually bound nature of scientific knowledge, a constructivist approach presents an alternative to forms of realism that for a long time dominated positivist/empiricist science. Rather than assuming that truth is something that is somehow 'out there', accessible in a pure, uninterpreted form via objective approaches within which the researcher distances him or herself from the object of research, this approach assumes the presence of multiple realities, and the inevitable involvement of the researcher in the research process, not simply as an observer, but also as a participant. Observation is assumed to be an interpretive process. Table 4.1 outlines the differences between the positivist and the constructionist assumptions about the nature of reality and the process of research.

Philosophically, this perspective is a movement away from what the pragmatic philosopher John Dewey has described as the *'spectator theory of knowledge'* (Harris 1996), or what one might describe as an empiricist model of language, that is, the assumption that any linguistic sign or symbol finds its meaning in its direct reference to an empirical reality. In other words, 'the idea that thinking refers to fixed things in nature, that is, the notion that for each idea there is a corresponding thing in reality' (Harris 1996). The constructivist perspective proposes that *all* meaning emerges from the shared interaction of individuals within human society. From this viewpoint, human behaviour and understanding is seen to be an active process of construction and interpretation in which human beings together endeavour to define the nature of their particular social situations and encounters and in so doing try to make sense of and participate appropriately in their social, psychological, physical and spiritual environments. The meaning and definition of reality is therefore flexible, and as such open to negotiation, depending on circumstances, perception, knowledge, power structures and so forth. If there is controversy over particular meanings, for example where several definitions exist for the same piece of reality, then the meaning of that reality is *negotiated*, and defined according to the interpretative framework which the individual uses to make sense of their experiences of reality (Eaton 1986, p.2). The relevance of this observation to the context of mental health care will become clear as we move on.

This approach is postmodern in as much as it refuses to be bounded by the idea that there is only one narrative that can explain reality. If there are multiple realities it becomes totally valid to listen to the myriad of mini-narratives within which a variety of explanations of human experience is expressed, each of which is considered valid according to its own criteria. Whilst the approach of positivism assumes that truth is researcher-defined, the approach used here assumes that truth is subject-oriented (Sandelowski 1986). To adopt such a stance does not mean that one needs to assume there is 'no such thing as reality'. What it *does* emphasize is that our ability to understand and define what reality is is always a process of interpretation and construction that is influenced by a number of social, cultural and interpersonal factors. Consequently truth is seen to be dialogical rather than propositional, emerging from listening to and dialoguing with the various narratives and constructions of reality that surround a particular phenomenon. Each story reveals a different dimension/perspective on the specific reality that is being examined.

Table 4.1. Contrasting positivist and naturalist axioms

Axioms	Positivist Paradigm	Naturalistic Paradigm
The nature of reality	Reality is single, tangible, and fragmentable	Realities are multiple, constructed, and holistic
The relationship of knower and known	Knower and known are independent, a dualism	Knower and known are interactive, inseparable
The possibility of generalization	Time- and context-free generalizations are possible	Only time- and context-bound working hypotheses are possible
The possibility of causal linkages	There are real causes, temporally precedent to or simultaneous with their effects.	All entities are in a state of mutual simultaneous shaping, so that it is impossible to distinguish causes from effects
The role of values	Inquiry is value-free	Inquiry is value-based

Lincoln and Guba 1985, p.37.

There are of course some proponents of this perspective who would argue that reality is inaccessible and that constructivism is *all* that there is. However, for the purposes of this book it is perhaps more useful to think in terms of a continuum between a naive realism that accepts that truth can be fully accessed through human endeavour, that is, that theoretical concepts find direct correlates within the world, and a form of mediated or *critical realism* that accepts that reality can be known a little better through our constructions while at the same time recognizing that such constructions are always provisional and open to challenge. The central thing that needs to be drawn from this perspective is that the idea of value-free, objective truth becomes unsustainable. All truth is formulated through an interpretative process within which the researcher is inevitable enmeshed. The quest is not for objectivity, but for *understanding*, brought about by the critical utilization of the observer within the research process: a *fusion of horizons* between the observer and the subject of her research. Human beings are recognized as actively creative agents who are constantly interpreting situations and ascribing meaning and purpose to events; constantly creating explanatory narratives. These meanings and interpretations form the 'maps of reality', which individuals (and cultures), use to interpret their experiences and decide upon appropriate forms of action. It is therefore not enough simply to observe what a person is doing or how they are behaving in order to assess what is actually going on within any given situation. To understand persons, it is necessary to understand the *meaning* of their actions and the reasons for their acting in a particular manner. This was highlighted previously in the discussion on religious orientation and the importance of the meaning of a person's spirituality. This being so, it is necessary to maintain a critical tension between action, context and meaning, as well as a balance between objectivity and subjectivity, when attempting to ascertain and correctly assess the significance of human behaviour. The method and philosophical perspective outlined below is designed to enable such a task.

Hermeneutic Phenomenology

The particular method deemed most appropriate for exploring the lived experience of spirituality in enduring forms of depression was hermeneutic phenomenology. The intention of this approach is to allow the researcher access into the inner experiences of research subjects. Although it has not been used extensively in the study of spirituality, significant studies have begun to emerge that explore the lived experience of spiritual distress (Smucker 1996), spiritual relationships (Styles 1994), recovery from alcoholism (Bowden 1998), and the essential elements of spirituality (Tongprateep 2000). These studies provide rich insights into human experience and vital understandings that can significantly inform the practice of care. To date, this approach and methodology has not been used to explore the experience of spirituality within the context of depression.

The use of this method has emerged from a growing dissatisfaction with a realist philosophy of science based on the study of material entities with no reference to cultural or social context (Ryan 1996). Hermeneutical phenomenology presents a significant challenge to the positivism that, as has been suggested, has been so influential in the development of contemporary health care practices within the Western world.

Phenomenology

Phenomenology is a philosophy of experience which attempts to understand the ways in which meaning is constructed in and through human experience. This perspective views a person's *lived experience* of and within the world as the foundation of meaning. Phenomenology is concerned with the strange tensions between the personal and social nature of experience. Whilst there are aspects of experience which are deeply private and 'not for sharing', other aspects are intersubjective and developed in community. The aim of phenomenology is to determine what an experience means to a person quite apart from any theoretical overlay put on it by the researcher, and to provide a comprehensive and rich description of it (Moustakas 1994).

> [P]henomenology is the study of the lifeworld – the world as we immediately experience it pre-reflectively rather than as we conceptualize, categorize, or reflect on it... Phenomenology aims at gaining a deeper understanding of the nature or meaning of our everyday experiences. Phenomenology asks, 'What is this or that kind of experience like?' It differs from almost every other science in that it attempts to gain insightful descriptions of the way we experience the world pre-reflectively, without taxonomizing, classifying, or abstracting it. (Van Manen 1990, p.9)

Unlike the perspective of positivism, phenomenology does not attempt to build theory that can be used to explain all instances of a given phenomenon. Rather it seeks to present plausible insights that bring us in more direct contact with the world (Van Manen 1990, p.9).

> Transformative experience alters action. Knowledge resulting from phenomenological inquiry becomes practically relevant in its possibilities of changing the manner in which a professional communicates with and acts towards another individual in the very next situation he/she may encounter. Phenomenological knowledge reforms understanding, does something to us, it affects us, and leads to more thoughtful action. (Van der Zalm 2000, p.213)

Hermeneutics

Phenomenology, as it has emerged as a way of doing research, has taken on varied forms. Rather than being a specific method, it might be better to describe it as a family of methods, all connected by certain understandings and presumptions, but yet differing in significant ways in their practice. The form used within this study is *hermeneutical* phenomenology. This form of phenomenology displays both descriptive and interpretive elements. It is

> *descriptive* (phenomenological) methodology because it wants to be attentive to how things appear, it wants to let things speak for themselves; it is an *interpretive* (hermeneutic) methodology because it claims that there are no such things as uninterpreted phenomena. The implied contradiction may be resolved if one acknowledges that the (phenomenological) 'facts' of lived experience are always already meaningfully (hermeneutically) experienced. Moreover, even the 'facts' of lived experience need to be captured in language (the human science text) and this is inevitably an interpretive process. (Van Manen 1990, p.181)

The Hermeneutics of Hans Georg Gadamer

Prejudice

The particular form of hermeneutic phenomenology that was used within this study was drawn from the thinking of German philosopher Hans Georg Gadamer. For Gadamer, understanding things is not something that can be done by separating subject from object in the way that the natural sciences assume. Both subject and object are bound to and mediated by a common cultural and historical context, and *effective history*, that is, personal exper-ience and cultural traditions. Gadamer refers to these pre-understandings as *prejudices*. However, his use of the word 'prejudice' does not have the negative connotations applied to it in common parlance. Our prejudices are fundamental to the way in which we interpret and make sense of the world. Gadamer argues that prejudice is not something that is negative or some-thing that we should try to eliminate. In fact, we can only access the world through our prejudices (Thomson 1999, p.241). Prejudice is

> a forestructure or a condition of knowledge in that it determines what we may find intelligible in any given situation. [Gadamer] replaces the opposition between truth and prejudice with the assertion that prejudice – our situatedness in history and time – is the precondition of truth, not an obstacle to it. (Hekman 1986, p.117)

In order to understand and assimilate new experiences it is necessary to draw on this pre-understanding. Thus, the basic structure of a person's or community's effective history constrains and to an extent defines the range of possible interpretations, excluding some possibilities and calling forth others. It is therefore necessary for a person to be aware of their own historical situatedness and the ways in which it influences their interpretations of those texts, objects, people, and events we choose to seek to understand. The *historically effective consciousness* (Gadamer 1981 pp. 204 ff.) is one which is truly open to experience, and which is aware of the influence of a person's pre-understandings. Thus in Gadamer, the image of the researcher as separate from the object of study is replaced by a dialectical understanding that suggests the need for dialogue and conversation between the text and the researcher; conversation that does not exclude the researcher's pre-understandings, but constructively draws them into the dialogical process.

Bracketing?

Gadamer's hermeneutical perspective contrasts with certain other phenomenological perspectives that assume the necessity of bracketing for authentic phenomenological research (Beech 1999). Bracketing refers to the suspension of a person's beliefs and preconceptions in the outer world. By adopting a stance of objectivity and neutrality, the phenomenon can be seen and understood for what it essentially is (Corben 1999). Instead, Gadamer argues that our pre-understandings or prejudices as he calls them, are necessary for us to make sense of the world. In order effectively to interpret a text, it is necessary to enter into dialogue with it, that is, to bring one's own 'horizon' into fusion or constructive dialogue with the horizon of the text. Out of this dialectical movement, fresh insights and new interpretations emerge which may even transcend the meaning originally intended by the author.

The fusion of horizons

Gadamer's position is that it is naive to believe that one can ever be truly detached from the object of interpretation. In order to understand a text we need a fusion between the horizon of our world and the world of the text. From this perspective, the task of the researcher is not to bracket their prejudices, but to fuse their horizons with the horizons of the research participants in a way that will deepen and clarify the meaning of the experience being explored. Horizons are closely connected with prejudice in that they contain an individual's and a society's underlying assumptions about the way the world is and how people and things should function within it.

Thus, the task of the researcher is to enter into a constructive, critical dialogue with the text within which a fusion of the two horizons is brought about. The fusion of horizons is a version of the hermeneutic circle (Weinsheimer 1985) in that it is a crucial dialogical process that takes place between interpreter and text. 'Understanding occurs when the horizons of the scholar intersect or fuse with the horizon, context or standpoint of the objective enquiry' (Smith 1996). Hekman (1986, p.104) likens this process to Buber's idea of the 'I–Thou' relationship in the sense that it demands a radical openness to the experience of the other and a respect for experiences that transcend one's own horizons.

Gadamer explains the metaphor of the horizon as

the wide superior vision that the person who is seeking to understand must have; to acquire a horizon means that one learns to look beyond what is close at hand – not in order to look away from it, but to see it better within a larger whole and in truer proportion. (1975, p.272)

This means that the horizon of the interpreter includes their entire forestructure, that is, what we find intelligible given our specific cultural perspectives and our place in history (Thomson 1990). Understanding occurs when the horizon of the scholar intersects or fuses with the horizon of the object of inquiry (Smith 1996).

Thus interpretation and understanding is more than simply adopting an empathic stance with the text's author. Rather it is a creative process within which even the author's original assumptions concerning the meaning of the text may be challenged and deepened.

The hermeneutical circle

The final concept that is central to this way of approaching research is Gadamer's idea of the hermeneutical circle. The hermeneutical circle refers to the interpretive process wherein the scholar moves backwards and forwards from 'whole to the part and back to the whole' (Gadamer 1981, p.259). Single words only make sense within the context of a wider linguistic pattern. Likewise that wider pattern is determined by the specific meanings of individual words. It is out of this interpretive, dynamic movement that meaning and understanding emerge. For example, the word 'football' on its own can have a variety of meanings according to the context within which it is used. It is only within the context of a sentence that one can assess whether or not the word 'football' is referring to the sport as a whole, or simply the leather ball that is used as part of the sport. Whether it is prefixed with the word 'American' or 'British' will to an extent determine the precise nature of the sport being referred to. If one introduces the word 'rugby' this again changes the meaning and shifts our understanding of the word football. Thus the meaning of the word emerges from its interaction with its wider context of other words or sentences. Similarly a sentence only provides partial information if it is viewed within a paragraph. A paragraph only makes sense within the context of a chapter, the chapter finds its full meaning within a book, and so forth. This circular exercise is an ongoing process, moving from whole to part and then back to whole. In order to make sense of the whole situation, it is necessary to move backwards and forwards between the meaning of the words and the meaning of the wider text. This is the type of movement that is present within the hermeneutical circle.

Method

The hermeneutic phenomenological method used in this study was an adaptation of the exploratory frameworks developed in the work of Smith 1996; Diekelmann, Allan and Tanner 1989; and Van Manen 1990. The research process moved through a series of ten stages that can be outlined as follows:

1. The interviews with participants were recorded on mini-disks which were then transcribed by the researcher, thus creating a text which could become the locus of the interpretive process.

2. The texts were then entered into MARTIN, a software program specifically designed to assist in phenomenological research. MARTIN is a Windows tool aimed at facilitating analyses rather than generating new theories. In this sense it differs from other similar software packages such as NUD*IST which is designed for grounded theory and theory generation. (NUD*IST stands for Non-numerical, Unstructured, Data: Indexing, Searching and Theorizing. Put simply, it works with textual documents, and facilitates the *indexing* of components of these documents; is able to *search* for words and phrases very quickly; and claims to support *theorizing* through enabling the retrieval of indexed text segments, related memos, and text and index searches; and through the construction of a hierarchically structured tree to order index

categories. MARTIN was designed to reflect the ways a researcher thinks about and interacts with written texts. 'Utilizing object-oriented programming and Windows' graphics interface, MARTIN offers researchers an alternative to fixed labeling schemes by using the computer screen as the electronic equivalent of a desktop. Documents and interview texts are displayed in windows that can be moved, stacked, tiled, resized, or reduced to icons. Each text occupies its own window, and multiple texts can be displayed simultaneously, making it easy to work across texts. Notes can be attached freely and discarded at any time' (UW–Madison School of Nursing 2000).

3. The researcher then began to immerse himself in the texts that had been created (Moustakas 1994). This involved reading them over and over in order to get a feel for the content and for the subtle nuances of the interactions with research participants.

4. During this process of immersion, and of moving between individual phrases, sentences, chunks of narrative and the entire text and context (the hermeneutical circle), themes began to emerge that appeared to incorporate something of the essence of the experience of depression and the role of spirituality in living with it. Van Manen (1990, p.79) describes phenomenological themes as 'structures of experience'. In searching for and seeking to analyse a phenomenon, 'we are trying to determine what the themes are, the experiential structures that make up that experience.' Themes are not objects of generalization. Rather, they are 'like knots in the webs of our experience, around which certain lived experiences are thus spun and thus lived through as meaningful wholes. Themes are the stars that make up the universe of meaning we live through. By the lights of these themes we can navigate and explore the universes' (Van Manen 1990, p.90). Themes do not necessarily represent the experience as initially interpreted and understood by the person themselves, but are a constructive product of the fusion of the researcher's horizons with those of the participants as together they embark upon the quest for meaning and understanding. All of the participants within this study commented on the way in which the themes that emerged from their transcripts made them aware of aspects of their experience that they had not reflected on or recognized previously.

This being so, the emergent themes may participate in a process of consciousness-raising within which research participants discover new aspects of their situation.

5. These themes were then collected and organized using MARTIN, and representative phrases and statements were collected to illustrate and elucidate the various themes and their meanings (Van Manen 1990, p.30). The various themes were grouped together and the researcher embarked upon a process of dialogical reflection, moving between the extrapolated themes (the parts) and the text as a whole (the hermeneutical circle) in order to check the authenticity of the themes, and to develop a deeper, fuller understanding of the meaning that was being expressed by the research participants.

6. The researcher then constructed a thematic analysis of each of the research transcripts. This involved structuring the themes in line with the various emphases within the text and developing an initial interpretation of the lived experience of each of the participants. Relevant extracts were taken from the text and used to illustrate and elucidate the various themes.

7. These reconstructed, thematized narratives were then given to the participants for validation. The author then spent time with the research participants, working through the transcript and making any alterations necessary due to misunderstanding or misinterpretation. At this stage the person becomes a co-researcher, actively participating in the shaping and interpreting of the data. A copy of the original transcripts and their thematic analyses was also given to independent expert nurses who were asked to validate the themes identified by the researcher.

8. All of this data was collated, and the final process of interpretive reflection and narrative construction was embarked upon. This involved a return to the process of immersion within which the texts were compared and contrasted in a search for 'constitutive patterns…which unified all of the texts' (Smith 1998).

9. Writing is fundamental to this form of research. 'Creating a phenomenological text is the object of the research process' (Van Manen 1990, p.111). Through the process of writing and

re-writing, the interpreted accounts were brought together and a final account constructed.

10. The research product was fed back to the research participants and their thoughts and comments were taken into consideration prior to the final draft of the account being produced.

Ethical Issues

Permission was granted by the local health care ethics committee to approach people with long-term mental health problems with a view to exploring the subject matter of the project.

Research Participants

It is clear from the previous methodological discussion that those participating in this study were not the *objects* of research. Rather they were co-researchers who were deeply and proactively involved in the process of research. The research process was, in a very real sense, a mutual journey of exploration and discovery. The research was based on six in-depth interviews with a purposive sample of three men and three women who had experienced depression for at least two years. All were currently living in the community, and all were regularly in contact with the mental health services. As the purpose of the investigation was to create a rich description of their experiences, rather than to explain or generate theory about them, a small sample was deemed appropriate. The participants were volunteers who responded to the invitation of the researcher and a call for volunteers put out at a local day centre for people with mental health problems.

The Interviews

Data was collected using unstructured interviews. This was deemed most likely to elicit rich data that enabled participants freely to relate their personal narratives in ways that were uninhibited by the researcher's personal agenda and the boundaries of fixed questions. All interviews were initiated with the question: 'What is it that gives meaning to your life?' The interviews lasted for 45 minutes to an hour and took place at a number of locations: within Aberdeen University, at the local drop-in centre and in the participant's own home.

As well as these primary interviews, the researcher also spent time with the participants at the various stages of feedback and reconstruction. These feedback sessions also provided useful information and clarification that proved invaluable to the overall research process.

Issues of Validity

Bearing in mind the differences between the scientific/positivistic paradigm of research and the constructivist approach developed above, it is obvious that the criteria for validation cannot be the same (Kuhn 1970; Koch 1996, 1999; Lincoln and Guba 1985; Sandelowski 1989). The question of validity in qualitative research is a matter for continuing debate. It is not possible to review the various arguments here. (Readers interested in following this line of discussion are referred to Koch 1994, 1996, 1998a and b, 1999; Lincoln and Guba 1985). The object of hermeneutic phenomenology is to gain *understanding* of the experience of research participants, rather than to *explain* the experience of the objects of research. Any form of validation will necessarily have to reflect this different perspective. For the purposes of this study the author chose to draw on certain validational processes that are well established within the literature and accepted as appropriate ways of validating a study such as this.

Lincoln and Guba (1985) put forward the term 'trustworthiness' to indicate the nature of rigour within qualitative research: 'Qualitative rigor emerges from three components; credibility, auditability and fittingness (whose quantitative analogues are validity, reliability and generalizability' (Smith 1996, p.24; cf. also Lincoln and Guba 1985; Sandelowski 1986). In order to be trustworthy in this sense, the study drew upon a number of suggestions that are present within the literature.

A thick, rich description

For a study to attain credibility it must be able to present a thick, rich and recognizable description of the subject matter.

> A qualitative study is credible when it presents such faithful descriptions of a human experience that the people having that experience would immediately recognize those descriptions of interpretations as their own. A study is also credible when other people (other researchers or readers) can recognize the experience when confronted with it after having only read about it in a study. (Sandelowski 1986, pp.32ff)

A thick description seeks to capture the essence of a phenomenon in a way that communicates it in all of its fullness. It is therefore rich, vivid and faithful (Koch 1998a). The implications of this for the research process as a whole is that the process of writing, reflecting and accurately interpreting the data is not simply epiphenomenal to data presentation and analysis. It is a crucial part of the process.

Participant validation

The transcripts and the interpretation of the data were returned to the participants for validation. In each case the themes were talked through and any suggested adjustments incorporated in the final draft of the text. This demonstrates the type of *credibility* that Lincoln and Guba (1985) highlight as fundamental to the trustworthiness of a research project. Without such credibility in the eyes of the 'information sources', 'the findings and conclusions as a whole cannot be found credible by the consumer of the inquiry report...credibility is crucial and...cannot be well established without recourse to the data sources themselves' (Lincoln and Guba 1985, p.213).

The final draft of the research product was fed back to selected participants to see if the text as a whole resonated with their own experiences of depression. Comments were noted and taken into the final process of reflection and text construction.

Participants also formed a vital part of the validation process in so far as their own words and narratives formed a prominent aspect of the final text. Thus the participants were given a voice and a 'shop front' within which their experiences could be expressed in their own words and the possibility of misunderstanding reduced.

Independent validation

The interview texts were read and the themes checked by independent researchers with knowledge of the particular research process being used. Comments were noted and discussed. In order to experience the fusion of horizons, it is necessary to 'tolerate the ambiguity of relaxing (not eliminating) one's own pre-conceptions' (Thomson 1990, p.246). The process of independent validation enables the researcher to reflect on and monitor his or her own prejudices and to ensure that the way in which the horizons are being fused is not to the detriment of the text as a whole. There were no major discrepancies in the interpretation and the themes that emerged from the various texts. One theme was questioned and further reflection was carried out before the theme was finally rejected.

Auditability

Auditability refers to the decisions made by the researcher at every stage of the process (Koch 1998b). This aspect is achieved when

> another researcher can follow the 'decision trail' of a study from beginning to end... In this way, readers of a report may not agree with the author's interpretations, but at least they should be able to understand how he arrived at those interpretations. (Smith 1996, p.25)

This means recording the decisions and experiences encountered at each stage of the research process and recording them in the form of an 'audit trail' that can be followed through by others (Koch 1998b). To this end, the researcher's reflexive journal is of great importance.

A reflexive journal

In phenomenological research 'the researcher not only collects data, but also serves as the primary instrument through which data are collected' (Smith 1996). Consequently it is necessary that the researcher is constantly in touch with their own horizon and the ways in which that may be influencing the continuing research process. Thus in order to enter into the hermeneutical circle in a way that is authentic and effective, the researcher maintains a reflexive journal. '[T]he daily journal is essential in recording the way in which my horizon is working... credibility is enhanced when researchers describe and interpret their experiences as researchers' (Koch 1996). It is important to be aware of the ways in which the researcher is constructing their reality and the possible ways in which these interpretations are affecting the overall interpretive process. 'The use of a reflexive journal can provide some evidence of the researcher's continuing engagement with the participants and reveals how the self of the researcher enters into the stages of the research process' (Smith 1996). The following journal extract illustrates this process in action.

> At one point during the interview she describes her suicidal tendencies and states that *'one day I will kill myself.'* This is powerful! I can begin to experience something of the deep tragedy that *is* depression. I feel awkward, challenged, yet in a sense honored at her honesty and her willingness to trust me with such deep and personal experiences. I am tempted to wonder if she is simply saying this for effect; attention seeking? But as I listen to her whole story and see the brokenness in her eyes, my therapeutic bias wanes. This is real.

The journal enables the researcher to remain aware of their own horizons and to work with them in interpreting and understanding. By keeping a journal of what the researcher encounters within the context of the interviews and as they work with the text, a rich and holistic understanding of the research process can be developed that enables the two horizons to merge creatively. Extracts of this journal may well be incorporated into the final research product, thus increasing the sense of participation and dialogue that is so central to a Gadamerian hermeneutical approach.

A recognizable final product

Finally, the end product of the research process should be recognizable as reflecting something of the essence to the experience being described (Lincoln and Guba 1985). To this end, the final product of this study was fed back to participants for discussion and further reflection.

Limitations of the study

Before moving on to examine the results, there are certain limitations of the study that need to be taken into consideration.

First, all of the participants in the study were committed to the Christian faith tradition. There were two main reasons for this, one cultural and the other semantic. At a cultural level, Aberdeen, where the study took place, does not have a high ethnic, multi-religious population. Consequently, the faith which overwhelmingly predominates is Christianity. The population of the particular day centre where the initial call for volunteers went out reflects this lack of cultural diversity in so far as those who attend are predominantly white and of Christian orientation if not commitment.

Second, the call for volunteers was aimed at people who had an interest in spirituality. In my later discussions with various day-centre attenders, it appeared that spirituality had been interpreted specifically in religious terms. Consequently, it was people with an interest in religion who responded. This may reflect a general confusion over what spirituality is, and the uncertainty about its wider dimensions. Although the results of this study are applicable beyond established religion, there is a need for a similar study aimed at exploring the spirituality of people with depression from the perspective of the wider definition that has been worked out previously.

Finally, there may be issues of gender, power and spirituality that were not addressed within this study. There was no attempt made to discern between female and male spiritual experiences, or to reflect upon how issues of gender and power influence the relationship between spirituality and mental health. However, as this was not an exercise in critical or feminist hermeneutics this was not deemed to be a serious omission within the general intentions of the study. Again, there may be scope for a study that focuses specifically on these particular issues.

Central Themes that Emerged from the Data

The meaningless abyss of depression

For the participants in this study, meaning and the ways in which it can be lost and regained within the context of depression were central to their experience of both their spirituality and depression. Meaning has been acknowledged by a number of writers as a fundamental aspect of both spirituality and mental health (Frankl 1964; Karp 1996). Burnard (1990), writing from a nursing perspective, suggests that the concept of meaning provides a common definition of spirituality that encompasses it in both its religious and non-religious dimensions. According to Burnard, it is the quest for meaning that provides the defining criteria for what spirituality is and what the primary focus of spiritual care should be. Psychoanalyst Victor Frankl also stresses the significance of meaning for human well-being. He suggests that the primary motivating force that drives human beings onwards towards mental health is the quest for *meaning* and *purpose*. Frankl argues that the quest for meaning is the fundamental dynamic force that motivates and guides the human person. For Frankl, meaning is foundational for the development of mental health. If a person has no meaning in their lives, they have nothing to motivate them towards the future. If they have no hope, then they will die, either physically or emotionally.

The great significance of meaning was central to the experience of depression in all of the participants. If life has meaning, then it is possible to cope with the considerable difficulties that depression imposes upon a person's life.

> I don't depend on there being direct, individual meaning in my particular circumstances or situation and all the bad things that happen to me. I'm quite happy to live with the idea that, you know, in a fallen world there are things that happen to people just sort of through chance and circumstance. But what one does need to believe is that all of that is happening in an ultimately meaningful framework.

However, if that 'ultimately meaningful framework' collapses, as is the case when the person tumbles into the depths of depression, they are is catapulted into a deep dark void that is deeply disturbing and spiritually devastating.

> *When I'm in a phase that I am able to believe that there is a God who gives meaning to that universe, then I have hope. But there have been spells when I haven't been able to believe that, and that has been absolutely terrifying. That's been falling into the abyss. That is seriously nasty!*

The imagery of the abyss powerfully symbolizes the terrifying black pit of meaninglessness into which a person slides during the experience of depression. The only foothold out of the abyss is the possibility that there is meaning beyond one's own situation. If this foothold is torn away, there is *'nothing but "nothingness" and darkness.'*

> *You would go to bed at night and it was dark outside, and it felt dark inside. All creative energy was gone, it just wasn't there. When I woke in the morning, although it was dawn, inside nothing had changed and it was still dark.*

The abyss is filled with doubt about self, others and the order of the world. It is a meaningless void within which strength, hope and light are drained, leaving the person in a dark and lonely place.

Questioning everything

Depression initiates a frightening form of unbelief which challenges everything that previously gave life meaning and purpose.

> *Well, when I was younger, my sister said to me – we were only about 12 or 13 at the time, in fact maybe younger – and she said something like, 'I don't really know what the point is in living, 'cause at the end of it we die.' And I was horrified because I thought, how can you feel like that? You know, at such an early age. She wasn't ill or depressed or anything, she was just stating how she felt about it, and it was like, gosh! I'd never thought of it before. To me it was just get on and live kind of thing. . .so it made me stop and think then. I never really. . .I didn't actually consider it properly until I got depression, because when my mood was low, and my thought processes were wrong, that made me question really everything about myself and about life and about the whole thing.*

The meaningfulness of this participant's youth, and her amazement at her sister's inability to grasp the meaning of life, are powerfully contrasted with the change of worldview brought about by her own experiences of depression.

The movement from a meaning*ful* universe to a meaning*less* one is startling and presents as a common feature in all of the participants.

> You're going along living your life as normally as you can when suddenly all your assumptions, presuppositions and in some cases values are called into question, so that everything gets tossed up in the air.

Suddenly the world looks different. The old familiar maps and landmarks no longer make sense. You look out on the world and it looks so different as to be almost unrecognizable.

> It was like looking out on a landscape that was total desolation; where once there had been growth and possibilities, now there was just nothing! Just nothing but desolation. Words can't really describe it. Like, I was looking at things that I had seen a hundred times before and they looked different. I could see them but I couldn't feel them.

The experience of depression causes a person to question everything that they once held dear. In questioning, one begins to doubt everything; in doubting that which gives one meaning in life, one slips even deeper into the desolation of the abyss. Depression is an experience which brings about a profound change in the way the person views themselves and the world around them. It is an experience which literally sucks the meaning out of life, leaving the person staring out on a panorama of meaninglessness; stranded deep within an abyss within which meaning, purpose, hope and possibility are banished and replaced with questions for which there appear to be no answers and no possibility of answers.

Abandonment

A common theme that ran through the interviews was the experience of feelings of abandonment; abandonment both by God and by those around you.

> I know that God is in control, but, when one's emotions and mood and everything are up for grabs, it's actually exceedingly hard to feel that. That then gives rise to a conflict, because what you feel and what you know are not saying the same things. So you get…what I probably got a lot of was a sense of abandonment and the feeling that God's walked off and left me. Where is He now? What use is this faith thing anyway? So that then becomes an inner conflict.

The essence of this man's faith has to do with his perception of engaging in a loving relationship with God. *'Faith to me is not religion as such. It's a personal relationship with God.'* Such a relationship cannot be maintained by intellect alone. As with any other personal relationship it demands emotion and feeling. Yet, during times of depression he cannot feel his relationship with God in the way that he has done in the past. This conflict between intellectual and experiential knowledge leads to a sense of abandonment by God. Like a lover who knows in his head that his partner cares for him, but in his daily life does not experience that care in either words or actions, so also this man finds himself caught up in a conflict between what he knows in his head and what he does not feel in his heart. If his faith were purely legalistic this might be easier. However, as his faith is deeply experiential and relational, this is a serious problem for him. He no longer *feels* loved by God. This experience is much more than a theological crisis. It is a crisis of *being* and *identity*.

Scottish philosopher John Macmurray in his trenchant critique of Cartesian dualism (MacMurray 1961) points to the ways in which human beings are 'created' in and through their relationships with others. In a very real sense we are persons-in-relation. We depend on one another for our identities and understandings of the world. I am only a father because of my children, a husband because of my wife, a lecturer because of my occupation and so forth. My personal identity and the way I view the world and my place within it is not a pre-set given, but rather the product of my relational interactions with other human beings and my social and cultural context, including the ways in which I interpret and utilize God.

This observation is helpful in interpreting and understanding the feelings of abandonment experienced by the research participants. All of the participants in the study appeared to have an intrinsic form of spirituality; that is, their religious/spiritual tradition was considered to be a fundamental part of their lives, the foundational bond that they used to bind themselves to the world. Depression destroys this bond and leaves the person with a serious crisis of identity and spirituality. The sense of being abandoned by God is more than just a negative cognition. It is indicative of a serious existential crisis. *'If God has abandoned me, then what and who am I?'* If a person can no longer relate to God, and if their self-image and interpretation of the world is dependent on their experience of God, then to experience such abandonment is, in a very real sense, to lose a part of themselves. The experience of being abandoned by God leaves them with a wide, gaping wound where once there had been a powerful source of hope, love, meaning and purpose. Thus the person is thrown into a void of unknowing that is much more profound and devastating than simply the lowering of their mood. In the midst of the sadness of depression, there is a significant loss of self which the person has to struggle to understand and come to terms with. Depression destroys that which is most dear and significant to a person. It challenges a person at the very core of their being and forces them to reconsider who they are and what their life is really about.

Clinging on

> *My faith is probably the main thing that gives me meaning and purpose in the midst of all this. Without that I would find it difficult to know why we are here. Faith to me is not religion as such. It's a personal relationship with God which helps me to cling on... em... I suppose* [pause] *it holds you up sometimes and gives you a reason to be.*

The idea of clinging on was present in the experience of all of the research participants. In the midst of the meaninglessness, confusion and desolation that marks the experience of depression, a person's spirituality appears to have a crucial role in enabling them to '*cling on*' to life and the possibility of a hopeful future. While depression may strip the meaning from a person's life, leaving them in a place of utter desolation, their spirituality helps relocate them within the world of meaningful experiences and enables them to find identity, worth, purpose and hope. In the midst of the hopelessness and helplessness that depression brings into a person's life, spirituality provides a '*reason to be*', a purpose and sense of meaning that reaches beyond their immediate situation. This 'reason to be' enables a person to cling on in the midst of the darkest storms.

> *When things were just at their absolutely hellish worst, that was just the only thing I could hold onto... I don't think I could've, I just couldn't have survived without having the faith to hold onto at that point. I've had it where I clung on to my faith as if... if I let it go I was going to completely die. It was like I've got to hang on to this because I've got nothing else that I feel secure in. But at the same time, the feeling about faith was, 'is it real?... if I let go, what's going to happen?' Do you know what I mean? It was that kind of... there was a need in me for clinging on to what was in the Bible. You know, the fact that God was there for you, protecting you and you just hung on to that.*

The metaphor of 'clinging on' expresses well the desperate desire to retain a connection with God when everything else is being eroded and undermined by the effects of depression. For the woman who made the above statement, God is personal, intimate and persistently present, in the midst of all of her struggles. The idea of 'clinging on' expresses well the intimacy o relationship with God. God is her protector. In times of deep distress, God is the one to whom she clings for protection and hope. With this intimacy of relationship comes the fear that she will lose her grip on her spirituality and tumble out of control into the emptiness of a meaningless universe within which God no longer exists.

The above statement illustrates well this woman's feelings of desperation as she reaches out to the only source of hope and comfort that is available to her. She can keep her head above the water just as long as her fingertips don't lose their strength or become powerless because of the paralysing effects of her depression. There is an ever-present, deep fear that her grip is loosening; that her fingers are becoming numb because of the relentless cold seas of depression that constantly wash over and threaten to engulf her.

The erosion of faith brought on by her depressive episodes means that she is frequently drawn towards an abyss of meaninglessness and nothingness. The fear of God and the knowledge of God's protecting presence revealed to her through scripture provides a means whereby she is enabled to cling on to life and the possibility of hope and meaning. She can only cling on to life as long as her spirituality is strong enough to prevent her from letting go. To let go is to risk the possibility of dying, not just metaphorically but also physically.

The desire to relate and the failure of relationships

Depression not only sucks the meaning out of life, leaving a person abandoned and desolate, it also drains the physical and psychological strength that is required to fight against it.

> The image that comes to mind is that, everything about life was like wading through thick treacle. Really just heavy going, and a struggle just to take a step forward. You know, everything just slowed down and was very exhausting. A fearfulness of...em...sometimes of meeting people, particularly people who were not close to me. That was very difficult.

This physical and psychological exhaustion makes relationships very difficult, not necessarily because they are not desired, but because the person simply does not have the strength, confidence or inner motivation to reach out to another human being in the way that they might desire. Under such circumstances, people tend to withdraw from company. This does not however mean that they lose their desire to relate to others. It was clear from the experiences of all of the participants in the study that there is a strange paradox at work in the midst of the experience of depression. On the one hand, the person inwardly desires to relate to others. Yet at the same time they experience a need to distance themselves from others.

> *People are very important to me…The problem that happens with depression is that when I get depressed, I withdraw from people, and so everything that I would normally be becomes the opposite from the way I am normally…And it's sort of, then you've got to re-learn, to get back into being what you normally are. And it's like, 'what is normal? I don't know what my normal is!' It's not that I don't want other people, it's just that I don't know how to deal with them at the time. What I really want is them all to come and go [gestures an embrace] you know, but that's irrational and you can't expect that of people, and so it's easier just to say, 'go away until I'm better.' What I really want is not what I do!*

Depression disconnects people from themselves, from God and from those around them. It destroys fundamental social and spiritual ties and leaves a person isolated, lonely and unable to find a foothold back into relationship and community. Even though they may desperately desire the company of others, the nature of depression means that they are unable to express this desire and reach out for the very thing that might bring healing.

At times such as these the sustaining faith of others and their persistent caring presence is of fundamental importance. A person's spirituality can sustain them in the midst of their depression and provide a significant source of meaning and hope. However, there are times when the darkness of depression is simply too dense to allow the person to access their spirituality directly. During these times it is the faith and the hope of others that sustains a person. '*All I had was other people's faith that God knew what he was doing, when everything in me was screaming "you don't know what you're doing!"*' This need for relationships and the empathetic support of others was very important for the spiritual sustenance of all of the participants, and was frequently expressed both in terms of their own experiences of social support and through reflection on their spiritual tradition.

> *In my mind there's the sort of picture story in the gospel of the paralysed man being unable to get to Jesus under his own steam, and it was four friends who basically did everything in their power to get that guy right down under Jesus' nose. That to me is a kind of parable that needs to happen when someone is really paralysed, whether it be physical or mental.*

Here we are presented with an image of a paralysed person, unable to walk or move towards the only source of healing that is available to them. He is lifted, sustained and drawn towards a source of healing by the faithful presence of his friends. This image reflects powerfully the experience of psychological paralysis experienced by the study's participants; a form of paralysis within which they could see the healing potential of relationships, but simply did not have the strength to move towards it. In the midst of depression, when a person cannot sustain their spirituality and desires, yet cannot hold onto meaningful relationships, there remains a possibility of hope and meaning through the faithful presence and the sustaining faith of others. Such care cannot be initiated by the person themselves. It is very much a work of 'grace' in the sense that it is brought about and sustained by others quite apart from the active participation of the person with depression. What is required is that 'the friends' understand the experience of depression and choose to sit with the 'paralytic' in the midst of their darkness, being with them and in a sense living their experience with them; reaching into their darkness and drawing them into the light, even if that presence is not always welcomed.

> *The friends have to come and they actually have to take the initiative and say, 'this is what we're doing chaps!' In a sense almost whether you like it or not, 'this is what you need!' ...People to see possibilities when you can't see them yourself.*

In this way people's repressed desire for relationship in the midst of depression can begin to find expression in the caring actions of others.

Grinding me down

A person experiencing depression finds himself or herself physically and psychologically exhausted, alone and often lonely, and without the ability to turn to others for support and friendship. In the long term this loss of strength and the thought of the continuing battle against depression can become profoundly demoralizing, persistently grinding a person down, even to the point where it threatens their will to carry on living.

> *It feels like each time I get depressed, it's more soul destroying each time, because you know you've got to get out of it again.*

Q. Because you've been there before?

> *Uhuh. It just grinds me down. The first time round I didn't know what I was dealing with. It was like I didn't know what I was aiming for when I was trying to get well. It was a case of 'have therapy, deal with all of this; get it sorted', and I had to trust the people that were dealing with me to get me well again. But the more it happens, you*

know, I find it's much more difficult to fight it, because it's like I haven't got the energy, and I'm just so tired of it. I know what I've got ahead of me. What's difficult is the fact that you know what you've got to get through, what you've to do to get yourself up again. And it's like Ugh! I say to my doctor, the thought of going through my life like this, it's too much. Because it's just a hellish illness. And it's a bit frightening, living with that thought... Your thoughts become, you know, wanting to die and kill yourself is like the most logical thing out, and it's gonna be the best for everybody. And you can't understand why people are trying to not let you do that! I do feel that one day I'll kill myself, because of depression. And that's a frightening thought. It feels like each time I get depressed, it's more soul destroying each time, because you know you've got to get out of it again.

This statement is a powerful revelation of the dark tension that forms a significant part of this woman's day-to-day life; the tension between the joy of experiencing the love of God and her anger about being prevented from killing herself provides an insight into the depths of pain and suffering she experiences during times of depression. Spirituality helps to ease this tension, but it does not take away the pain.

Trapped into living

Connected with the theme of 'grinding me down' is the idea of being 'trapped into living'. Spirituality plays a double-edged role in the context of the frustration and desire to end one's life. On the one hand, it gives the person the strength to cling on in the midst of the experience of depression. In this sense it is beneficial to the person's survival and to the development and maintenance of mental health. On the other hand, it can also be perceived as trapping people into living, that is, preventing them from doing that which they consider to be the most logical and rational way of ending their psychological pain.

The idea of suicide is the most rational thing in the world when you are going through all that pain. It's the people who try to stop you that you think are off their heads. Why would you want to go on living if you felt like that?

Suicide may be perceived by others as an irrational response to the experience of depression. However, from the perspective of the depressed person, it makes perfect sense. So much so that spirituality and its palliative effects may be looked upon quite negatively.

I've had experiences where faith was, at the time, the last thing I wanted, because I felt it trapped me into living, because I...I suppose it was when I was most suicidal, and... the only thing that I could think of was killing myself and so the fact that I knew God and had a faith made it very difficult for me because I knew deep down that God wouldn't particularly want me to kill myself, so I would be going against his word I suppose, to actually do it. And so it was like a trap [laughs] because I couldn't get out of that; I couldn't... I suppose in a way it was fear, fear of the consequences of doing it, eternal damnation or whatever. You know this fear of, I've got to meet and...I've done this, what's going to say to me? [laughs] You know? So that's probably what's going on in my brain at the time – the fact that my greatest need and wish was to be dead, but I couldn't do it because God was there and I shouldn't, I suppose.

Here we encounter a strange tension between the positive benefits of spirituality that enable people to cling on in the midst of depressive experiences, and the restraining aspects of belief structures which at times frustrate suicidal intentions and prevent a person from taking their own life. This tension engenders mixed feelings of relief at still being alive, and anger at being prevented from doing the one thing that it is felt would provide freedom from the psychological agony of depression.

It's a very strong feeling of... it's anger really, that comes out, it's like 'this is hell!' and it's like, I don't want to fight it any more. I haven't got the energy to fight it any more, so just let me go. I think it is a fear of God in many ways, which is an unhealthy thought, to be afraid of God, because God is love.

The knowledge of being loved by God provides the strength to cling on in times of deep distress. However, at the same time, the fear of that same God acts to prevent self-harm, even though self-harm may be the desire of the individual and the best perceived solution. Life with depression is lived in the midst of this tension between being pleased about being alive, and a feeling of being *'stuck in life'*, an experience which can be both frustrating and at times annoying.

It's a bad thing [not being able to commit suicide] *when you're feeling incredibly depressed and your stuck in life. It's like... em... I just wish I didn't know about God. You know? 'Cause then it would be easier to actually just say 'that's it! I can't take any more!' But in the end when I feel better, I feel probably... that, well it's probably just as well* [laughs] *that I knew him. You know? But I think there's always this em... it's a double edged sword I think.*

The phrases *'stuck in life'* and *'a double-edged sword'* highlight something of the ambivalence that can be experienced towards spirituality when a person is plummeted into the dark, meaningless abyss of depression. The tension between the joy of experiencing the love of God and the anger at being prevented from committing suicide, provides a deep insight into the depths of pain and suffering which people experience during times of depression. Spirituality helps to ease this tension but it does not take away the pain. The pain of depression can darken even the most profound experiences of God's love, even to the point where that experience of love becomes meaningless. The good times are good, but they don't always make the bad times, or even the fear of recurring bad times, any easier to live with. One gets the impression that, for some people, at times, the pain of the darkness may slightly outweigh the times of relief.

The crucible of depression

While depression was certainly not deemed to be desirable by any of the participants, for some it appeared to be a catalyst for a degree of positive change. Despite the soul-destroying experience of depression, for some, the journey through darkness brought about new spiritual insights and fresh possibilities even in the midst of deep sadness. This suggestion was captured by one participant in the metaphor of the *crucible*. A crucible is a melting-pot used to purify metals. Metal is put into a crucible and heated to extremely high temperatures. That which is impure comes to the surface and is sloughed off. That which is pure remains and is used for its proper purpose. A similar process of refining and cleansing can also occur within the context of depression:

> *A crucible…I suppose I use that image, because that's what it feels like, it feels as though, em…everything feels as though it's been put in a melting-pot; feels as though there's nothing solid, and the heat's turned up, and everything boils away, and you don't know what's going on, you haven't a clue what's going on, and somehow stuff comes to the surface, and it can be skimmed off and you know there can be a purifying process going on… That's how I felt depression, and my experience of it. But I think there's a much broader picture, that any kind of suffering is like that. It kind of dispenses with a huge amount of rubbish, and you don't value things the same in the end. Everything's different.*

The experience of depression has radically changed this man's perspective on life. His priorities, his values, what is and what is not important to him, have all been altered as they have been thrown into the 'refiner's fire' of depression.

> *I found [this image] was right there in scripture, you know the kind of bit in Malachi, the refiner's fire, the kind of purifying the gold and all that stuff. It kind of made me*

hold onto the fact that it wasn't some kind of strange twist of fate, but actually it was peculiarly and unbelievably sometimes an act of God, and therefore if that bit was an act of God, then the ultimate deliverance from it would be an act of God, and so there was hope. Sometimes not very much. [laughs] *When people told me it was there.* [laughs]

The metaphor of the 'crucible' and the 'refiner's fire' offers powerful images of the potential reconstructive process that can come about through the experience of depression. By relating his experiences to the image of the 'refiner's fire' drawn from his spiritual tradition, the meaningless and hopelessness of his depression is reframed as a necessary part of his spiritual journey. Instead of depression being a pointless and confusing affliction, it becomes an act of God, designed to teach him new things about life, and to make him ultimately into a better, more spiritual person. Using his spirituality as an interpretive hermeneutic which can enable him to make sense of his situation, he concludes that all suffering has a purpose, even though that purpose may not be immediately obvious. In this way, his depression is reframed as part of his spiritual journey which whilst painful and deeply disturbing is nonetheless necessary in the grand scheme of things.

As he reflected on these things, this participant felt that he had reached a place and discovered spiritual and personal insights that he might never have discovered if he had not had the experience of depression.

There's a peculiar thing goes on when you're in the crucible, and that is that...em...I felt I could see things much more clearly, my kind of understanding of what's going on in the world, and my understanding of things church, and what was going on in relationships. All that actually was quite heightened in the depths. And that would go too for sort of insight into the understanding of scripture and the kind of immediacy of it, and so, that was all kind of heightened at the same time as everything else was terribly depressed, which I think was quite an interesting kind of...em...that you tend to think of depression as being completely down, with, you know, it's all valley, there are no mountains and there is no light. But there were very significant kind of points popping through that that wouldn't have come otherwise.

The suggestion that depression had brought positive benefits was echoed by some, though not all of the participants. One participant described herself as going through an 'Eriksonian Moratorium' a time-out for reflection, questioning, reconsideration and a reconstruction of certain fundamental assumptions about herself, God and the world.

The process of therapy causes you to question motives and reasons and assumptions behind everything that makes you up, including the faith bit of you...you can't take anything for granted anymore. And also it makes you aware of how some parts of your faith can...well...either be unhelpful and tie in with unhelpful parts of your mental makeup.

Her experiences with depression have led her into a period of transition, within which she has found herself moving from one way of understanding the Christian tradition, which she finds legalistic, proscriptive and guilt-inducing (conservative evangelicalism), to another as yet undefined understanding of Christianity based within the Roman Catholic tradition.

I find that Catholicism is a type of faith where questions and doubt and struggle are recognized as a legitimate part of the spiritual journey and experience, rather than things that you need to repent of and trust more, pray more, read the Bible more.

Thus her experience of depression has forced her to embark upon a fresh spiritual quest within which she has distanced herself from what she perceives as the more destructive aspects of her spiritual tradition, enabling her to move towards the possibility of a form of spirituality that will enable her to cope more effectively with her experience of depression.

In a sense I have learned to almost sit lightly to everything else in the spells of turmoil. I find that much more helpful than flagellating myself about not believing and in the end the pieces do come together.

What emerges from this process of exploration and rebuilding is a movement towards liberation and the possibility of a 'new spirituality' that can hold in tension the new insights gained through her experiences of depression and her subsequent therapy, and the established doctrines of her faith tradition.

Part of my ongoing task is to try to find a way of integrating the changes in attitude and value that contribute to growing mental health, with what are sort of recognized as spiritual values, either by the church and other areas where they can seem to be in tension...So trying to seek an overall framework that can integrate the attitudes which just...I'm finding so liberating, so health giving, with attitudes and values that can enable me to have a place within the church. And that is an ongoing struggle.

This woman's experience of depression has forced her to question many of her previous assumptions and in so doing, create a new spirituality that includes, but is not defined by, parts of her previous spiritual history. In the dialectical interchange between new and old, her vision for the future is emerging and taking on a new shape; a shape that is filled with new possibilities and fresh understandings. This movement towards liberation and a more fulfilling form of spirituality might legitimately be described as a 'fruit' of her experience of depression.

Restoring Meaning

Participants found a variety of ways of using their spirituality to restore meaning, purpose and hope to their lives.

The healing power of understanding

For all of the participants, *understanding* lay at the heart of their perceptions of what they would want in terms of 'spiritual care'. Part of the sense of abandonment and loneliness experienced and expressed by all of the participants related to the inability of others to understand and cope with the things that they were experiencing. This inability to understand and to accept the reality of their situation in a therapeutic manner was something that was particularly clear in their encounters with church communities. To varying degrees, all of the participants found the Christian church wholly unprepared to deal with their mental health problems. At one level, the teaching and approaches to worship were very intellectually oriented and failed to meet the experiential needs that emerged in the midst of depression.

> *I was involved in the Christian community in practical terms, but that involvement didn't touch. Yeah, I found it very, very difficult being part of a Christian fellowship where the teaching was very cerebral, and the worship was very... when I say worship, I mean the kind of prayers and the hymns and so on, was very cerebral, there was very little scope, either for space or for feeling.*

At another level, the church community was found to be uneducated about mental health problems and unable to cope with the situation of people with severe long-term depression in a way that was creatively helpful for either party.

> *There were one or two people who did, but these people had experienced it, either first or immediately second-hand. Otherwise there was just a kind of... distance. And everybody would ask 'how are you doing,' but actually wouldn't be able to handle, 'I'm not doing well!' And in a sense it almost opened up how true a question are you asking, then? Actually, is this just a form of greeting or is it serious? And, you can draw your*

own conclusions. It may be that it was a sincere thing. I believe it probably was. But it's just fear, kind of 'help, I don't know how to handle this either theologically or emotionally!' I found Christian people who I probably had thought were fairly mature in faith terms, actually had…well either they had an incredibly imprisoned view of God, or they had no experience of suffering, and probably the combination of the two made it actually very lonely, in the sense that there wasn't any…there wasn't a place really for me. I was a sort of misfit… [laughs] That's precisely what a Christian church is about: having space for misfits.

It is not insignificant that those who cared most effectively were those who had experienced suffering themselves. This highlights the importance of empathy and understanding as vital aspects of the caring process.

However, poor as the church communities appear to be, the mental health care professionals were often not much better when it came to acknowledging and understanding the significance of spirituality in the lives of the participants. While generally tolerant of spirituality, none of the participants had experienced any active spiritual support or intervention from the professionals. While fellow patients often recognized the need for spiritual care and intervention, mental health care professionals frequently failed to understand or acknowledge this dimension as an important aspect of care.

The last time I was in hospital it was more the patients who actually said 'you know there's a church service on Sunday. I'm going, so if you want to come…' It wasn't particularly the staff. They accepted that you went, but there was no discussion about it. I think it was purely a case of this is what's happening and she's gone to church. I don't feel there was any relationship between that and the care you were given, if you see what I mean. As a nurse myself, in training you're told that spirituality is an important issue and it's something that you should aid. But as a patient I think it was very much seen as something that they can't get involved with or that they don't particularly discuss with you, and it's just a wee extra bit that's added on to the person I'm dealing with. [laughs]

Although the participant's spirituality was not necessarily pathologized, it was often considered a bit odd, '*you know "she's gone religious on us" kind of thing which you hear a lot of people saying. "she's a wee bit religious" you know, "a bit dodgy!"'* For all of the study's participants, spirituality was considered to be an 'added extra' by their carers. Although the carers may have considered their mental health care to be adequate, in fact it was often deficient in significant ways.

However, this was not always the case. One participant spoke of a notable encounter with her community psychiatric nurse.

I've been in the depths of despair where it's like 'I'm sorry, but I don't believe this anymore.' In fact I said that once to my community nurse. He wasn't a Christian. I talked a lot about faith and Christianity then, and…eh…you know, I was at the state when I was suicidal, and he was basically trying to keep me going. [laughs] I said 'I don't believe it anymore.' And he said, 'you know that's not true, because you do believe it, and that's what's kept you going and you've got to hang onto that.' And I found that quite…em…amazing, that somebody who really didn't believe in religion was able to use that, 'cause he knew I did…he didn't agree with me. He didn't say yeah there's nothing there, because that wouldn't be what I would need to hear at the time. [laughs]

Here we gain some vital insights into what this woman feels spiritual care should be. Her community nurse did not share her belief. Nevertheless he recognized the significance of her spirituality, and encouraged her to cling on to that which was most important to her. The attitude of the psychiatric nurse is enlightening. He did not pathologize the situation, or withdraw because he did not share her beliefs. Nor did he refer her to the 'religious expert'. Rather, he was able empathetically to enter into her situation and recognize the most appropriate form of action for her at that moment in time: pointing her back to that which he had observed to be most important to her. This reflective process and the resulting cognitive realignment enabled her to see her situation differently and remember the significance of her spirituality. *'If he can see how important it is to me, maybe I should think again.'* Thus the situation was changed and spiritual care effectively carried out, not by what the nurse *did*, in any kind of formal, psychological terms. Rather the situation was transformed by the nurse's *therapeutic understanding* of the situation and his ability to communicate that understanding effectively, irrespective of his own belief systems.

The suggestion that understanding and empathy are in themselves effective forms of therapy emerges again in the following extract. When asked what he perceived as effective spiritual care, another participant replied:

You don't have to believe what I believe to give me spiritual care, but you have to have empathy and the understanding that this person requires this…its part of her… [carers need to be able to say] 'I may not believe it but because she needs it then we'll try and provide that for her.'

The implication here is that it is not the amount of 'spiritual knowledge' that a carer has that makes for effective spiritual care. Rather, it is their ability imaginatively to enter into a person's experience in a way that communicates empathy and care, and opens up the possibility for their experience to be valued and understood. In this way the carer, implicitly or explicitly, models God to the other.

> I lost all confidence in myself and in God. I couldn't see where it was all going. I couldn't believe in a God who loved me, but let me go through all of this crap! The thing about therapy was that it enabled me to experience value and to begin to accept the possibility that I am worthy of being loved, and that maybe, just maybe there is a God after all and that the understanding, love and acceptance I feel in therapy might be transferable to something beyond myself or my therapist.

The interpersonal encounter between carer and cared for, whether in therapy or whether in the less formal situation of day-to-day encounter with carers, is thus seen to be potentially a spiritual experience. Meaningful connection at the temporal level may well move a person towards the possibility of a reconnection at the level of the transcendent. If this is so, irrespective of the particular belief structures of the carer, the art of mental health care in all of its dimensions is inevitably a profoundly spiritual task.

Liturgy and worship

Another important source of meaning and hope was found by participants in the liturgy and the worship of the church community. One of the primary experiences of all of the participants was the inability to grasp and hold onto their faith when they were in the midst of depression. When their lives were filled with crushing sadness, intellectually they found it very difficult to hold onto their faith. When a person's intellect can no longer hold onto faith, their other senses can enable spiritual contact through the symbols, hymns and sacraments of the church.

Consequently, the non-cognitive elements of ritual and symbol become, for some, extremely important.

> Even though, intellectually and emotionally you may have all sorts of doubts and turmoils, you are able sort of outwardly to share in the liturgy of the mass, and by that, em… it's kind of an acted out statement of faith even when your mind and your emotions may not be able totally to provide faith.

The act of worship, even in informal circumstances, appears to offer sustenance and a way of binding a person to the religious community that transcends the boundaries of their intellectual struggles over the question of truth. Even though a person may be journeying and is not able to believe and accept the things that once offered security and hope, through the liturgy and the mass they can find a way of binding themselves to the church community. In the actions of the mass, the participant who made the above statement finds herself enabled to express her spirituality and hold onto her spiritual community, even though, intellectually, she is struggling to believe. The mass seems to provide a safe space where she can bring her doubts and questions and express them to God within the shared context of worship. Though her intellect may be struggling, her whole person can still find sustenance through the symbolism, language, music and literature of the mass, which reaches beyond the boundaries of reason and intellect. Her doubts can be expressed in the context of a worshipping community within which she is fully included in spite of her struggle to believe and her continuing quest for truth.

This healing power of worship is again evident in the following narrative extract.

> *When I was in hospital and particularly the evenings were the worst time of day, and it was literally like being tormented in your mind and you know, almost incapable of stringing a thought together. Sometimes what I would do just to help me through the agonizing, agonizing endless hours and minutes till it was Temazepam time, was to read the words of hymns. I was not capable of stringing together any prayers of my own so each night I said to myself the words of a song from junior praise: 'Father I place into your hands the things that I can't do.' And the words of the first two verses of that just sort of said everything that I needed to say and I don't think I could've, I just couldn't have survived without having the faith to hold onto at that point.*

Here the words of the hymn express the inner longings of this woman when her intellect will not allow her to grasp the truth of her beliefs. In her darkest hour, when she does not have the words to express her agony, she allows these simple words to become a vehicle for the expression of her psychological pain and deep spiritual need.

A similar use was made of the Psalms by some of the participants; particularly the Psalms of lament.

> *I think that what I got a lot of help from on that was just reading the Psalms. That was precisely the conflict that the Psalmist came up against. Almost every Psalm has got something in it about 'where have you gone God?' 'Why aren't you answering me?' 'Have you walked off and left me,' you know, 'am I on the scrap heap?' You know? It's all that, the feelings of the heart, and yet the same Psalm has got something about 'I*

praise you God because you're faithful and wonderful,' you know, and 'look what you've made,' and there's just that tremendous kind of conflict in the Psalms of 'I know it's true, but I can't feel it.' I found that very, very helpful that I wasn't the first person to...[laughs]... *to have that dichotomy and inner struggle. And to know that it's in God's word for a purpose, you know, for people like me to say 'right, OK, I'm not peculiar here, this is normal.' 'This is OK! This isn't actually a crisis of faith in any way.' In fact it's just discovering what faith is really about, and that's when things...when the chips are down and you can't actually make any sense of it, believing that God is still there and you know, just get on with it.*

The way in which this participant reads the Psalms is *personal* and *relational*. He uses scripture in a very particular way. He does not read the Bible propositionally, that is, seeking to 'mine' it or a set of propositions which he can then apply to his life. Rather, he reads and interprets it *relationally*, i.e. he seeks to identify with and relate to the spiritual figures he encounters in scripture, reflecting on their experience in the light of his own experience of mental health problems. It is the experience of relating to and identifying with figures within scripture that provides him with the template for making sense of his own situation and his current relationships with God, self and others. The act of reading scripture is as much an emotional/relational experience as a cognitive learning task.

In the experiences of the Psalmist he finds a similar conflict between knowledge and feeling, and a resolution that involves a return to God and the possibility of restored relationship and new perspectives. In identifying with the Psalmist he experiences the possibility of hope and a radical reframing of his experience. Rather than being a crisis of faith, his experience is now seen as a 'rite of passage'; a necessary part of his spiritual journey that will ultimately enhance his relationship with God who has in fact never left him. In this way he is able to reframe his situation in a way that moves it from a perceived crisis of faith towards an understanding that is fully in line with his definition of faith as '*trusting in what you do not see, and being in relation to what you cannot see, but you can know*'.

The emotional turmoil and conflict between the intellect and the emotions moves a person away from the stability of their faith and spiritual beliefs, leading to deep experiences of abandonment and a feeling of being lost. As we have seen, this sense of abandonment is existentially and spiritually shattering. However, it is to an extent overcome by this man's ability to reassess his situation in the light of the experience of the Psalmist. In this way the experience is drawn into a deeply meaningful framework which acknowledges the reality of his pain, but also offers the possibility of meaning beyond it. In this way, the Bible provides the language and formulates the boundaries within which he understands and expresses his experiences of depression.

Conclusion

As we have reflected on the experience of the participants in this study, it has become clear that depression is much more than simply a lowering of a person's mood. Depression is a profoundly spiritual experience. It is a condition that affects a person in their entirety, producing a deep spiritual, existential, physical, psychological and relational crisis that embraces them in all five dimensions. Irrespective of whether its roots lie within a person's biology, psychology or trauma within their social experiences, the experience of depression relates to the whole experience of the person. It is a truly holistic form of psychological distress that demands a fully holistic response. Although the participants in this study all had specifically religious forms of spirituality, the spiritual nature of their experiences of loss of meaning, desolation and abandonment are spiritual crises that apply to everyone who encounters the experience of depression.

Spirituality is a dimension that appears to be overlooked or marginalized by certain approaches to and assumptions about mental health care. However, if one listens to the experiences of the participants of this study, it becomes clear that spirituality has the potential to offer meaning in the midst of meaninglessness and hope in the face of extreme hopelessness. As such it is a resource of which mental health carers should be aware as potentially available and of importance to the process of caring for and recovering from depression.

The approach of hermeneutic phenomenology opens up a dimension on the relationship between spirituality and mental health that supplements and enriches the type of research reviewed in the previous chapter. It provides us with a fuller picture of the experience of depression that takes seriously the various ways in which depression is experienced and interpreted. In terms of developing effective mental health care practices, this perspective is vital inasmuch as it focuses specifically on the individual and seeks to introduce the voice of the client into the process of care planning and understanding. As such it has much potential as a source of empowerment and in enabling care that is genuinely person-centred.

This approach has allowed us to gain a rich insight into what it feels like to experience depression. In assuming the existence of multiple realities, and by listening intently to and offering deep respect for the reality expressed by sufferers, the study has enabled us to move beyond medical, psychological and sociological interpretations of depression towards an understanding that incorporates the inherent spiritual dimensions of depression. While it is neither possible nor desirable to attempt to apply the insights uncovered by this study as generalizable principles, the insights provided alert us to potential understandings and insights that can enable us to care more thoughtfully, appropriately and insightfully when we encounter people experiencing depression and other forms of mental health problems.

Drawing Together the Threads

The type of phenomenological approach that has been developed in this chapter also has much to offer the actual practice of mental health care. This suggestion will be worked out more fully in the following chapter. However, before moving on it will be useful to draw together the various strands that have been developed within the book thus far. Figure 4.1 presents a diagrammatic outline of what has been developed and worked through. Spirituality has been defined as a wide-ranging concept which includes the quest for meaning, purpose, value, hope, connectedness and transcendence. Spirituality, whether in its religious or its non-religious form, contributes to the particular set of concepts and ideas that make up a person's or a community's belief systems or worldviews. The way in which a person views the world can have a significant effect on the way they react to their illness experiences.

Spirituality is a basic human need which manifests itself in various ways according to culture, context, and so forth. It may work itself out through religious structures, but it may also become apparent in a personal quest for meaning, hope, value and transcendence that has no necessary connection with institutionalized religion. Although both religious and non-religious forms of spirituality are human responses to the same basic needs, the way in which these needs are worked out differs in focus. Religious spiritualities centre on some concept of a transcendent God, who is perceived in various ways as being an active presence within the person's life experience. Also, religiously oriented spirituality gives a person access to a religious community, with the various potential benefits of social and spiritual support that the literature has suggested are beneficial for mental health and spiritual well-being. The significance of religion for mental health depends on the particular orientation of the person.

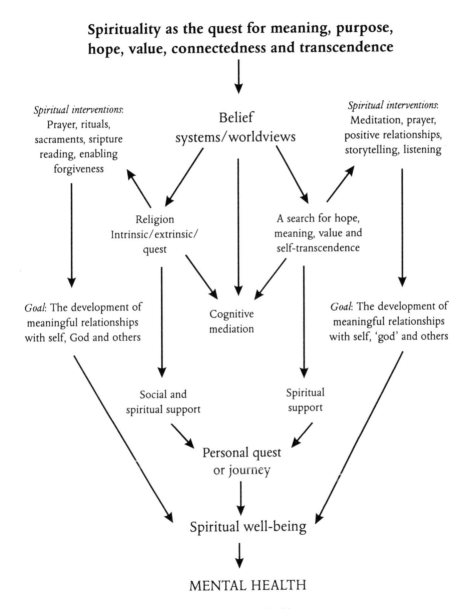

Figure 4.1. Spirituality and its relationship to mental health

The 'god' of the non-religious person may not be external but may revolve around a quest for that which is most significant to the individual. Social and spiritual support here centres on the development of meaningful relationships with people who will respect and listen to the spiritual beliefs of the individual. Although the specific area of non-religious spiritual orientation has not been a source of research activity, it is probably safe to surmise that the intrinsic/extrinsic, quest dynamic may well apply to the non-religious person's spiritual quest. As the diagram suggests, the forms of intervention necessary to care for religious and non-religious people are similar, but different in certain ways. All of these factors contribute to the spiritual well-being of the individual and to the development and maintenance of mental health.

CHAPTER 5

Enabling Spiritual Healing

Developing an Understanding of
Spiritual Care

You don't have to believe what I believe to give me spiritual care, but you have to have empathy and the understanding that this person requires this . . . it's part of her. [Carers need to be able to say] 'I may not believe it but because she needs it then we'll try and provide that for her.'

One thing that has emerged from the research presented in the previous chapters is the desire of many people with mental health problems to have their spiritual experiences accepted as both real and significant within the process of care. Carers need to have the necessary skills to be able to recognize, respect and deal effectively with this aspect of their clients' lives. Even if they personally cannot identify directly with the experience, carers are called upon to enable spiritual development within those whom they care for. This will require much more than simply knowing the central tenets of Islam, Buddhism, Judaism, atheism, secular humanism or Christianity. Knowledge of spiritual labels on its own tells us little about what a person's religious or spiritual beliefs actually *mean* to them and the ways in which they function in a person's life. In order genuinely to grasp the importance and meaning of the spiritual experience of people with mental health problems, we need to develop an approach that will enable carers in a real sense to *enter into* the life-worlds of people with mental health problems, and to seek to *understand* their experiences rather than simply *explain* their conditions. This will require not only the acquisition of new skills, but more importantly, the development of a fresh way of viewing the task of caring and a revised understanding of the experience of mental health problems.

This chapter will not attempt to present a model of spiritual care in the strictly systemic, conceptual sense normally associated with studies of this kind. Instead, in line with the ideas associated with the type of methodological approach outlined in the previous chapter, it will develop a series of themes that underlie effective spiritual care; themes that, when reflected on by carers, can inform their current practices in significant ways. As will be argued more fully below, the intention is to develop a form of practical wisdom that will allow mental health carers to develop the type of practical knowledge and intuition necessary to care for those dimensions of human experience that in some senses defy strictly rationalist approaches. The chapter will inform carers as much on what they should *be* as to what they should *do* if they are to care effectively for the human spirit although of course in practice, being and doing are inextricably interconnected.

Care that takes seriously the spiritual dimensions of human beings requires an approach that draws carers into the deepest, most mysterious realms of human experience and allows them to function empathetically within a context that is often strange and alien. The question is, how best can such a caring movement into the life-world of people with mental health problems be enabled?

Developing a Hermeneutical Approach to Spiritual Care

The hermeneutical-phenomenological perspective developed in the previous chapter opened up new possibilities for understanding spirituality and its relationship to mental health care. When taken over from research into the practice of mental health care, such a way of viewing mental health problems provides a basic perspective that can help to highlight the importance of the spiritual dimension of mental health problems. A hermeneutical approach to understanding mental health problems differs in emphasis from the biomedical approach in that its primary focus is not on pathology, but rather on the significance of meaning and the semantics of illness and disease. Table 5.1 presents some of the primary distinguishing features that mark the biomedical approach and the hermeneutic-phenomenological approach. This table compares and contrasts psychiatric/biomedical and hermeneutic perspectives on clinical practice. While accepting the reality of pathology and the significance of appropriate medical and psychiatric interventions, the hermeneutical model, as it is used in this book, takes seriously the fact that mental health problems are never merely biological or psychological. Mental health problems are human experiences that occur within the lives of unique, spiritual, meaning-seeking individuals. A person's wider social and semantic context is not simply a backdrop to the *real* task of dealing with pathological entities. Rather, it is an important aspect of the caring process. A person's illness experiences, the things they experience, the way they interpret what is happening and the potential impact this has on the process of care are accepted as a fundamental reality which must be taken seriously as being of integral importance to the overall process of caring. Symptoms and experiences are not simply constructed as pathological entities that require to be cured or excised. Rather, they are viewed as significant aspects of the living human document (Boisen 1962) that need to be read, interpreted and understood in order that the person as a whole can be cared for in a way which recognizes and respects them in all of their fullness. When our focus falls on this meaning dimension, issues of spirituality are found to be of central importance.

Table 5.1. The semantics of mental health problems: a hermeneutical model of mental health care	
Psychiatric (biomedical) Model	**Hermeneutic Model**
Pathological entity: somatic or psychological illness or dysfunction	Meaningful construct, illness reality of the sufferer
Structure of relevance: relevant data that reveal psychological or biological disorder	Relevant data that reveal the meaning of the illness
Elicitation procedures: psychiatric assessment	Evaluate explanatory models, decode semantic network
Interpretative goal: diagnosis and explanation	Understanding
Interpretative strategy: dialectically explore relationship between symptoms and psychological processes	Dialectically explore relationship between symptoms (text) and semantic network
Therapeutic goal: intervene in psychopathological process.	To treat patient's experience: to bring to understanding hidden aspects of illness reality and to transform that reality

Adapted from Goode and Goode 1981.

It is very important to stress that juxtaposing the two approaches to understanding mental health problems in this way is *not* intended to suggest an antipathy between the two perspectives. The introduction of a hermeneutical dimension to the process of mental health care is not intended to replace the biomedical approach, although it will challenge it and force it to move on and develop in new ways. Both perspectives are important dimensions in the process of understanding and seeking to care effectively for people with mental health problems. Like our previous use of Trent's two-continua model of mental health, the suggestion here is not that one way of looking at mental health problems should be replaced by another. Rather, what is required is that a practical working dialogue can be brought about between the two perspectives which will help to draw our understandings of mental health problems into a framework that incorporates but is not defined by the biomedical dimension.

Asking new questions

A hermeneutical perspective on the practice of mental health care enables carers to ask different questions about what is going on within the experience of their client. These questions do not begin with the person's pathological condition (although they acknowledge and are fully aware of it). Instead they begin with the person themselves and seek to discover what is of most significance to that person quite apart from the formal identification of their mental health problem and the assumed implications of their diagnosis. Rather than beginning by asking 'what is wrong with this person', we begin our questioning from a different perspective and ask different questions: 'What gives this person's life meaning?' 'What is it that keeps them going, even in the midst of their psychological pain and turmoil?' 'Where is this person's primary source of value?' 'What can be done to enhance their well-being?' In asking such questions, the person's situation is reframed in a way that reveals hidden dimensions.

A good example of the significance of asking different questions is provided by Blise (1995, p.18) in her exploration of radical reframing within the context of long-term mental health problems:

> I met one young man with his face red, eyes wide, and gaze fixed, after being literally dragged into the clinic by his family. 'Uncooperative, hostile, and paranoid,' had been the description from the admissions clerk. He began with the statement that his family was plotting against him, that he did not need psychiatric care, and that there was nothing wrong with him.

He leaned forward, gripping the arms of the chair until his knuckles blanched. 'How would *you* like it if the FBI was following *you* around, messing with your mind, knowing everything you do?' The answer was spontaneous honesty. 'I'd hate it. I don't even like it when the Highway Patrol is following me. I'd be a wreck if it was the FBI.' At that response, he sat back in his chair, his affect relaxed, and he said, 'You would?'

The standard questions that one might ask of a situation like this would include: what identifiable symptoms is this young man manifesting? What is the cause of his distress? Is his behaviour abnormal according to the criteria for psychiatric standards of assessment? How best can this condition be treated? However, it is clear from this short vignette that the questions that underlay Blise's approach were of a different order: how would it feel to experience what he is going through?; What is the meaning of his reaction and behaviour? What is the impact of his condition on his life? How might we see and understand his situation differently?

Blise's approach, although informed by the biomedical approach, appears to be closer to the hermeneutical model. She clearly entered into the experience of the young man in a way that was empathetic and therapeutic. However, her focus was not on the pathological nature of his delusions. Rather, her focus was on the young man as a sentient being, the nature of the experiences he was encountering and how it was affecting him, quite apart from psychiatric assumptions.

Such a way of understanding enabled her to see the situation in a different light. Few would argue that delusions are not the product of some sort of pathological activity. They are false, fixed beliefs or ideas that cannot be disconfirmed by logical reasoning. However, although they may not relate to an external reality, they are very real and logical for the person who is experiencing them. From this young man's perspective, his experience of being followed by the FBI was not a delusion but a frightening reality. On its own, the language of psychiatry can often overlook this vital fact. His experience may have been delusional, but his reaction and general behaviour was not illogical. When viewed through his eyes, his anxiety and paranoia are perfectly understandable. His heightened anxiety and aggressive manner was a normal response to being followed; a normal response to an abnormal and unexplained experience (Blise 1995). It may well be that he required medication to help him cope with the worst manifestations of his delusional experiences. However, as well as medication, *therapeutic understanding* was of vital importance to him.

Spiritual care?

The interesting point is that, when different questions were asked, what appeared to be a straightforward clinical situation in fact turned out to be a deeply spiritual encounter. If we reflect back upon the secular definition of spirituality worked out in Chapter 1, it is clear that the young man's distress was spiritual in nature. His immediate experience was of confusion, fear and perceived rejection by both his family and the mental health professions (relational disconnection). He was dislocated from all around him, afraid, and one might surmise, feeling abandoned, betrayed and perhaps even lonely. These are spiritual needs that require an appropriate spiritual response. Blise's empathetic understanding of his situation enabled her to *enter into* his situation, to *be with* the young man in a meaningful way and to communicate that she was understanding something of his experience. In this way she began to reconnect him to the human community and to draw him back to a position where the possibility of meaningful relationship and a revised future (hope) became real. When all around him, including his family, saw him as 'uncooperative', 'hostile', and 'paranoid', Blise saw something deeper and was able to connect with his inner experience and form a bond of trust and understanding. To describe this as spiritual care is fully in line with the humanistic/secular understanding of spirituality outlined in Chapter 1. In fact, such entering into the experience of the other and communicating understanding and a willingness to *be with* the other, is of the very fabric of spiritual care.

Spiritual care as therapeutic understanding

The type of therapeutic understanding highlighted in the previous example is central to any understanding of spiritual care. The idea of therapeutic understanding refers to the carer's ability to cross 'over' into a client's experience and to develop and communicate understanding, compassion and empathy. It is a form of understanding that in itself initiates a degree of healing. Therapeutic understanding is not a technique. Rather, it is a way of seeing the world and being with people which is sensitive to their inner experiences and to the significance of these experiences for the therapeutic process. It is an approach, or perhaps better an attitude, that seeks to *enter into* the experience of people with mental health problems and in so doing focus on ways in which that experience can be *understood* rather than simply *explained*.

Phenomenology and spiritual discernment

Psychiatrist Andrew Sims (1994) suggests that the approach of phenomenology may well be a way of enabling psychiatrists to develop a form of therapeutic understanding that acknowledges and seeks to work with the spiritual dimension of clients and discern the meanings they attach to their spiritual experiences. Phenomenology

> directs the practitioner not only to explore how the patient feels inside himself through detailed questioning, but also to use her innate characteristics as a human being, and the experience acquired through learning empathy as a skilled activity, to feel for herself what the subjective experience of the patient must be like. (Sims 1994, p.441)

At the heart of such an approach to understanding mental health problems is the concept of *empathy*:

> an intentional affective response to another's feelings experienced on the basis of perceived differences between the observer and the observed... In empathy, the process of 'feeling with' the other is focused on the imagination by which one is transposed into another, in self-conscious awareness of another's consciousness... In empathy, I empathetically make an effort to understand your perceptions, thoughts, feelings, muscular tensions, even temporary states. In choosing to feel your pain with you, I do not own it; I share it. My experience is the frame, your pain the picture. (Augsberger 1986, p.31)

Empathy is a learned skill that refers to the mental health carers' ability to utilize their common bond of humanness and to therapeutically draw upon their own experiences of thinking and emotion in a way that allows them to access and understand the experience of the other. To cross spiritual boundaries and in some sense enter into the experience of a spirituality that may be alien to oneself requires the development of empathy.

Sims (1999, p.98) describes empathy as a method which

> implies using the ability to feel oneself into the situation of the other person by proceeding through an organized series of questions; rephrasing and reiterating where necessary until one is quite sure of what is being described by the patient.

This view of empathy might be seen as the practical equivalent of the type of methodology that was used in Chapter 4. As a basic underpinning for spiritual care, such an approach makes a good deal of sense, not simply in the light of the phenomenological research presented earlier, but also in terms of what we have learned about the many variables that are involved with religious and spiritual commitment, such as religious orientation, cognitive sets and assumptions, the way a person relates to the recipients of their spiritual adoration and so forth. Spiritual assessment and understanding can only accurately be achieved when one is prepared to enter into the experience of the person with a mental health problem in a way that enables empathy and understanding. It is only when we *cross over* into their life-worlds that we can begin to assess the role and significance of spirituality. The term 'empathy' is therefore useful and in many ways appropriate, for the task of moving across into the life-world of those to whom we are seeking to offer care.

Crossing over Spiritual Boundaries:
Interpathy as a Mode of Spiritual Care

However, the radical difference in perception and experience that is a feature of certain forms of mental health problem means that feeling oneself into the situation of another can be very difficult. Within a mental health context, where the life-world and belief systems of those in need of care may be radically different from those of the carer, the moving-across of the carer into the life-world of the cared for is perhaps more akin to moving across cultures than therapeutic empathy in the way that Sims highlights. When we cross cultural boundaries we enter into strange lands where new languages are spoken, interpreted and learned and new and alien landscapes need to be negotiated. When we encounter mental health problems, we face a similar situation as we are confronted with different belief structures and worldviews, and language with which we are uncomfortable and unfamiliar. This is particularly so if the carer has no personal knowledge of the particular belief systems or spiritual language of the other. In such a situation, it is very much a matter of entering into a foreign land where the possibility of miscommunication, alienation and misunderstanding is high.

Crossing over

David Augsberger, in his work on cross-cultural pastoral care and counselling offers another concept which helps develop Sims's proposition regarding the importance of entering into the experience of mental health problems: *interpathy*. Interpathy is an expansion of empathy that relates to

ENABLING SPIRITUAL HEALING / 143

'thinking with' and 'feeling with' a person whose cultural context is very different from one's own. It requires

> an intentional cognitive and affective envisioning of another's thoughts and feelings from another culture, worldview, and epistemology... In interpathy, the process of knowing and 'feeling with' [that is central to empathy] requires that one temporarily believe what the other believes, see as the other sees, value what the other values... In interpathy, I seek to learn a foreign belief, take a foreign perspective, base my thought on a foreign assumption, and feel the resultant feelings and their consequences in a foreign context. Your experience becomes both frame and picture. (Augsberger 1986, p.31)

Interpathy involves genuinely entering into the experience of the other and viewing their worldview *as if* it was the only way in which the world could be understood.

The skill of interpathy is central to a number of other disciplines. As Lartey points out, the art of moving across and entering into different life-worlds is a basic skill for historians, anthropologists and those seeking to translate one language into another (Lartey 1997, p.66). Likewise, 'anyone who reads a novel set in a different time, period or country has, to some extent, to exercise "interpathy"' (p.66). Interpathy is more than empathy, in that it does not simply attempt imaginatively to enter into the experience of the other. It is the ability to discern and explore the lived experience of someone whose view of the world may be very different from one's own. Interpathy asks the carer temporarily to suspend his or her own beliefs and actually, in a meaningful sense, *share* the experience of the other person or culture. It is an attempt genuinely to enter into the experience of another culture or worldview; to sit down within an alien world and look around.

Utilizing our prejudices

There are difficulties with Augsberger's formulation of interpathy, in particular his suggestion that carers should 'bracket off' their own beliefs, values and assumptions. For reasons made clear in Chapter 4, the idea that one can totally bracket off one's prejudices in the way that Augsberger seems to suggest is of course neither possible nor desirable. If an interpathic approach to spiritual care is to be effective, it must learn from the insights of hermeneutics.

All research and practice takes place within a particular interpretative framework or paradigm which predisposes us to 'looking for certain aspects and away from others in the situation' (Addison 1989). This pre-understanding, for the most part, remains in the background as the taken-for-granted way that the world is. For example, this book has suggested that the biomedical model provides a significant part of the pre-understandings and prejudices of mental health professionals. This in turn leads them to particular explanations of mental health problems and particular forms of mental health care practice. The interpathic spiritual carer who takes seriously the insights offered by hermeneutics, recognizes the nature of their prejudices and uses them to enhance their understanding of particular situations. So, for example, a psychiatrist might use their specialized knowledge of psychological distress to understand aspects of their clients' behaviour and experience. However, the search for understanding does not end with the detailed identification of symptoms. A hermeneutically oriented interpathic approach requires the carer to acknowledge and constructively utilize their prejudices. It requires that they have enough critical self-awareness to be able to enter into the experience of the other and learn to understand and respect aspects of their situation that are not encapsulated by psychiatric language, and which may in fact challenge current understandings and assumptions. Carers therefore need to recognize their own prejudices and to feel secure enough with their own cultural/professional identity that they need not feel threatened when they encounter another way of viewing the world. When this occurs, rather than being threatened, they will discover that they can be transformed as they enter into the experience of the other and realize that there may be more ways to viewing their situation than they had previously assumed. Bracketing may be impossible, but, with a little insight and some critical self-reflection, it is possible to bring together the various horizons within the caring context in a way that will enable effective therapeutic understanding and truly interpathic spiritual care.

Practising Spiritual Care

It will be useful to continue to develop this approach to spiritual care within the context of some prevalent forms of mental health problems. We will begin with one of the most challenging areas for our understanding of spirituality and mental health: *schizophrenia*. Psychotic disorders like schizophrenia form a context within which spirituality is frequently pathologized and misunderstood. An exploration of this area of spirituality and mental health care will raise a number of questions and draw out some significant issues that have relevance to all of our caring encounters and help put this particular form of mental health problem into a slightly different frame.

Listening, hearing and understanding

UNDERSTANDING DAVID

David is 26 years old. He is diagnosed as having schizophrenia and has been on various psychotropic medications since he was 17. He hallucinates quite frequently and hears voices that tell him to do various things. Sometimes his voices can be quite helpful and reassuring, at other times they can be destructive and can cause him a good deal of distress. David has a great interest in spirituality and religion. He reads his Bible avidly, along with the scriptures and tracts from various other religions such as the Koran and the Jehovah's Witness magazine *Watchtower*. He has a great knowledge of spiritual things and a desire for what he describes as 'spiritual enlightenment'. At times he believes that the voices he hears are the voices of spiritual leaders such as Mohammed, Jesus or Ghandi. At other times he claims to *be* Jesus Christ and tells all around him that he has come to save the world. However, bizarre as his behaviour may appear at times, as one watches the concentration on his face as he worships, and the tears in his eyes as he participates in the eucharist at the hospital chapel, one cannot help but be touched by the obvious genuineness of his beliefs.

David suffers from schizophrenia, a form of mental health problem that is often chronically disabling. Briefly stated, schizophrenia is a psychotic illness, characterized by basic distortions of thinking and perception. A person may experience auditory or visual hallucinations that may comment on the person's behaviour, character and so forth. They may experience delusional thinking – that is, false, fixed beliefs. For example, a person may believe themselves to be a historical figure such as Napoleon, or a famous media personality such as James Bond. They may also feel that their most intimate thoughts, feelings, and actions are known or shared by others and transmitted to the world via television sets, radios and so forth. Other symptoms would include paranoia, withdrawal and social isolation. The course of the disorder is variable. Some people make a full recovery, whilst others have to live with this condition for the remainder of their lives. (Readers wishing to develop a deeper understanding of this condition should consult: Barham 1993; Barham and Hayward 1995; Strauss 1992, 1994; Swinton 2000b.)

As we reflect on David's situation, a number of things emerge. First, and most obviously, he suffers from a particularly demoralizing form of mental health problem for which the prognosis is not encouraging. At one level, David's diagnosis of schizophrenia could easily lead one to assume that his spiritual experiences may be *nothing but* a manifestation of his psycho-pathology. If one concentrates only on the form in which some of his experiences are manifested, and ignores the wider context and relevance of spirituality within David's life, his spiritual experiences could very easily be written off as nothing more than pathological symptoms. There is a real temptation simply to translate David's experiences into the narrower, but more familiar, language of psychology or psychiatry. Doing this enables one to hold his situation within a linguistic framework that is both familiar and professionally legitimate. Within such a framework it is possible to make sense of David's experiences without the necessity of taking his spirituality seriously. If we think back to Trent's two-continua model of mental health (Figure 2.1), the primary focus would be on the mental illness continuum without any necessary reference to the mental health continuum.

However, if we take the time interpathically to cross over into David's life-world, we discover another dimension to his experience. Without denying the reality and the pain of his mental health problems, in crossing over, we discover a young man with hopes, dreams and expectations, who, whilst experiencing a good deal of disturbance, continues to search for meaning, purpose and spiritual fulfilment. Viewed from the mental health continuum of Trent's model, David's spirituality provides us with the common ground upon which the foundations of his spiritual care can be built. With regard to religious orientation, and the meaning of his spiritual beliefs to his life, David's spirituality appears to be of the intrinsic type, and as such, provides a foundational epistemological framework around which he interprets and makes sense of his life experiences. Yet at the same time, his spiritual journey appears to involve a *quest* for meaning and a continuing inquiry into the purpose of his life and how best that purpose can find its fulfilment.

Spirituality as Language

Words create worlds and profoundly affect those who inhabit these worlds and the ways in which these worlds are inhabited.

(Swinton 1999b)

To suggest that there are various ways in which aspects of David's situation can be interpreted is *not* to suggest that his mental health problem in some way does not exist (Szasz 1973, 1979). It may however exist in a form that is different from certain commonly held assumptions. There are elements of David's experience which would certainly indicate the presence of psychopathology. For example, the times when he insists that he *is* Jesus (rather than speaks with Jesus, which in itself is not an uncommon religious experience), indicate some kind of delusional activity. David clearly is not Jesus, and his belief does not fit in with the culture and belief systems of mainstream Christianity or the particular church community that he is involved with. In other words, the form of this aspect of his spiritual experience would indicate the presence of psychological disturbance.

However, even here it is necessary to be cautious. The fact that this belief appears to be the symptom of psychological disturbance does not necessarily lead to the assumption that his religion either causes or exacerbates his psychological condition. As has been suggested, the content of psychotic disturbance is not free floating, but is in fact deeply tied in with the social context of the individual. It is true that there was a time when religious delusions were common amongst people with psychotic disturbance. However, in a context where institutionalized religion is losing its grip on the public psyche, delusions are as likely to be about pop stars, science fiction, or any other culturally popular phenomena.

This observation tells us something important, not only about delusions, but also about the way in which we should understand David's spiritual experience. Whereas it is tempting causally to associate spirituality with mental health problems, the observation of the culturally bound nature of delusional beliefs presents another possible way of interpreting and understanding the role of spirituality in the context of disturbances like David's.

When one hears a person express religious delusions and hallucinations, it is not difficult to see why, from a certain frame of reference, a direct cause-and-effect association could be drawn. However, if one takes a slightly different perspective, it becomes apparent that a simple cause-and-effect explanation of the relationship between religious and psychotic experience may be overly simplistic and may well miss the point in serious ways.

In their hermeneutical exploration into the role of religion in mental health and ill-health, Williams and Faulconer (1994) present a useful framework for understanding the role of religion and spirituality in the lives of people with mental health problems. They emphasize the role of language in the ways in which human beings construct their worlds. Language and the meaning of language are closely connected to culture, context and belief structures. Religion and spirituality offer specific cultural context which provides a language for the expression of inner longings and meaningful interpretations of the world and a person's experiences within it. Religion provides a language which gives a person a very specific perspective on and account of the world.

Likewise, psychopathology is not simply the final stage of a chain of previous causes. Rather it is 'an interpretive act which discloses the way or manner of one's situatedness in the world. Psychopathology is an "expression" of one's situation, an expression necessarily occurring in some language' (pp.339–40) In other words, psychopathology, in all its various forms, is not something that occurs apart from the influence of the person and their context. A person therefore expresses their psychopathology through language which gains its meaning from its context within the whole person-in-the-whole-of-their-world. This is true of delusions, but it is also true of other symptoms such as depression, anxiety and obsessive thoughts or actions which may have a ritualized, religious expression.

In the phenomenological study that was presented in Chapter 4, it was clear there that the participant's religious beliefs provided a specific language which they used to interpret, express and make sense of their experience. In like manner, in David's situation, his spirituality provides the language he uses to express his experiences. David's spirituality provides the lens through which he sees the world and the language and concepts that enable him to make sense of it. Consequently, when he experiences psychological disturbance, he expresses it in the same language that he uses to make sense of the rest of his existence.

Given the fundamental importance of religion to the lived experience of religious people, they are likely to articulate all of their struggles and tensions in the language of religion because it is the central expression of their life in the world. Therefore, even when the tensions faced by those people are not specifically religious tensions, we should not be surprised to find them expressed in religious language... Indeed, religious language may be the language in which some people most carefully and passionately articulate human being. In other words, people whose pathology (from a certain abstract and objectivized point of view) may have nothing at all to do with religion may articulate their pathology and express the tensions inherent in their lived world in religious terms. (Williams and Falconer 1994, p.339)

For David, his spirituality is the form of language he uses to express his inner search for meaning, purpose and value. Both his normal and his delusional experiences are expressed in the language of spirituality, that is, the language which he uses to express that which is of most importance to him. Even David's delusions may be more that 'mere pathology'. Roberts (1991) in his study of chronic delusions in people with enduring schizophrenia showed that there are certain people for whom delusional structures provide a sense of purpose and meaning for their lives, which can be protective against depression and suicidal ideation. For certain people, delusional beliefs protected them against the devastating effects that realization and acknowledgement of their actual situation would bring. Before treating David's delusions it is worth while reflecting on what they mean within the context of his life experience.

David's spirituality thus offers both a language to express his situation in a way that is framed more positively, and a form of cognitive realignment that allows him to find hope, meaning and purpose even whilst he is trapped in a situation that might be perceived as profoundly hopeless. David gains spiritual support through his interactions with the various spiritual traditions and religious figures that he draws upon to construct his understanding of spirituality, self and world. In this way he is enabled to find a sense of well-being and an important source of hope and value and connectedness which will ultimately benefit his sense of self-esteem and mental health.

Symptoms on Beliefs

Form and content

Nonetheless, although we might want to be constantly asking new questions of David's illness experience, in order to offer him effective spiritual care it is necessary to be able to discern what within his experience is primarily the product of illness experience, and what relates to his spiritual experience as a whole. It is at this point that Sims's approach to phenomenology is of particular importance. Sims (1992, 1994, 1997) presents a useful perspective that can help in the process of discerning between spirituality and pathology. In line with the principles of Jasperian psychiatric phenomenology (Jaspers 1959), he suggests that it is helpful to think in terms of *form* and *content* when attempting to discern the actual nature of religious and spiritual experience in those suffering from mental health problems.

> [T]he form reveals the nature of the illness whilst the content arises from the social and cultural background. Only the study of the form can reveal whether a symptom is present or not and this can be explored by finding out what is the meaning of experience for the individual. (Sims 1992, p.44)

If the religious belief manifests itself in the form of commonly acknowledged psychiatric symptomatology, such as delusions or hallucinations, and the belief holds no connection to the religious or social culture from which a person comes, then it may well be that the particular belief *is* in fact a part of the person's illness experience, in the sense that it does not connect with reality as it is perceived and interpreted within the regular experience of the individual or the experience of their own religious or spiritual community.

Content is relevant in so far as the content of a person's experiences of mental health problems is not free floating, but emerges from their cultural context, including their spiritual belief systems.

Delusional beliefs that are true?

Sims's approach is useful and offers a helpful perspective that allows us to explore and examine the nature of a person's spiritual experience. However, it is important to be aware that the division between form and content is not as clear cut as it might first appear to be. As a basic guide, the utilization of context, previous beliefs and the closeness of a strongly held belief to the spiritual norm of particular religious communities are undoubtedly helpful. However, even though a belief may be appropriately correlated with the spiritual context of the individual and firmly in line with their spiritual or religious tradition, it can still be a symptom. It is not enough to ask, 'is this belief a false, fixed, unshakeable delusion, or is it a belief that is appropriate to the person's religious tradition?' It may be that the person's belief is delusional, but at the same time true. For example, a man may have a delusion that his wife is having an affair. He might justify this by saying that he is certain because he heard a voice from the television set telling him that this was so. Now, it may turn out that his wife *is* actually having an affair, that is, that his delusional belief is true. However, the process by which he reaches such a conclusion is indicative of psychological dysfunctioning and calls for a deeper reflection on the wider context of his experience. Another example would be a woman who believes that Jesus Christ is the Son of God, that he died and rose again and is coming to take her to heaven at some point in the future. This of course is a very standard, mainstream Christian belief. However, if she claims to know this because the snow on her windowsill has been disturbed by angels, rather than through an affiliation with a Christian church or by reading the Christian Bible, one might consider the possibility that this belief although true according to the tenets of this religious tradition, may well be abnormal.

The question of cults

A second difficulty with the form/content dichotomy emerges within the context of cults, or institutional religions which indulge in cult-like practices. When a person enters into a cult, or an institutionalized religion that indulges in cult-like practices, they enter into a highly controlled situation. Leaders will attempt to isolate the person from the outside world by limiting all forms of communication with anyone other than fellow cult members. Within such a situation, a person may not be allowed to be ill, in the sense that the concept of mental illness is not an accepted framework for explaining their experiences and behaviours. Here, delusional and hallucinatory experiences may be validated and even venerated as being highly spiritual, irrespective of the distress that such symptoms may cause the individual. In other words, both the form and the content of the person's experience are validated as normal by the particular spiritual community they belong to.

Disorganized or normal?

Even if we use a framework such as that of Sims to discern the nature of a person's spirituality, we need to be careful to be fully informed about the subject matter that we are reflecting on and attempting to assess. What might appear to be symptomatic of illness experience may, on further reflection, be normal; the difference being that we assume it is not because of its context within mental health problems. To return to David's situation, it is apparent, even from the small amount of information that is available, that spirituality is a significant aspect of David's total life experience. In other words, it is not something that has suddenly appeared during a period of illness. His spiritual beliefs do not adhere to any one religious or spiritual tradition. His expressed spirituality is an eclectic mishmash of a number of different and diverse contemporary spiritualities. Here, we are faced with a choice of interpretations. His eclectic gathering of various spiritualities *could* be interpreted as indicative of a general disorganization, confusion and lack of focus caused by his schizophrenia. However, the *form* of his belief system, at least when he is not disturbed, is not identifiable as pathological. Also, his use of various spiritual traditions in constructing his spiritual outlook is not in itself unusual. Such an eclectic form of spirituality is very typical of the way that many people within Western societies pick and mix their spirituality within a postmodern context. The decline of institutionalized religion and the rise of secular forms of spirituality highlighted previously suggest that adherence to a single religious system is being replaced by a gathering together of various forms of spirituality, the so called pick-'n'-mix approach to spirituality. This being so, the way in which David constructs his spirituality is not in itself atypical of the way many people within society work out their spirituality. Therefore, David's eclecticism does not necessarily indicate psychopathology.

There is thus found to be an interpretative tension between a pathological reading of his situation and one which interprets his experiences as genuine manifestations of spiritual desire. What is required is a multidisciplinary approach which incorporates, for example, the chaplain's knowledge of spiritual trends, David's own feelings and how his spirituality works itself out in his life, as well as the opinions of nurses, psychiatrists and other members of the team who relate to him and spend time with him. This approach will enable carers to collate all of the necessary information required to make a fair and adequate assessment of the role of David's spirituality in his life, and its relationship to his mental health problem.

A Multidisciplinary Approach to Spiritual Care

It has become clear that in order to assess the nature of a person's spiritual beliefs, it is necessary to develop an approach that takes full consideration of the multiple domains of the person that are affected by mental health problems. This being so, the separation of symptoms from beliefs, like any other aspect of holistic care, can only be truly worked out within the context of a multidisciplinary, multidimensional (in the sense that it seeks to develop its understandings in the light of the way in which mental health problems affect all five dimensions of the person) approach which includes the person's family and their religious communities.

The acknowledgement of the holistic nature of persons and recognition of the importance of multidisciplinarity are two of the central premises that underlie effective spiritual care and assessment. Assessment of the person's spirituality, and the implementation of appropriate forms of spiritual care, require not only in-depth interviewing, but also collaboration with people from other disciplines who hold different perspectives and forms of knowledge, such as nurses, chaplains, social workers, occupational therapists, family and friends, all of whom can provide invaluable information.

The personhood of the individual

One of the most important things that can be drawn from Sims's phenomenological approach to discerning symptoms from beliefs is that he begins by listening to and taking seriously the patient's own story. Without denying the possibility of distortion and illness experiences, by beginning with a serious and comprehensive account of the person's personal narrative, one adopts a position which fully respects the personhood of the individual and remains open to the possibility that their experience may be valid and relevant to the caring process. In fact, their experiences and perceptions of reality may be *more* valid than those developed by the mental health professional, who may be fully inculturated into the worldview of science and the medical model.

The medium of story, used in the ways that have been highlighted in this book, can bring together the objective and the subjective aspects of the experience of mental health problems. By contextualizing the clinical picture within the narrative experience of the individual, it is possible to 'personalize' psychiatric diagnoses, or at least sensitize carers to the possibilities of an alternative interpretation of a person's experience that can be gained by a serious acknowledgement of the epistemological relevance of a person's experience to them as an individual rather than in terms of their illness.

Psychiatry

Within such a multidisciplinary context, the task of the psychiatrist, as Sims correctly points out, is to recognize the pathological nature of certain

ind belief structures. The psychiatrist's knowledge of psy-
rocesses and psychiatric diagnostic criteria, combined with the
nomenological approach suggested by Sims, enables her to
explore significant aspects of the form and the content of the particular
belief structures of the person. In this way, a hermeneutically informed
psychiatrist will have a significant contribution to make to the overall
assessment of the person's spirituality.

Chaplaincy

Chaplains have a vital role to play in the provision of spiritual care and the
accurate discernment of spiritual experiences. They bring specific expertise
of religions and spirituality and as such, are in a perfect position to make a
major contribution to the process of care and assessment. For example, they
are in a position to provide the multidisciplinary team with vital information
as to whether or not a person's specific belief structures bear any
resemblance to accepted forms of religion or spirituality. As we have seen,
the fact that they do, does not necessarily make them 'normal'. It does
however contribute significantly to the overarching assessment process.
Similarly, the fact that it may not concur with established practices does not,
in itself, prove the belief to be pathological. Most people have views and
opinions that may be idiosyncratic and to a greater or lesser extent at odds
with the majority opinion of our spiritual communities. However, radical
difference from an established spiritual tradition *may* be indicative of
pathology and can be used as part of the accumulation of data required for
the accurate assessment of the person's spiritual state.

Chaplains also have time to spend with clients over a prolonged period
giving them the opportunity to get to know and understand the person and
how their spirituality functions in the midst of their mental health problems.

They also provide vital conduits into the religious and spiritual communities to which a person may belong. They therefore have access to and
understanding of the particular belief structures of religious communities, as
well as the types of cultish belief systems which, it has been suggested, can
be problematic.

Nursing

Nurses are perhaps best placed to assess and understand the role of
spirituality in those they offer care to. The basic task of the nurse is to
provide a therapeutic presence that can empower and enable change. Their

continuing, round-the-clock contact with clients places them in a unique position to observe, explore and reflect upon the role of spirituality within the full context of a person's life.

Social work

Social workers have an important role within this process of multi-disciplinary spiritual care and assessment. As a group of carers who are involved with client, family and other mental health care workers, social workers are a vital link which ties together hospital, family, and particular services within the community. They are therefore able to offer a wider contextual understanding of the person that includes the person's family and social situation. They can also be a vital conduit for the family in situations where they might be unable or unwilling to participate formally in the assessment process.

Family and friends

Family and friends can inform the caring team on the person's normal beliefs and behaviour, how they function, and what their normal level of involvement might be. Only when the various disciplines and parties enter into constructive dialogue can effective and accurate assessment take place. Such an approach helps avoid confusion and misinterpretation of what is actually going on within a person's life experience.

By bringing together these parties in constructive dialogue around spiritual issues such as those that have been highlighted above, effective assessment and understanding that is informed by all five of the dimensions of the person can be achieved, and genuinely person-centred forms of spiritual care can become a possibility. There are a number of established formal models of assessment that could be used within such a team context. Appendix 1 presents a representative cross-section of established models for spiritual care and assessment.

CARING FOR DAVID

When we begin to ask different questions of David's situation and begin to see things from his perspective, it becomes clear that he is in a very vulnerable position. His spirituality, one of the primary things that appears to give him purpose and meaning in his life, can very easily be misinterpreted and translated into the language of pathology. This can lead to a form of professional misunderstanding that could easily result in a medical response to what are basically spiritual issues. The danger is that his voice is swallowed up by the biological and psychiatric discourse, thus silencing aspects of his situation that are of vital importance to David-as-a-person, as opposed to David-as-a-'schizophrenic'. As Gleeson (2000) astutely observes: 'A service user is often in a position of vulnerability, and may thus disregard their familiar form of expression, taking on that of the helpers, to find "common" ground.' The power of the medical model not only impacts upon the ways in which mental health professionals view clients, it also affects the ways in which clients view themselves. It is very easy for the powerful voice of the biomedical discourse

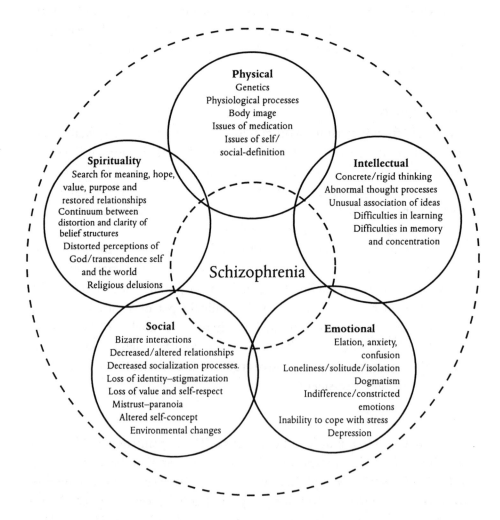

Figure 5.1. Spirituality and schizophrenia

fragile voice of those who are vulnerable and open to persuasion that their spiritual experiences are *nothing but* manifestations of their illness: 'Explaining away symptoms can deal a blow to the individual's integrity, especially if the punch is thrown by someone with the backing and prestige of professional expertise' (Gleeson 2000).

What David needs in terms of spiritual care is to be understood, supported and empowered to hold onto the importance of his explanatory narrative, even if others may wish to offer an alternative framework of explanation. He also needs his spirituality to be recognized as important to him as a *person*, quite apart from his schizophrenia. In order for this to happen, carers must take time to enter into his life, *be with* him in a meaningful sense and learn to take aspect of his life with the utmost seriousness and respect. In other words, to show him *therapeutic understanding.*

We might conceptualize David's situation as in Figure 5.1. This diagram points out the particular ways in which psychotic disorders such as schizophrenia can impact upon all five dimensions of the person identified by Peplau (1952). It is important to note that within this diagram, the area of spirituality, and the particular experiences associated with it, are viewed as a discrete though connected aspect of the whole person. These experiences are not psychological, intellectual or emotional needs (although they affect and are affected by all of these areas). They are distinct forms of need that require specific attitudes, understandings and forms of intervention.

People with schizophrenia have the same spiritual needs as any other human being. There may be profound differences in the way these needs are expressed, but they are nonetheless of the utmost significance to the individual concerned. Thus we begin to explore schizophrenia, as with all forms of mental health problems, from the basic assumption that the search for meaning, hope, value, purpose and transcendence is present as a valid aspect of the person's experience, and as such deserves to be treated with understanding and respect. This is the common ground that locks us together when there appears to be no obvious point of connection.

Certainly there will be times when this spirituality will be distorted and chaotic, as will the person's perceptions of God, self and the world. Such distortions in certain aspects of a person's spirituality at certain times do not mean that the whole of their spiritual experience is *nothing but* the product of distorted thinking or biology. Spiritual care means developing ways of crossing over into the life-world of people with schizophrenia, attempting to understand the world as they see it and learning to understand the language they use to describe it.

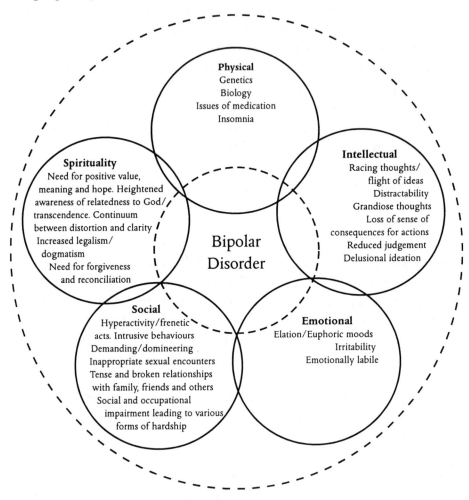

Figure 5.2. Spirituality and bipolar disorder

Our exploration of David's situation has thrown up some useful insights into the way in which spirituality functions within the life of a person with a psychotic form of mental health problem. It has also provided an understanding of some of the ways in which pathology and spirituality can be distinguished from one another and worked with within the context of a multidisciplinary team. David's experience has highlighted some useful points of contact between for example, psychiatrists, with their diagnostic skills, nurses with the ability to spend time with a client and enter into their lived experiences, relatives with specific knowledge about the client's context and previous belief structures, and chaplains with their specific expertise within the realms of spirituality and formal religion. If these groups can be brought together around issues of assessment, care and understanding, new possibilities for spiritual care will emerge in fresh and potentially exciting ways.

Widening Our Vision

Although the focus here has been specifically on psychotic disorder, the general approach to spiritual care and the reframing of mental health that has developed can be carried over into the spiritual care of other forms of psychological distress and disorder. Although there are experiences and difficulties that are specific to particular forms of mental health problems and particular people who are experiencing them, in significant respects, the themes presented below provide a framework for the interpathic spiritual care of mental health problems in all of their varied forms. A few examples will serve to show how the insights gathered above can contribute to our understanding of spiritual care within the context of a variety of mental health problems.

Bipolar disorder

Bipolar disorder is a form of mental health problem that has a widely recognized biological etiology (Rosenhan and Seligman 1995). Yet a closer examination reveals it to have significant spiritual dimensions. Like depression, bipolar disorder is a form of mental health problem that profoundly impacts upon a person's mood. It is characterized by mood swings within which the person cycles between periods of extreme elation and episodes of deep depression. During a manic phase a person may, for example, become highly uninhibited and promiscuous; they may give up their occupation or spend all of their savings on expensive cars, gambling or overly ambitious business ventures. Because of the speed of the person's thought processes and actions whilst in a manic state, people can become inappropriate in their social encounters, talk incessantly, or have ideas of grandeur that do not reflect their normal self-perception, all of which serve to alienate them from those around them. During these periods the person may be offensive to family and friends, and as a result find themselves isolated and alone, even though they may feel that they are the most sociable person imaginable.

Spiritually, this manic phase can have a variety of effects such as heightened awareness of God or a person's own self-transcendence, or delusional ideas that the person is a religious messenger or spiritual figure. The person may also become dogmatic and fixed in their beliefs and frequently alienate themselves from their religious or spiritual community. This dogmatism may be a genuine attempt to be faithful to their spiritual tradition; that is, their commitment to their faith is concentrated and heightened by the manic process. Consequently, when their actions appear to be condemned or rejected, this can lead to serious confusion and added spiritual distress.

Thus, even though the particular difficulty may be the product of malfunctioning biology or chemical imbalance, when we begin to explore the spiritual dimensions of the person's experience it becomes clear that bipolar disorder requires more than simply biomedical intervention in order for the person to receive effective care. A case study will illustrate some of the features of spiritual care within this context.

UNDERSTANDING ELAINE

Elaine is 44 years old. She has suffered with bipolar disorder for the past ten years. She has no specific interest in religion. She finds herself seriously confused and her life knocked out of focus by her condition.

> I have been sad for a long time. It's OK when I'm high. You couldn't care less then. The world's a great place, and you are in control! But then you always have to come down. Sometimes I think, there must be more to life than this! I've got a husband, two lovely boys, a nice house yet...[sighs]...I always let them down. I don't know how Doug [her husband] puts up with me. The things that I've done... I don't deserve him... I don't deserve any of them. I had hoped that the last change in my medication might sort me out, but I don't feel much different. I don't know...I just can't see the future.

As we reflect on this brief vignette at least two key themes emerge. We can draw them out under the headings of *faith and hope*, and *forgiveness and reconciliation*.

FAITH AND HOPE

Elaine's experience of bipolar disorder has been particularly discouraging and demoralizing. Her constant cycles of depression and mania have made it very difficult for her to gain any sense of stability or security in her life. When she is in a manic phase, she finds her life filled with meaning and purpose, so much so that she feels that she can break the social and relational ties with family and friends that, in reality, offer her what little stability she has. She has been unfaithful to her husband Doug on several occasions, which has put a tremendous strain on her marriage. Doug accepts the fact that her behaviour is the product of her disease processes, but this does not make it easier for either of them. When Elaine's mood begins to even out, she is filled with genuine remorse for the things she has said and the ways in which she has behaved. Yet at the same time, she is aware that it is likely to happen again the next time she becomes ill. The persistent threat of illness has gradually worn away much of the hope and expectation that she had for her future.

Elaine's comment regarding her expectations of medication is highly significant. In the midst of the turmoil and desolation that her condition inflicts upon her, one primary source of hope has been medication. Although she may be resigned to having bipolar disorder for the remainder of her life, there remains the hope that medication can bring a degree of control and the possibility of relief. Inextricably connected with this source of hope are the mental health professionals in general, but in particular her psychiatrist, the 'dispenser of hope'. She has no formal religious beliefs and no contact with a religious or a spiritual community. Her source of hope does not lie in God, but, in a very real sense, in her psychiatrist and the possibility that his or her pharmacological expertise may bring relief and release from the relentless momentum of her illness. When her faith in the psychiatrist is shaken by the fact that medication has not been as effective as she had hoped for, she is faced both with a crisis of faith and with an overwhelming feeling of hopelessness. Certainly the sadness she expresses may well be part of the depressive phase of her illness experience, but that is not *all* that it is. If we reflect a little deeper and take seriously the spiritual implications of her situation, it becomes clear that there is a logical and deeply spiritual dimension to her experiences of disappointment and hopelessness which makes sense quite apart from any form of disease process that may be affecting her thinking. If medication is not doing what she had expected and hoped it to do, then an important source of faith and hope is no longer available to her.

FORGIVENESS AND RECONCILIATION

A second spiritual dimension that emerges from reflection on Elaine's experience revolves around issues of forgiveness and reconciliation. Elaine's life has been marked by bizarre incidents and episodes where she has behaved in ways that have embarrassed and deeply saddened both herself and her family. If one reflects on Elaine's statements of remorse, it would appear that one of the things she may well need to achieve is forgiveness and reconciliation, both with herself and with those around her.

There is no doubt that forgiveness and reconciliation are central to the survival of her marriage. This would suggest the need for support, education and possibly family intervention to enable the family to come to terms with the nature and effects of her condition. Here the work of such community-oriented mental health carers as community psychiatric nurses and social workers is of great importance. Carers working within these contexts function at the interface of the social and the spiritual dimensions of the person highlighted in Figure 5.2. In recognizing forms of spiritual need that exist within her wider interpersonal and social context, community mental health carers can learn to work with the interpersonal levels of spiritual care, as well as the more intimate intrapersonal elements. There is a good deal of useful literature available that can instruct mental health carers in ways of enabling forgiveness and bringing about reconciliation within individuals, families and communities (Stutzman and Schrock-Shenk 1995).

Elaine also needs to find mechanisms whereby she can forgive herself for the ways in which she behaves and the things she does. It is important to recognize that while there are features of her sadness that may be the product of biologically produced depression, her guilt is often based in the reality of her own actions. Gordon (2000) highlights three forms of guilt:

- *Transgression guilt* – here the person has actually done something wrong and the feelings of guilt are justifiable and understandable.

- *Perfection guilt* – comes from falling short of one's own or other people's standards and expectations. In other words the person fails to achieve idealistic standards.

- *Rejection guilt* – is the product of serious rejection by significant others. This form of guilt stems from 'serious emotional rejection marked by emotional deprivation and verbal and physical abuse. Because the treatment they received was undeserved, the guilt feelings were false.'

Gordon argues that while forgiveness is an appropriate response to transgression guilt, it is inappropriate for the other two forms of guilt in so far as it may well serve to confirm the undeserved feelings of guilt. Perfection and rejection guilt require affirmation of the positive things that have been done and integration into welcoming, accepting forms of relationship.

Elaine's guilt combines transgression guilt and elements of rejection guilt. Clearly she does transgress when she is in a manic phase, and experiences the need for forgiveness and reconciliation when she 'comes down'. Yet at the same time she frequently experiences rejection and misunderstanding from many people who assume that her condition is a *trait* rather than a biological *state*. Spiritual care for Elaine will mean creating a context within which she can feel accepted, irrespective of what has happened in the past. In this sense the spiritual carer is called to embody forgiveness through their attitudes, approaches and communications with her. Spiritual care is thus seen to be a deeply relational encounter within which Elaine can experience forgiveness and reconciliation and discover the possibility of hope for the future.

Spiritual care for Elaine is also an *educational* task. As has been mentioned, bipolar disorder is recognized as biological in origin. Forgiveness and self-acceptance can be initiated by constructively utilizing the biomedical explanation of bipolar disorder in a way that abrogates her of the responsibility for and by implication the guilt of, her manic actions. This involves an educational process within which carers can draw upon the available evidence that points towards the biological roots of this condition, and in so doing help to absolve her of guilt and blame for things that, in many senses, are outwith her control.

From this it can be seen that one of the primary ways in which such forgiveness can be communicated and experienced is through the mental health carer developing the type of therapeutic understanding that has been highlighted above. By entering into non-judgemental, interpathic relationships with Elaine it is possible for a carer to model forgiveness in a way that is meaningful and healing. This is achieved by providing a truly therapeutic relationship which embodies and acts out the possibility of forgiveness, and communicates clearly that, irrespective of what she may have done, Elaine remains valued and worthy of relating with.

Stress and anxiety

Stress and anxiety disorders can be disturbing and devastating for the lives of those who suffer from them. There are well-established ways of viewing such conditions, and effective modes of intervention designed to alleviate suffering and bring peace and relief, some of which are outlined in Figure

5.3. However, the spiritual dimensions of stress and anxiety are much less well considered, researched and written about. Anxiety can bring about such things as a dread of death and a morbid fear of the afterlife, the loss of meaning and purpose, unhelpful reflection on past sins or perceived sinful actions, as well as obsessional religious thoughts and actions. Anxiety and stress can therefore bring on serious existential crises that threaten the very spiritual being of those who are experiencing them. There is evidence to suggest that interventions that include a spiritual perspective can be beneficial in enabling a person to cope with anxiety (Suess and Halpern 1989).

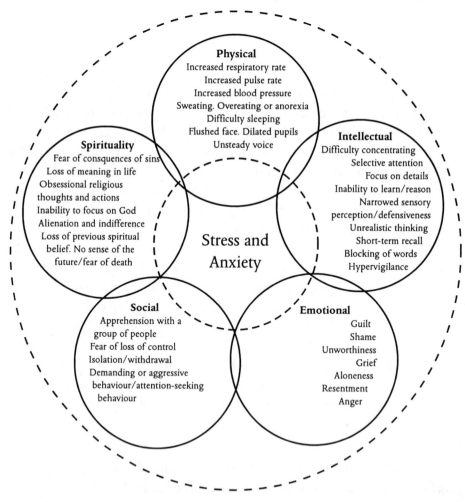

Figure 5.3. Spirituality and anxiety

In order to deal with such difficulties, it is necessary:

1. To recognize them as spiritual difficulties that may need to be understood and cared for in particular ways.

2. To be able to separate that which is the product of the person's illness experience and that which is real. For example, as has been suggested, certain forms of guilt and anxiety may be normal and justifiable reactions to particular events in the person's life, whilst others may be the product of pathological thinking or biological disturbance.

3. To utilize specific spiritual interventions that may be appropriate in enabling the person to cope with their difficulties. There is evidence that certain religious practices can be helpful in alleviating stress and anxiety, for example, prayer and meditation (Brown-Saltzman 1997; Rees 1995); forgiveness and absolution (Gordon 2000), which facilitates relationships with God, self and others, encouraging affirmation; and meditation on religious scriptures. Also, in line with the previous observations on social support and its relationship to coping with stress and anxiety, the possibility of support from a religious or spiritual community offers much potential as a useful form of intervention and support structure. There is a growing literature on the introduction of spiritual interventions specifically within the context of counselling and therapy which relates well to some of the difficulties encountered by people experiencing excesses of stress and anxiety (Steketee, Quay and White 1991).

This is a field of spirituality and mental health that is underresearched and should be considered as an area to be targeted for future research purposes.

Dementia

Dementia provides a particularly good example of the possibilities of reframing from a spiritual perspective. When we ask the question, *what does it feel like to have dementia?* rather than simply *what is dementia?* we begin to see this particular condition in a very different light. The important work carried out by Tom Kitwood (1997a and b) from the perspective of psychology and Stephen Post (1995) from the perspective of moral philosophy have shown clearly the importance of recognizing the continuing personhood of people with dementia, even in the midst of terminal neurological degeneration. When viewed from the perspective of the person experiencing it, dementia is found to have 'hidden' (in the sense that they are not prioritized or noticed within the dominant biomedical discourse surrounding dementia) psychological and spiritual dimensions that are unnecessarily subsumed by the dominance of the medico-biological discourses.

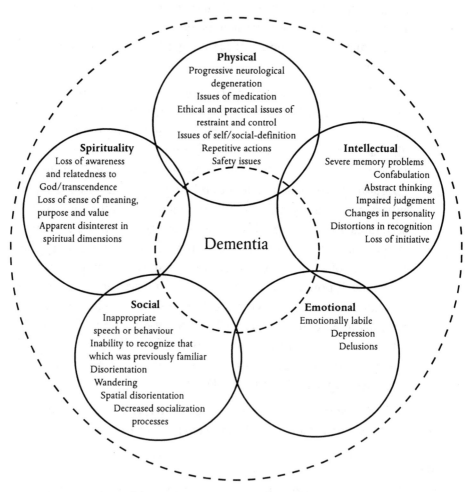

Figure 5.4. Spirituality and dementia

Consequently a focus on psychological and spiritual interventions offers new possibilities of rehumanization for people with this form of mental health problem. A concentration on spiritual interventions such as the use of spiritual music, scripture readings, therapeutic presence that reconnects the individual to themselves and to their particular religious or spiritual communities, shared prayer and so forth can contribute to the redefinition of the person in terms that capture their fullness without subsuming some vital aspects of the person to the biomedical discourse. Such forms of intervention help reconnect those who are by definition in the process of being disconnected from self, others and God.

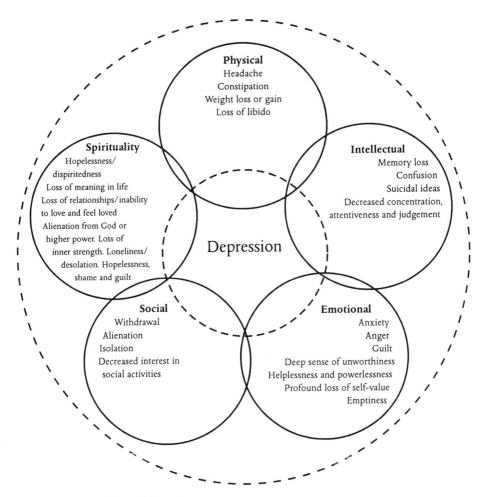

Figure 5.5. Spirituality and depression

Depression

Depression is a profoundly spiritual illness that digs into the heart of a person's spirit and forces them to face experiences of meaninglessness and hopelessness that are devastating in their consequences. Our previous discussion of depression clearly showed some of the ways in which this mental health problem impacts upon the spiritual dimension. Yet at the same time, it has the potential to reframe and enable people to reinterpret their experiences in ways that are therapeutically helpful and can enhance mental health.

A Framework for Spiritual Care

This chapter has presented a number of important thoughts and insights into the nature of spirituality and the form that spiritual care should take within a mental health context. The various threads that have been presented thus far are drawn together in Table 5.2.

Table 5.2. Caring for the spirit:
the primary themes that underlie effective spiritual care

1. Developing a hermeneutical perspective

2. Spiritual reframing

3. Spiritual interpathy

4. Acknowledging and affirming the significance of the person as a unique individual with hopes, dreams and expectations, rather than as a universal diagnostic category

5. Therapeutic understanding

6. Acknowledging and affirming both the unique and the shared aspects of a person's spirituality

7. Being open to the possibility of entering into dialogue with perspectives and worldviews that may differ radically from one's own

8. Being alert to, respecting and striving to understand the person's own account of their illness experience and the ways in which this explanatory narrative relates to and differs from the explanatory narrative provided by mental health professionals

9. Developing a multidisciplinary approach that will enable carers to discern that which is mental-health enhancing from that which is primarily (although not necessarily solely) the product of pathology

10. Learning and becoming fluent in the language of spirituality

1. Developing a hermeneutical perspective

By introducing a hermeneutical dimension to the practice of mental health care and the assessment of mental health problems, it is possible to open up new and challenging aspects of care that previously might have gone unnoticed. The hermeneutical perspective takes the spiritual dimension from the margins into the centre of our thinking and enables us to ask new questions which open up the possibility of revised forms of practice that care for human beings in all of their fullness.

2. Spiritual reframing

As we ask new questions of situations and current practices, so fresh dimensions of what goes on within our care come to light. As we begin to look at mental health problems from a slightly different perspective, so our understanding of what they are and how they affect the life experiences of those who suffer from them alters. The introduction of a spiritual dimension enables us to reframe mental health problems and mental health care in a way that places the person at the centre of our thinking and enables us to offer care that seeks to meet not only professional expectations, but also the perceived needs of clients. This is called reframing, that is, changing the frame in which a person perceives events in order to change the meaning of the event. To reframe a situation, concept or experience is to change the conceptual and/or emotional setting or viewpoint in relation to which a situation is experienced and to place it in another frame which fits the 'facts' of the same concrete situation equally well or even better, and thereby changes its entire meaning (Govig 1994, p.78). When the meaning changes, the person's responses and behaviours also change (Capps 1990, p.10). Reframing increases life choices by offering a different perspective on a situation and presenting an alternative structure of meaning by which to interpret it. Thus, changing the frame in which a person perceives events can change the meaning the person associates with the events (Pesut 1991, p.9). In reframing, both the situation and therefore the consequences are changed. The effect is changed even though the concrete facts remain the same (Blise 1995, p.18). When something is reframed, we look at it in the same way we have always done, but we are suddenly forced to see that it is not quite the way that we thought it was. Taking a hermeneutical perspective on mental health problems which fully incorporates the spiritual dimension enables us to reframe them in a way that emphasizes certain aspects and de-emphasizes others. When we reframe our understanding of mental health problems, they remain pathological entities that are in need of varying degrees of professional intervention. Schizophrenia remains schizophrenia with all of the medical discourse that surrounds this diagnosis. Depression remains a socio-biological condition that frequently needs specific psychiatric interventions. These conditions do not cease to exist because we might choose to look at them from a different angle. However, in reframing them from a spiritual perspective, we discover new priorities and fresh possibilities for intervention that do not fall within the remit of a purely materialistic psychiatry. If the focus is placed on a person's spirituality rather than on their biological or psychological difficulties, their situation can be reframed from one of inevitable loss to the possibility of hope, purpose and a meaningful existence, even in the midst of severe psychological disturbance.

3. Spiritual interpathy

This provides a way of understanding mental health problems and spiritual care within that context which enables carers to enter into people's spiritual experiences and work with them within a frame of reference which is the client's own and not imposed by preconceived theory or assumptions. To adopt such a stance requires a movement towards a more hermeneutical approach to understanding mental health problems. Such an approach focuses on meanings and semantics, and seeks to enter into and understand the lived experience of people with mental health problems.

4. Acknowledging and affirming the significance of the person as a unique individual with hopes, dreams and expectations, rather than as a universal diagnostic category

Diagnosis and the development of appropriate pharmacological or therapeutic interventions are of course important in developing our understanding of mental health problems and improving methods of treatment. Most would agree that increased knowledge with regard to drugs and therapy have brought significant relief and release for many people experiencing psychological distress. However, *a person is not their diagnosis.* Psychiatric diagnosis and categorization are 'explanatory frameworks that are used by the mental health professions to explain, understand and correlate constellations of signs and symptoms for the purpose of explanation, prediction, and control' (Pilch 2000, p.25). They are specifically focused on particular aspects of a person's *pathology*. As such, by definition, they are oblivious to certain other dimensions of the person's *experience.* At best diagnoses are useful organizing concepts that enable effective intervention and appropriate care. At worst they are labels that determine the social identity and life trajectory of those to whom they are ascribed. One of the most serious problems that people have to deal with is often not the constellation of signs and symptoms that make up their diagnostic category, but the constellation of negative associations and assumptions that cluster around their particular diagnostic label. Mental health problems are human experiences that happen to unique individuals with hopes, dreams and aspirations, and they can profoundly affect the course and manifestations of their difficulties. The humanness of a person's experience cannot be fully expressed in the technical language of the mental health professions. In order effectively to care for persons in all of their fullness, it will be necessary to begin by resurrecting the language of humanness as we reflect on people's life experiences, and in so doing, begin to acknowledge the significance of the spiritual dimensions of their situations. A focus on the spiritual dimension of clients emphasizes shared humanity and a common spirituality rather than particular diagnostic labels. As such it provides common ground upon which carer and cared for can stand, even in the midst of the most severe symptoms.

5. Therapeutic understanding

The idea of therapeutic understanding is basic to all spiritual care. If we do not understand what a person is going through, we cannot offer meaningful care. It has been suggested that spirituality is a form of language. If this is so, then it is a language that carers must learn. This does not simply mean learning what concepts such as prayer, forgiveness or reconciliation mean in a technical sense. It refers to developing an understanding of what the spiritual language of our clients actually means in terms of their life experience and the ways in which they structure that experience.

6. Acknowledging and affirming both the unique and the shared aspects of a person's spirituality

While spirituality is a universal human phenomenon, it is also personal and unique. A person's spirituality provides a very particular way of negotiating, interpreting and understanding the world. Spiritual carers must learn to discern the universal from the particular in order that the way in which a person's spirituality functions in their lives is acknowledged and worked with. The perspectives of phenomenology and the development of the skills of empathy and interpathy provide a way of being for mental health carers and emphasize the important point that interventions need to be grounded not in dislocated theories or theologies, but in the particular spirituality of the person being cared for.

7. Being open to the possibility of entering into dialogue with perspectives and worldviews that may differ radically from one's own

Spiritual care can only begin if one is prepared to open oneself to the other in such a way that they experience affirmation and understanding, even if the carer does not accept or fully understand their experiences, views or spiritual paradigms. The object of spiritual care is not to persuade the other that one's own views or understandings of reality are correct. Rather, its aim is to find ways in which, together, both carer and cared for can explore and negotiate the complexities of their spiritual journey and be enabled to move closer to that which provides the person's source of meaning, value, hope and transcendence. What is required is that in approaching the task of spiritual caring, the carer accepts the coexistence of different worldviews and manifestations of spirituality, and seeks to work through the implications of this for the continuing process of mental health care. Such an attitude enables a form of dialogue, a two-way conversation within which both parties search for common ground and explore ways of understanding the other's point of view that respect the views and opinions of both parties without compromising the values and beliefs of either.

8. Being alert to, respecting and striving to understand the person's own account of their illness experience and the ways in which this explanatory narrative relates to and differs from the explanatory narrative provided by mental health professionals

Even that which appears to be grossly pathological, may in fact be deeply meaningful (and indeed is always so from the perspective of the sufferer). In certain circumstances, that which is assumed to be negative can in fact be helpful for the individual. Spiritual care means carers learning how to *notice, understand,* and *act* in accordance with the spiritual experiences of others rather than their own preconceptions of how the other *should* be thinking or acting. It involves moving beyond the expectations of a personal or professional worldview and opening one's self and one's worldview to the possibility of becoming sensitized to those dimensions of human experience that, for reasons previously outlined, are often hidden from many contemporary approaches to the practice of mental health care.

9. Developing a multidisciplinary approach that will enable carers to discern that which is mental health enhancing from that which is primarily (although not necessarily solely) the product of pathology

Accurate assessment of mental health problems and the effective practice of spiritual care requires cooperation and dialogue between the various members of the multidisciplinary team, as well as the incorporation of understandings drawn from family and friends. Spirituality that manifests itself as commonly accepted forms of pathological symptoms should be treated as any other symptoms of forms of psychological distress would be. However, that which is of fundamental importance to the person's life as a whole, i.e. not just in times of exacerbated distress, should be respected, understood and focused on with equal verve. This can only come about if the members of the team understand and acknowledge the spiritual dimension, and effective liaison and dialogue is encouraged between the various team members as well as with family and friends. In this way therapeutic understanding can be nurtured and the possibility of spiritual care that reflects the reality of people's experience can become a possibility. Such an approach listens intently to all of the voices within the multidisciplinary team, including the personal narrative of the client. It is from within this constructive dialogue that the possibility of accurate assessment of spiritual needs can arise.

10. Learning and becoming fluent in the language of spirituality

It has become clear that in order to care for the spiritual needs of people with mental health problems, spiritual carers will have to become fluent in two languages: the language of spirituality and the language of psychiatry and psychology. Hunsinger (1995) calls for mental health carers to become *bilingual* in their approach toward care-giving and therapy. She suggests that there is one language of pain and distress which 'speaks' in a language of depth psychology (and by implication any discipline that focuses on the identification and treatment of psychopathology), and another language which 'speaks' of these same things in the language of the spirit. Being able to discern which language is 'spoken' by the client and being able to 'speak' in response, contributes to more effective therapy, and prevents those aspects of the therapeutic encounter which belong to the spiritual from being translated into the language of psychology or psychiatry. Hunsinger's point is an important one. In order to develop an approach that cares effectively for the spiritual needs of people with mental health problems, it is necessary for mental health carers to become fluent in two languages:

- *The language of psychiatry and psychology*, which seeks to enable a better understanding of a person's pathological condition and offers appropriate therapeutic interventions and forms of rehabilitative activity pertinent to the person's diagnostic condition (the illness continuum of the model of mental health presented in Chapter 2).

- *The language of spirituality* that focuses on issues of meaning, hope, value, connectedness and transcendence (the mental health continuum of Trent's model of mental health), all of which have a secondary role within the dominant medical paradigm but which the previous research has suggested hold a central place within the experience of many people with mental health problems.

The suggestion that mental health carers need to become bilingual highlights the need for balance, understanding and critical dialogue between spirituality and the particular perspectives of the other mental health disciplines along the two continua. Only when both languages are learned, internalized and brought into critical dialogue can therapeutic understanding be achieved and the possibility of genuine spiritual care become a reality. The development of such bilinguality will not be easy. Mental health professionals tend inevitably to be much more comfortable with the categories and perceived diagnostic 'certainties' encountered along the illness continuum, than with the openness, uncertainty and mystery that is encountered along the spirituality–health continuum. They tend to feel at home with the language of biology, genetics and psychodynamics, but they are much less comfortable when dealing with spiritual matters. It is much easier to translate people's experiences of spirituality into the language of psychology or the emotions than face the challenge of opening ourselves and our therapeutic language and practice to new possibilities and forms that may well change significantly the way in which mental health problems are understood and mental health care is carried out. However, if we are to take seriously the insights developed in this book, then learning and using the language of spirituality is really not an option, it is a necessity.

Conclusion

Spiritual Care as Practical Wisdom

As we contemplate the journey that this book has taken us on, it is clear that spiritual care is much more than simply an added task to be done or an extra skill that has to be learned. Rather, it has to do with seeing the world differently, and in seeing it differently, acting differently within it. Spiritual care has to do with asking different questions of those to whom we offer care and, equally as importantly, being equipped and prepared to respond appropriately and openly to the answers one receives. Spiritual care is as much a way of *being* as a way of *acting*.

It is important to be clear that what has been developed within this book in general and the previous chapter in particular, is not a *theory* of spiritual care. As we reflect on the ideas that have been developed as the book has progressed, it becomes clear that spiritual care is not simply the application of theoretical knowledge to particular situations. The ten themes presented in the conclusion to the final chapter are not intended to provide a formal, systematic model of spiritual care in the way that we are used to understanding such things. What this schema provides is a series of insights, understandings and therapeutic attitudes towards others that is designed to inform the continuing *praxis* of mental health care. Reflection on these insights will not tell carers what to do in every situation. It will however, contribute to the development of a form of *practical wisdom* a kind of 'knowing that guides being and doing'(Swinton 2000a) that will enable carers to recognize, respect and deal with spiritual issues as they arise in the midst of their daily practices. Such practical wisdom is

> a knowing in which skill and understanding co-operate; a knowing in which experience and critical reflection work in concert; a knowing in which the disciplined improvisation, against a backdrop of reflective wisdom, marks the virtuosity of the competent practitioner. (Fowler in Ballard 1986, p.60)

Aristotle divided human knowledge into three forms: *theoria*, *praxis* and *poesis*. While each of these elements of knowledge is relevant for spiritual care, here we will focus on the relationship between *theoria* and *praxis*.

Theoria roughly concurs with contemporary understandings of theory. It is the type of knowledge that is developed from the types of research reviewed in Chapter 3. Theoria is a vital part of understanding and knowing, but it is only one component and not the whole of knowledge. One of the difficulties with the scientific paradigm is that it has come to assume that theoria is *the* primary source of knowledge that is adequate to underpin all forms of practice and intervention.

Praxis is action saturated with meaning. It refers to the reflective movement between theoretical premises and human action within particular situations.

> Praxis is practical knowledge-in-action. It is the reflective practice of a specific community as it seeks to work out the essence of right living and correct practice. Praxis is not a substitute for theoretical knowledge, but is a complementary form of knowledge required for true and faithful living. (McKie and Swinton 2000)

Praxis assumes that actions and theory are inseparable aspects of the same process. However, praxis is more than simply the passive embodiment of theoretical structures. Rather it is the *critical* embodiment of theory. Praxis refuses to accept the primacy of theory or to accept the assumption that good practice emerges simply from the application of preconceived theoretical premises.

The praxis of mental health professionals is the embodiment of its theoretical underpinnings. This became clear when we explored the impact of the biomedical model on the mental health professions. The materialism that frequently underlies this theoretical perspective has had a great impact on mental health care practices. Consequently, when embodied within the practices of mental health professionals, the spiritual dimension is frequently overlooked and rarely taken seriously as a significant theoretical premise. The introduction of the hermeneutical dimension that has been laid out in Chapters 4 and 5 draws in and legitimates the dimension of human experience within the praxis of mental health care. By allowing the voice of the person critically to dialogue with established theoretical perspectives, mental-health care praxis will inevitably be enriched, and the pertinence of the spiritual dimension to the process of care will become more and more obvious.

Spiritual care is therefore not simply the application of predetermined principles. Spiritual care emerges from the interplay between the types of theoretical knowledge presented in the initial chapters of this book, and the experiential knowledge that has been developed in the proceeding discussion. The insights developed in the final chapter are intended to contribute to such critical praxis and to enable mental health problems to participate in the process of spiritual praxis and authentic, holistic mental health care. Practical wisdom within a mental health context emerges from the constructive interplay between theory and practice as it is worked out within the life-worlds of people with mental health problems.

Spiritual Care as Poetry

In a sense, spiritual care is like poetry. It is the kind of knowledge that you get as you enter into a poem. Poems are not things to be explained, they are things to be shared and grasped with the heart rather than the head. Explaining a poem communicates something of its essence, but not all of it. As you are swept up into the mystery and the rhythm of the words, you experience something new about life; a deep revelation of aspects of reality that were previously shielded from your gaze. It is not always possible fully to articulate that 'newness', but it *is* possible to allow that experience to change the way you view the world and your actions within it. Spiritual care contains a necessary element of poetry which strives to understand and express those deep aspects of human experience that defy words, yet which are fundamental if we are to live fully and humanly.

Human experience contains as much poetry as prose. As such, understanding the complex dimensions of experience requires a form of practical wisdom that holds in tension the aspects of theoria, praxis and poesis. Spiritual poesis moves us beyond the boundaries of concepts, categories and fixed definitions; spiritual praxis locates care, not within the world of abstract concepts, but firmly within the life-worlds of people with mental health problems.

The object of the insights presented within this book is to enable mental health carers to learn not only what they should *do* in terms of effective spiritual care, but more importantly what they should *be* if they are to recognize and deal effectively with the spiritual needs of people with mental health problems.

Looking to the Future: Becoming Spiritual Healers

The aim of this book has been to point towards ways in which mental health carers can become spiritual healers. Spiritual healers have the ability to discern the things of the spirit, to recognize the need for meaning, purpose, value and hope, and to be able to work with these dimensions even in the midst of the most painful psychological distress. In order for this to happen, there will need to be changes in the ways in which mental health carers are educated. We need to begin to recognize these issues at an early stage. We need to learn to think along the two continua of mental health at a very early point in our learning in order that the language of the spirit can become our second, or perhaps even our first language. Mental health carers need to be introduced to the types of evidence that have been presented within this book in order that they can wrestle with the data and reflect critically on its implications for their own understandings and practices. They need to be given experiential, practical education that will enable them to overcome the uncertainty regarding personal spiritual and religious beliefs and values that has been highlighted as a major barrier to the provision of spiritual care.

In the face of community care, we need to reflect on the relationship between the hospital and the religious and spiritual communities, in order that we can find ways of dialoguing with those within the community who seek to care for the spiritual needs of people with mental health problems. If spiritual communities have as much healing potential as the literature appears to suggest, we need to ask piercing questions as to why it is that so few people with mental health problems can actually find a valid and valued place within such communities. This is a critical area of care on which I have written extensively elsewhere (Swinton 2000b).

This book has begun to open up some of these issues and has at least contributed to the initiation of a movement towards spiritual healing within the mental health care professions. There is much to do, but, where there is a will there is a way. It is the task of all of those who have had their eyes opened to the reality of the spiritual dimension to begin to shift the paradigm in a way that will enable people with mental health problems to discover care in all of their dimensions. When the spiritual domain is taken seriously, so is the wholeness of all persons. As a basic goal for genuine caring, it is difficult to do better than to seek to care for our fellow human beings in all of their fullness.

Appendix

Models for Assessment
and Intervention

A number of writers have pointed to the importance of assessment in the meeting of spiritual needs. Accurate assessment, it is suggested, is central to the development of effective spiritual care and intervention that meets the genuine spiritual needs of clients. A variety of models of assessment have been developed from this premise within a number of different contexts. These models aim to assess the spiritual needs of clients in a way that is in line with current assessment practices of other aspects of human beings. A representative selection are presented below.

Multidisciplinary Models

Assessing spiritual needs

A good example of a comprehensive model of spiritual assessment is presented by Farran *et al.* They present a holistic model of spiritual assessment designed to enable the accurate assessment of spiritual needs and interventions. This model is useful, comprehensive and holistic, aiming at exploring spirituality within the context of the person, their immediate family and their wider social and spiritual environment. Farren *et al.* develop the following guidelines for assessment based on what they identify as the seven primary aspects of assessment. These principles are outlined in Table A.1.

Table A.1. Assessing spiritual needs

Belief and meaning
What does a person believe and what do these beliefs mean to them?

Authority and guidance
Where does the person find authority for his beliefs, e.g. from religious writings, a direct connection with the divine, the medical profession and so forth?
Is there any clash between the person's spiritual authority and the medical or psychiatric authority of his or her immediate context?

Experience and emotion
Exploration of the person's history to assess their capacity for religious experience, emotions, moods and feelings and the impact the immediate illness experience has on these things.

Fellowship
Examines the extensiveness of the community of shared faith, i.e. what state the person's relational network is in, and whether or not there are any obvious conflictual connections that might impinge upon the caring situation.
The degree of affirmation received from the community.
The community's openness to discuss matters of health and illness.
The impact of the community on the illness experience of the person.

Ritual and practice
How do individuals use rituals such as group or private worship, prayer, sacraments, meditation, scripture reading and so forth?
How has their current illness experience impacted upon this practice?
Does the person have any special requests for rituals?

Courage (hope) and growth
What sources have provided courage (hope) in the past?
Can the person let old hopes die in order that new ones can emerge?
How has spiritual growth occurred for the individual in the past?
Is the current illness experience prompting a person to rethink previously held spiritual ideas and assumptions?

> **Vocation and consequences**
> How does the individual express the spiritual dimension in their everyday encounters?
> Has the individual's illness experience altered the way they express their spirituality on a daily basis?
> Has the individual been able to incorporate the illness experience into a sense of vocation and/or meaning?
> If not, what are the consequences on a psychological, sociological, or spiritual level?

This model is a good example of a comprehensive model of assessment that could be incorporated within a multidisciplinary team in a way that would enhance understanding and enable better spiritual understanding and care. Its structure enables carers to view their clients from a number of different perspectives, and acknowledges the wider dimensions of spiritual experience that were highlighted in Chapter 1 of this book.

This model could be criticized for its complexity. It demands a number of skills and competencies drawn from *inter alia* theology, philosophy and developmental psychology. As such it would demand a good deal of commitment to a multidisciplinary approach to care, and a caring context that accepted the validity of the various disciplines that are necessary for such an assessment to be effective. In this sense, it presents an idealistic model that may provide a strong and valid vision for the future, but which would be very difficult to implement within the current culture of health care as it has been outlined within this book. Nevertheless, it does provide a strong structure even if it can only be moved towards at the moment, rather than implemented immediately.

The Nursing Process

Ross's model

One model which has been used quite effectively to provide a structure for the incorporation of spiritual care within a hospital context is the nursing process. Ross (1994, 1998) argues that if nurses are to be enabled to meet the spiritual needs of patients, they will require a conceptual framework that will guide their practice. Her rational for using this approach is as follows:

> An individual entering hospital will do so with particular spiritual needs. Whether or not these needs are met may determine the speed and extent of

their recovery and the level of spiritual wellbeing and quality of life they experience. It is important, therefore, that they receive the necessary help to meet their spiritual needs. (Ross 1994, 1998)

She suggests that a way of ensuring that these needs are met is through the use of the nursing process, which provides a 'mechanism to deliver systematic individualized spiritual care' (Ross 1998).

She moves on to develop a model of assessment and implementation, using the nursing process as a mechanism for delivering systematic, individualized spiritual care (Table A.2).

Table A.2. The nursing process	
Aspect of the nursing process	**Nurse Requires Knowledge of**
Assessment	What spiritual needs (understood in their widest dimension) are, and the various ways in which they can be identified.
Planning and intervention	What spiritual interventions are and how best they might be implemented.
Evaluation	What indicators and assessment outcomes might best be utilised to show that the patient's needs have been met.

ASSESSMENT

Here the patient's spiritual state is assessed and their spiritual needs identified. This will involve exploring questions of religious orientation, specific belief structures, particular spiritual needs and so forth. All of this is designed to enable the nurse to gain a deeper insight into the spiritual experience of the patient.

PLANNING

This stage involves the planning of appropriate forms of intervention that may be required to meet the spiritual needs identified in stage one.

INTERVENTION

Intervention refers to the specific strategies employed to meet the identified spiritual needs.

EVALUATION

Here the interventions are evaluated as to their efficacy or otherwise, i.e. whether they enhance spiritual well-being or increase spiritual distress or leave it unalleviated.

In Ross's model, the nursing process provides an acknowledged and easily understandable framework within which spiritual care can be incorporated into the nurses' caring practices.

Govier's model of spiritual care

Another model based on the structure of the nursing process is presented by Govier (2000) in his development of a systematic model of spiritual care for nurses, based on the nursing process. Govier uses the structure of the nursing process to present a model for assessing spiritual needs that can be of assistance to nurses in assessing, planning, implementing and evaluating spirituality and spiritual care. His basic framework is similar to Ross's. However, he also proposes guidelines for spiritual assessment which will 'invite the nurse to inquire into intimate details of the patient's world'. Govier develops a helpful structure aimed at grasping the patient's spiritual experience in a way that is systematic and comprehensive. As the result of an extensive literature review (Govier 2000), he develops what he describes as the 'five Rs of spirituality'.

REASON AND REFLECTION

Human beings are essentially meaning-seeking beings (Frankl 1962). In the context of illness this meaning may be lost, and ways of restoring the quest after meaning need to be sought. Reason and reflection are necessary for people to draw themselves out of such a dilemma.

It is through the nurse taking a sincere and active role, and recognizing that the physical, psychological/emotional, social, cultural and spiritual realms are all interconnected, that he or she is in a position whereby he or she can help those who are suffering to reflect upon and find meaning in their experiences.

RELIGION

Religion is a significant form of spirituality which can provide the answers to many of the deep existential questions asked by people when they encounter sickness and ill-health. People often express their religion in their own way, with no necessary reference to traditional belief systems or institutionalized religions. 'Nevertheless such beliefs demand the respect of the nurse who seeks to listen to and respect the views and practices of patients, without always agreeing with them.'

RELATIONSHIPS

Relationships with self, God and others lie at the heart of spirituality. Spirituality may be expressed vertically towards God or horizontally towards other human beings. Both are authentic forms of spirituality that need to be respected and understood. Carson (1989) observes 'the need for a continuous interrelationship between the inner being of the person (the person's vertical relationship with the transcendent/God or whatever supreme values guide the person's life) and the person's horizontal relationships with self, others and the environment.'

RESTORATION

Restoration refers to the ability of a person's spirituality to have a positive influence on their physical aspects. Certain life events can cause an inability to 'restore' the body to a spiritual equilibrium, resulting in spiritual distress (Burnard 1987, 1988). These may be displayed through a change in a patient's disposition manifested by his or her mood, emotions or physical being. Whatever the alteration, the nurse should be able to recognize signs of spiritual distress and draw on either personal or adjunctive means to assist the patient in restoring spiritual well-being.

Govier suggests that these five dimensions provide a foundation for a systematic model of spiritual care. As a guide to assessment he presents the framework of questions shown in Table A.3, designed to enable nurses to access the inner regions of the person's spiritual beliefs and experience.

Govier's model is helpful in so far as, like Ross, he provides a working model and a systematic approach to dealing with spiritual needs which presents itself to health carers in a form that is familiar and compatible with current practices. However, there are aspects of Govier's approach which are problematic, particularly when transposed into a mental health context. For example, the question regarding the way in which the illness has affected a person's spiritual belief system may require deeper knowledge and understanding than can be conveyed by a simple question on an assessment form. Within a mental health context, such discernment requires sensitivity and the participation of the whole multidisciplinary team. Also, bearing in mind what has been learned about religious orientation and the significance of the meaning of a person's spiritual belief systems, questions such as 'does the patient have a religion?' provide little information in terms of the person's actual spiritual needs.

Table A.3. Govier's five dimensions of spiritual care

Reason and reflection

Does the patient take time to reflect on life's experiences? If yes, can he or she describe how?

What events in the patient's life have had an effect on him or her?

Are there any things that particularly motivate the patient? If yes, what are they?

Has the patient thought why the illness/trauma has happened to him or her? If yes, in what way?

Is there anything that frightens the patient about this illness/traumatic experience? If yes, in what way?

Religion

Does the patient have a religion? If yes, which one?

Is there a religious representative that the patient finds especially useful? If yes, who?

Would the patient like to see a hospital chaplain or religious representative during his or her stay in hospital?

Are there particular rituals or practices that are important to the patient? If yes, what are they?

How can the patient's religious beliefs and practices be accommodated while in hospital?

Relationships

What are the most influential relationships in the patient's life?

Does the patient have a belief in God or a higher being? If yes, can he or she describe this belief?

How does this belief in God or a higher being manifest itself?

Has the patient ever felt, or been, abandoned in a relationship? If yes, how did he or she feel? Have these feelings been rectified?

Restorations

Has the illness/trauma affected the patient's spiritual beliefs? If yes, in what way?

Does the patient feel at peace with him or herself? If no, what might be the reason for this?

Are there any signs of spiritual distress? If yes, what are they?

Govier 2000.

A much greater problem, and one which is highlighted by Ross in her research into nurses' perceptions of spiritual needs (1994, 1998), is the very basic fact that although the nursing process has much potential when applied to the area of spiritual care, it is wholly dependent on nurses having adequate knowledge to be able or willing to implement it. It would appear that this knowledge is not available to nurses, with the consequence that 'there is currently a lack of knowledge to enable [the nursing process] to be enacted' (Ross 1994). Once again we are faced with the previously mentioned educational gap, which presents a serious barrier to spiritual care being anything more than an honourable idea.

Govier's and Ross's approaches are nonetheless useful in that they present a framework for professionals to understand and work with aspects of spirituality in a form that is very much in line with the ways in which one might assess any other aspect of the person, from bowel habits to bed sores. Within these frameworks, spirituality is presented to nurses in a form that they can understand, identify with and, it is hoped, work with within a structure that is familiar to them. Spirituality is viewed as a specific *competency* that nurses should attain as part of their standard repertoire of caring practices.

However, in the light of our previous discussion on spiritual care as a practical wisdom rather than another competency that mental health carers have to learn, approaches such as Ross's and Govier's beg the question: *is spiritual care simply another competency, or is it first and foremost a basic principle that underlies our whole approach to mental health care?* It may be that the answer is that it is both a competency and a basic approach to human beings. If it is both, then models such as these deal effectively with the competency dimension of spiritual care, but may fail to deal adequately with the deeper ontological dimensions of spiritual care. In other words, they view spiritual care primarily as a series of caring actions, rather than as a way of being for both nurse and patient.

Exploring Meanings

Stoll's model

A set of guidelines for spiritual assessment which assumes the significance of the deeper, ontological, meaning oriented aspects of spirituality and spiritual care is presented by Stoll (1979). Stoll's model is intended to offer a conceptual framework within which health carers can systematically organize specific forms of information pertaining to the spiritual lives of patients. Unlike the more task-oriented models of spiritual care that emerge from understandings based on the nursing process, Stoll's focus appears to be on the meaning dimension of spiritual experiences. She presents a series of four headings carers can use to focus on the spiritual dimension of their clients. In appraising these four areas, carers can derive important information about the religious and non-religious spiritual needs of their patients.

Table A.4. The meaning of spirituality
• The person's concept of deity • The person's source of strength and hope • The significance of religious practices and rituals to the person • The person's perceived relationship between his or her personal beliefs and his or her state of health

Stoll 1979.

Within Stoll's structure it is possible to frame some very significant questions concerning the nature and function of a person's spirituality and spiritual experiences: does the person have a god concept? How does it function in their lives? Where does a person gain strength to cope with their experiences? What do religious practices *mean* to the individual? How do they interact with the person's illness experience? Do they have a positive or a negative influence on the progress of their condition? Using this structure as a framework for developing appropriate assessment questions can enable carers to assess such things as religious orientation, the personal meanings of spirituality, the relationship of the individual to a wider spiritual community, the relationship of their belief structures to their religious tradition and so forth. In this way Stoll's framework provides a way into exploring the deeper regions of a person's spiritual life.

Stoll's model is useful in that it is flexible enough to be easily transposed into the area of mental health care, and can enable carers to access the types of hidden dimensions of meaning and religious/spiritual orientation that it has been shown are so significant to the spiritual experience of people with mental health problems.

Stoll's model might be criticized for being too focused on specifically religious forms of spirituality, thus excluding all of those people who choose to express their spirituality in different ways. This is a fair criticism. If it is to be of use within a wider framework of spirituality, the second point would have to be rephrased to incorporate non-religious forms of spirituality. This model might also be criticized for being too time-consuming and as such impractical. However, one has to wonder whether (*a*) such criticisms might be better directed not at Stoll's model, but at health care systems which are unable to provide adequate resources to provide for an important aspect of care; and (*b*) whether the criticism of 'not enough time' reflects the particular priority-setting agenda of the health care professions. In the light of the research presented in this book, Stoll's model would appear to highlight some vital dimensions of human experience and spirituality within the context of mental health care practices, and allow carers to delve into some very important areas.

This model should not be understood as being in opposition to the types of models based on the nursing process. Rather, what may be required is a creative fusion between the two in order to build a model of spiritual care that enables both the task-oriented and the ontological dimensions to function harmoniously.

Physician Oriented Models of Spiritual Assessment

Maugan's model

One model of assessment which is worthy of note, and which is designed for general health care practice, is Maugan's (1996) model of SPIRITual history. This model provides a good example of a way of structuring and carrying out spiritual assessment. Maugan presents his model of spiritual assessment in the form of a mnemonic, 'SPIRIT', as a guide for identifying important components of a person's spiritual history. It is aimed at enabling physicians to understand spirituality in both its religious and non-religious forms. Maugan's sensitivity to the wider dimensions of spirituality is helpful. As he puts it himself, some 'will express no formalized religious orientation; by virtue of their humanness, however, atheists, secular humanists, and agnostics maintain personalized belief systems that can be explored by physicians equally well.' Table A.5 presents Maugan's framework.

Table A.5. SPIRITual history
S Spiritual belief system
P Personal spirituality
I Integration and involvement in a spiritual community
R Ritualized practices and restrictions
I Implications for medical care
T Terminal events planning (advance directives)

SPIRITUAL BELIEF SYSTEMS

Identify the formalized belief systems to which the person adheres (what we have previously identified as the cultural or shared aspects of a person's spirituality).

PERSONAL SPIRITUALITY

Assess the particular ways in which the individual understands and uses their spiritual perspective (what we have previously identified as the unique aspects of a person's spirituality).

INTEGRATION AND INVOLVEMENT WITH OTHERS IN A SPIRITUAL COMMUNITY

Assess the level of spiritual and social support available to a person from their religious community or spiritual connections.

RITUALIZED PRACTICES AND RESTRICTIONS

Assess which, if any, rituals, practices and restrictions a person may have. For example, prayer and meditation is central to many religions, and has been shown to be beneficial to health (Koenig 1997). Likewise, some religions have certain restrictions including,

> non-Kosher foods for orthodox Jews; animal flesh for Adventists, Buddhists, and Hindus; and alcohol and caffeine for many faiths. Well-known, medically relevant prohibitions include the receiving of blood products by Jehovah's Witnesses and all allopathic medical care by Christian Scientists. (Maugan 1996)

IMPLICATIONS FOR MEDICAL CARE

Certain beliefs and ways of living can be beneficial to health. Others can be detrimental, such as the specific prohibitions by Jehovah's Witnesses and Christian Scientists mentioned above. The task of the physician is to understand the person's belief systems and to approach their care with compassion and understanding.

TERMINAL EVENTS PLANNING

This aspect of Maugan's schema focuses on issues relating to terminal care, death and dying. He suggests that once the other aspects of the SPIRITual framework have been worked out and thought through, the physician is in a good position to deal with this final aspect, within which issues of spirituality and religion are commonly centre-stage.

Although primarily aimed at a general practice context, with some modification Maugan's model could be used to meet the needs of a mental health context.

Bibliography

Addison, R.B. (1989) 'Grounded Interpretive Research: An Investigation of Physicians' Socialization.' In M.J. Packer and R.B. Addison (eds) *Entering the Circle: Hermeneutic Investigation in Psychology.* New York: Albany University Press.

Adherents.com. (2000) [online] http://www.adherents.com

Allen, M.N. and Jensen, L. (1990) 'Hermeneutical Inquiry: Meaning and Scope.' *Western Journal of Nursing Research 12,* 2, 241–253.

Allport, G.W. and Ross, M. (1967) 'Personal Religious Orientation and Prejudice.' *Journal of Personality and Social Psychology 5,* 4, 432–443.

Althouse, J.W. (1985) 'Healing and Health in the Judaic-Christian Experience: A Return to Holism.' *Journal of Holistic Nursing 3,* 1, 19–24.

Annells, M. (1999) 'Evaluating Phenomenology: Usefullness, Quality and Philosophical Foundations.' *Nurse Researcher 6,* 3, 5–19.

Ashbrook, J.B. (1991) 'Soul: Its Meaning and its Making.' *Journal of Pastoral Care 2,* 144–163.

Augsberger, D.W. (1986) *Pastoral Counselling Across Cultures.* Philadelphia: Westminster Press.

Aye, J. and Robinson, K.M. (1994) 'Spirituality among Caregivers.' *IMAGE: Journal of Nursing Scholarship 26,* 3, 218–221.

Baker, M. and Gorsuch, R. (1982) 'Trait Anxiety and Intrinsic–Extrinsic Religiousness.' *Journal for the Scientific Study of Religion 21,* 2, 119–122.

Barbour, I.G. (1990) *Religion in an Age of Science: The Gifford Lectures 1989–1991* (Vol. 1). San Francisco: Harper and Row.

Barham, P. (1992) *Closing the Asylum: The Mental Patient in Modern Society.* London: Penguin.

Barham, P. (1993) *Schizophrenia and Human Value.* London: Free Association Books.

Barham, P. and Hayward, R. (1995) *Relocating Madness: From Mental Patient to the Person.* London: Free Association Books.

Barnum, B. (1998) *Spirituality in Nursing From Traditional to New Age.* New York: Springer.

Batson, C.D. and Schoenrade, P.A. (1991) 'Measuring Religion as Quest: 1. Validity Concerns.' *Journal for the Scientific Study of Religion 30*, 416–429.

Batson, C.D. and Ventis, W. L. (1982) *The Religious Experience: A Social Psychological Perspective.* London and New York: Oxford University Press.

Batson, C.D., Schoenrade, P.A. and Ventis, W.L. (1993) *Religion and the Individual: A Psycho-social Perspective.* New York: Oxford University Press.

Beech, I. (1999) 'Bracketing in Phenomenological Research.' *Nurse Researcher 6*, 3, 35–50.

Benner, P. (ed) (1994) *Interpretive Phenomenology: Embodiment, Caring and Ethics in Health and Illness.* London: Sage Publications.

Benson, H. (1996) *Timeless Healing: The Power and Biology of Belief.* New York: Fireside.

Berghash, R. and Jillson, K. (1998) 'Thoughts on Psyche, Soul, and Spirit.' *Journal of Religion and Health 37*, 4, 313–322

Bergin, A.E. (1980) 'Psychotherapy and Religious Values.' *Journal of Consulting and Clinical Psychology 48*, 1, 95–105.

Bergin, A.E. (1983) 'Religiosity and Mental Health: A Critical Re-evaluation and Meta-Analysis.' *Professional Psychology: Research and Practice 14*, 170–84.

Bergin, A.E. (1988) 'Three Contributions of a Spiritual Perspective to Counselling, Psychotherapy, and Behaviour Change.' *Counselling and Values 32*, 21–31.

Bergin, A.E. and Jensen, J.P. (1990) 'Religiosity of Psychotherapists: A National Study.' *Psychotherapy 27*, 1, 3–7.

Bergin, A.E., Masters, K.S. and Richards, P.S. (1987) 'Religiousness and Mental Health Reconsidered: A Study of an Intrinsically Religious Sample.' *Journal of Counseling Psychology 34*, 197–204.

Bernstein, R.J. (1983) *Beyond Objectivism and Relativism.* London: Blackwell.

Bhurga, D. (ed) (1996) *Psychiatry and Religion.* London and New York: Routledge.

Birney, M.H. (1991) 'Psychoneuroimmunology: A Holistic Framework for the Study of Stress and Illness.' *Holistic Nursing Practice 5*, 4, 32–38.

Blise, M.L. (1995) 'Everything I Learned I Learned from Patients: Radical Positive Reframing.' *Journal of Psychosocial Nursing 33*, 12, 18–25.

Boisen, A. (1962) *The Exploration of the Inner World: A Study of Mental Disorder and Religious Experience.* New York: Harper and Brothers.

Boiven, M. (1991) 'The Hebraic Model of the Person: Towards a Unified Psychological Science among Christian Helping Professionals.' *Journal of Psychology and Theology 19*, 2, 157–165.

Borbasi, S.A. (1996) 'Living the Experience of being Nursed: A Phenomenological Text.' *International Journal of Nursing Practice 2*, 4, 222–228.

Boutell, K.A. and Bozett, F.W. (1987) 'Nurses' Assessment of Patients' Spirituality: Continuing Education Implications.' *Journal of Continuing Education in Nursing 21*, 172–176.

Bowden, J.W. (1998) 'Recovery from Alcoholism: A Spiritual Journey.' *Issues in Mental Health Nursing 19*, 337–352.

Bown, J. and Williams, S. (1993) 'Spirituality in Nursing: A Review of the Literature.' *Journal of Advances in Health and Nursing Care 2*, 4, 41–66.

Brittain, J.N. (1986) 'Theological Foundations for Spiritual Care.' *Journal of Religion and Health 25*, 2, 107–121.

Brown, D.R., Ndubuisi, S.C. and Gary, L.E. (1990) 'Religiosity and Psychological Distress among Blacks.' *Journal of Religion and Health 29*, 1, 55–68.

Brown, G.W. and Prudo, R. (1981) 'Psychiatric Disorder in a Rural and an Urban Population: 1 Aetiology of Depression.' *Psychological Medicine 11*, 581–599.

Brown, L.B. (ed) (1994) *Religion, Personality, and Mental Health*. New York: Springer.

Brown-Saltzman, K. (1997) 'Replenishing the Spirit by Meditative Prayer and Guided Imagery.' *Seminars in Oncology Nursing 13*, 4, 255–259.

Burkhardt, M.A. (1989) 'Spirituality: An Analysis of the Concept.' *Holistic Nursing Practice 3*, 3, 69–77.

Burkhardt, M.A. (1994) 'Becoming and Connecting: Elements of Spirituality for Women.' *Holistic Nursing Practice 8*, 4, 12–21.

Burkhardt, M.A. (1998) 'Reintegrating Spirituality into Healthcare.' *Alternative Therapies 4*, 2, 128–129.

Burnard, P. (1987) 'Spiritual Distress and the Nursing Response: Theoretical Considerations and Counselling Skills.' *Journal of Advanced Nursing 12*, 3, 377–382.

Burnard, P. (1988) 'The Spiritual Needs of Atheists and Agnostics.' *The Professional Nurse 4*, 3, 130–132.

Burnard, P. (1990) 'Learning to Care for the Spirit.' *Nursing Standard 24*, 4, 18, 38–39.

Byrd, R.C. (1988) 'Positive Therapeutic Effects of Intercessory Prayer in a Coronary Care Unity Population.' *Southern Medical Journal 81*, 7, 826–829.

Byrne, C., Kirkpatrick, H., Woodside, H., Landeen, J., Bernardo, A. and Pawlick, J. (1994) 'The Importance of Relationships in Fostering Hope.' *Journal of Psychosocial Nursing and Mental Health Service 32*, 9, 31–34.

Campbell, A.V. (1985) *Paid to Care*. London: SPCK.

Capps, D. (1990) *Reframing: A New Method in Pastoral Care*. Minneapolis MI: Fortress Press.

Capra, F. (1983) *The Turning Point: Science, Society and Rising Culture.* London: HarperCollins.

Capra, F. (1998) 'The Emerging New Culture.' *Thinking Allowed: Conversations on the Leading Edge of Knowledge and Discovery* (with Jeffrey Mishlove) [online] http://www.intuition.org/txt/capra.htm.

Carson, V.B. (1989) *Spiritual Dimensions of Nursing Practice.* Philadelphia: Saunders.

Carter, T.M. (1998) 'The Effects of Spiritual Practices on Recovery from Substance Abuse.' *Journal of Psychiatric and Mental Health Nursing 5,* 409–413.

Chadwick, P.K. (1997) 'Recovery from Psychosis: Learning More from Patients.' *Journal of Mental Health 6,* 6, 577–588.

Charters, P.J. (1999) 'The Religious and Spiritual Needs of Mental Health Clients.' *Nursing Standard 13,* 26, 34–36

Chu, C. and Klein, H.E. (1985) 'Psychological and Environmental Variables in Outcome of Black Schizophrenics.' *Journal of National Medical Association 77,* 793–796.

Cobb, M. and Robshaw, V. (1998) *The Spiritual Challenge of Health Care.* Edinburgh: Churchill Livingstone.

Cohen, M., Kahn, D. and Steeves, R. (in press) *Hermeneutic Phenomenological Research.* Thousand Oaks, CA: Sage Press.

Constance Harris, S. (1998) 'Recognizing and Responding.' *American Journal of Nursing 98,* 1, 26–30.

Copp, G. and Dunn, V. (1993) 'Frequent and Difficult Problems Perceived by Nurses for the Dying in the Community, Hospice and Acute Care Settings.' *Palliative Medicine 7,* 1, 19–25.

Corben, V. (1999) 'Misusing Phenomenology in Nursing Research: Identifying the Issues.' *Nurse Researcher 6,* 3, 52–66.

Cotterell, P. (1990) *Mission and Meaninglessness.* London: SPCK.

Crawford, M., Handa, P. and Weiner, R. (1989) 'The Relationships between Religion and Mental Health/Distress.' *Review of Religious Research 31,* 1, 16–22.

Crossley, D. (1995) 'Religious Experience within Mental Illness: Opening the Door on Research.' *British Journal of Psychiatry 166,* 3, 284–286.

Currey, C. (1997) 'Religious and Spiritual Beliefs.' In M. Beeforth (ed) *Knowing Our Own Minds.* London: The Mental Health Foundation.

Davie, G. (1994) *Religion in Britain Since 1945.* Oxford: Blackwell.

Davie, G. and Cobb, M. (1998) 'Faith and Belief: A Sociological Perspective.' In M. Cobb and V. Robshaw (1998) *The Spiritual Challenge of Health Care.* Edinburgh: Churchill Livingstone.

Dawson, P.J. (1997) 'A Reply to Goddard's "Spirituality as Integrative Energy".' *Journal of Advanced Nursing 25*, 282–289.

Department of Health and Social Security (1972) *Report of the Committee on Nursing (Briggs Report)*. London: HMSO.

Department of Health (1991) *Research for Health: A Research and Development Strategy for the NHS*. London: HMSO.

Department of Health (1993a) *Strategy for Research in Nursing, Midwifery and Health Visiting*. London: HMSO.

Department of Health (1993b) *A Vision for the Future*. London: NHS Management Executive.

Department of Health (1993c) *Report of the Taskforce on the Strategy for Research in Nursing, Midwifery and Health Visiting*. London: HMSO.

Department of Health (1996) *Research and Development. Towards an Evidence-Based Health Service*. London: HMSO.

Department of Health (1997) *The New NHS: Modern, Dependable*. London: HMSO.

Department of Health (1998) *A First Class Service: Quality in the New NHS*. London: HMSO.

Diekelman, N., Allen, D. and Tanner, C. (1989) 'The NLN Criteria for the Appraisal of Baccalaureate Programmes: A Critical Hermeneutical Analysis.' In N. Diekelman and D. Allen, *The NLN Criteria for Appraisal of Baccalaureate Programmes: A Critical Hermeneutic Analysis*. New York: NLN Press.

Dominian, J. (1990) *Depression*. London: Fontana Press.

Donahue, M.J. (1985) 'Intrinsic and Extrinsic Religiousness: Review and Meta-Analysis.' *Journal of Personality and Social Psychology 48*, 2, 400–419.

Donahue, M.J. (1988) 'Aggregate Religiousness and Teenage Fertility Revisited: Reanalyses of Data from the Guttmacher Institute.' Paper presented at Society for the Scientific Study of Religion, Chicago, Illinois.

Dossey, B.M. and Dossey, L. (1998) 'Body–Mind–Spirit: Attending to Holistic Care.' *American Journal of Nursing 98*, 8, 35–38.

Dossey, L. (1993) *Healing Words: The Power of Prayer and the Practice of Medicine*. San Francisco: Harper.

Dossey, L. (1999) 'God in the Laboratory: A Look at Science, Prayer, and Healing.' *Oates Journal 2* [online] January: http://www.oates.org/journal/mbr/vol-02-99/articles/dossey-01.htm.

Doyle, D. (1992) 'Have We Looked beyond the Physical and Psychosocial?' *Journal of Pain and Symptom Management 7*, 5, 302–11.

Droege, T.A. (1991) *The Faith Factor in Healing*. Philadelphia: Trinity Press International.

Duke, S. (1998) 'An Exploration of Anticipatory Grief: The Lived Experience of People during their Spouses' Terminal Illness and Bereavement.' *Journal of Advanced Nursing 28*, 4, 829–839.

Dyson, J., Cobb, M. and Foreman, D. (1997) 'The Meaning of Spirituality: A Literature Review.' *Journal of Advanced Nursing 26*, 1183–1188.

Eaton, W.W. (1986) *The Sociology of Mental Disorders.* New York: Praegar Publishers.

Eisenberg, L. (1986) 'Mindlessness and Brainlessness in Psychiatry.' *British Journal of Psychiatry 148*, 497–508.

Elkins, D.N., Hedstrom, J.L., Hughes, L.L., Leaf, J.A. and Saunders, C. (1988) 'Toward a Humanistic-Phenomenological Spirituality: Definition, Description and Measurement.' *Journal of Humanistic Psychology 28*, 4, 5–18.

Ellis, A. (1980) 'Psychotherapy and Atheistic Values: A Response to A.E. Bergin's "Psychotherapy and Religious Values".' *Journal of Consulting and Clinical Psychology 48*, 5, 635–639.

Ellis, A. (1986) 'Do Some Religious Beliefs Help Create Emotional Disturbance?' *Psychotherapy in Private Practice 4*, 101–106.

Ellis, D. (1980) 'Whatever Happened to the Spiritual Dimension?' *The Canadian Nurse 76*, 42–43.

Ellison, C.G. and Levin, J.S. (1998) 'The Religion–Health Connection: Evidence, Theory and Future Directions.' *Health Education and Behaviour 25*, 6, 700–720.

Ellison, C.W. (1983) 'Spiritual Well-Being: Conceptualization and Measurement.' *Journal of Psychology and Theology 11*, 4.

Ellison, C.W. and Smith, J. (1991) 'Toward an Integrative Measure of Health and Well-Being.' *Journal of Theology and Psychology 19*, 1, 35–48.

Emblen, J.D. (1992) 'Religion and Spirituality Defined According to Current Use in Nursing Literature.' *Journal of Professional Nursing 8*, 1, 41–47.

Emblen, J.D. and Halstead, L. (1993) 'Spiritual Needs and Interventions: Comparing the Views of Patients, Nurses and Chaplains.' *Clinical Nurse Specialist 3*, 7, 175–82.

Ersek, M. and Ferrell, B.R. (1994) 'Providing Relief from Cancer Pain by Assisting in the Search for Meaning.' *Journal of Palliative Care 10*, 4, 15–22.

Fagan, P. (1996) 'Why Religion Matters: The Impact of Religious Practice on Social Stability.' *The Heritage Foundation Backgrounder* 1064 [online] http://www.heritage.org/library/categories/family/bg1064.html.

Farran, C.J., Fitchett, G., Quiring-Emblen, J.D. and Burck, J.R. (1989). 'Development of a Model for Spiritual Assessment and Intervention.' *Journal of Religion and Health 28*, 3, 185–195.

Fitchett, G. (1993) *Assessing Spiritual Needs: A Guide to Caregivers.* Minneapolis: Augsberg Fortress.

Fitchett, G., Burton, L.A., Sivan, A.B. (1997) 'The Religious Needs and Resources of Psychiatric Inpatients.' *The Journal of Nervous and Mental Disease 185*, 5, 320–326.

Fowler, J. (1981) *Stages of Faith*. New York: Harper and Row.

Fowler, J. (1986) In a paper by J. Wesson 'How Cinderella Must Get to the Ball: Pastoral Studies and its Relation to Theology.' In, P.H. Ballard (ed) *The Foundations of Pastoral Studies and Practical Theology*. Cardiff: Faculty of Theology University College.

Frank, J.D. (1991) 'Religious and Ethical Issues in Psychotherapy.' *Current Opinion in Psychiatry 4*, 375–378.

Frankl, V.E. (1962) *Man's Search for Meaning: From Death Camp to Existentialism*. Boston: Beacon Press.

Freud S. (1959) 'Civilization and its Discontents.' In J. Strachey (ed) *The Standard Edition of the Complete Psychological Works of Sigmund Freud*. London: Hogarth.

Freud, S. (1966) 'Obsessive Actions and Religious Pratices.' In J. Strachey (ed) *The Standard Edition of the Complete Psychological Works of Sigmund Freud* London: Hogarth.

Fry, A. (1998) 'Spirituality, Communication and Mental Health Nursing: The Tacit Interdiction.' *Australian and New Zealand Journal of Mental Health Nursing 7*, 25–32.

Gadamer, H.G. (1981) *Truth and Method*. London: Sheed and Ward.

Garrett, C. (1998) *Beyond Anorexia: Narrative, Spirituality and Recovery*. London: Cambridge University Press.

Gartner, J., Larson, D.B. and Allen, G.D. (1991) 'Religious Commitment and Mental Health: A Review of the Empirical Literature.' *Journal of Psychology and Theology 19*, 1, 6–25.

Gatchel, R.J., Baum, A. and Krantz, D.S. (1989) *An Introduction to Health Psychology*. New York: McGraw Hill Book Company.

Gibbs, H.W. and Achterberg-Lawlis, J. (1978) 'Spiritual Values and Death Anxiety: Implications for Counseling with Terminal Cancer Patients.' *Journal of Counseling Psychology 25*, 563–569.

Gilbert, P. (1992) *Depression: The Evolution of Powerlessness*. Hove: Erlbaum.

Gleeson, J. (2000) 'Psychiatry and Religious Experience: Room for Expansion?' *Bishop John Robinson Fellowship Newsletter 9*, 2–3.

Goddard, N.C. (1995) 'Spirituality as Integrative Energy: A Philosophical Analysis as Requisite Precursor to Holistic Nursing Practice.' *Journal of Advanced Nursing 22*, 808–815.

Goldberg, B. (1998) 'Connection: An Exploration of Spirituality in Nursing Care.' *Journal of Advanced Nursing 27*, 836–842.

Goode, B. and Goode, M. (1981) 'The Meaning of Symptoms: A Cultural Hermeneutic Model for Clinical Practice.' In L. Eisenberg and A. Kleinman (eds) The Relevance of Social Science for Medicine. Dordrecht: D. Reidal Publishing Co.

Gordon, H. (2000) 'Guilt: Why is it Such a Burden?' *Bishop John Robinson Fellowship Newsletter 9*, 4–6.

Gournay, K. (1996) 'Schizophrenia: A Review of the Contemporary Literature and Implications for Mental Health Nursing Theory, Practice and Education.' *Journal of Psychiatric and Mental Health Nursing 3*, 7–12.

Govier, I. (2000) 'Spiritual Care in Nursing: A Systematic Approach.' *Nursing Standard 14*, 17, 32–36.

Govig, S.D. (1994) *Souls are Made of Endurance: Surviving Mental Illness in the Family.* Louisville, KY: Westminster John Knox Press.

Granstrom, S. (1985) 'Spiritual Care for Oncology Patients.' *Topics in Clinical Nursing 7*, 1, 39–45.

Group for Advancement of Psychiatry (GAP) (1976) *Mysticism: Spiritual Quest or Mental Disorder.* New York: Group for Advancement of Psychiatry.

Hahn, R.A. (1995) *Sickness and Healing.* Newhaven and London: Yale University Press.

Hall, B.A. (1996) 'The Psychiatric Model: A Critical Analysis of its Undermining Effects on Nursing in Chronic Mental Illness.' *Advances in Nursing Science 18*, 3, 16–26.

Harrington, A. (1995) 'Spiritual Care: What Does it Mean to RN's?' *Australian Journal of Advanced Nursing 12*, 4, 5–14.

Harris, C.D. (1996) 'Symbolic Interactionism as Defined by Herbert Blumer.' The Society for More Creative Speech. [online] http://www.thepoint.net/~usul/text/blumer.html.

Harris, W.S., Gowda, M., Kolb, J.W., Strychacz, C.P., Vacek, J.L., Jones, P.G., Forker, A., O'Keefe, J.H. and McCallister, B.D. (1999) 'A Randomized Controlled Trial of the Effects of Remote Intercessory Prayer on Outcomes in Patients Admitted to the Coronary Care Unit.' *Archives of General Medicine 159*, 2273–2278.

Harrison, J. and Burnard, P. (1993) *Spirituality and Nursing Practice.* Aldershot: Avebury.

Hartz, G.W. and Everett, H.C. (1989) 'Fundamentalist Religion and its Effect on Mental Health.' *Journal of Religion and Health 28*, 3, 207–217.

Hay, M. (1989) 'Principles in Building Spiritual Assessment Tools.' *American Journal of Hospice Care* September/October, 25–31.

Hekman, S. (1986) *Hermeneutics and the Sociology of Knowledge.* Cambridge: Polity Press.

Highfield, M.F. (1992) 'Spiritual Health of Oncology Patients: Nurse and Patient Perspectives.' *Cancer Nursing 15*, 1–8.

Hill, W.E. and Mullen, P.M. (1996) 'An Overview of Psychoneuroimmunology: Implications for Pastoral Care.' *The Journal of Pastoral Care 50*, 3, 239–247.

Hillhouse, J. and Adler, C. (1991) 'Stress, Health, and Immunity Review of the Literature and Implications for the Nursing Profession.' *Holistic Nursing Practice 5*, 4, 22–31.

His Royal Highness the Prince of Wales (1991) '150th Anniversary Lecture.' *British Journal of Psychiatry 159*, 763–768.

Honer, S.M. and Hunt, T.C. (1987) *Invitation to Philosophy: Issues and Options* (5th edition). Belmont, CA: Wadsworth.

Horsfall, J. (1997) 'Psychiatric Nursing: Epistemological Contradictions.' *Advances in Nursing Science 20*,1, 56–65.

Horton, P.C. (1974) 'The Mystical Experience: Substance of an Illusion.' *American Psychoanalytic Association Journal 1* and *2*, 364–380.

Houldin, A.D., Lev, E., Prystowsky, M.B., Redei, E. and Lowery, B.J. (1991) 'Psychoneuroimmunology: A Review of the Literature.' *Holistic Nursing Practices 5*, 4, 10–21.

Hunsinger, D. van Deusen (1995) *Theology of Pastoral Counselling: A New Interdisciplinary Approach.* Michigan: Wm. B. Eerdmans Publishing Co.

Jacobson, D.E. (1986) 'Types and Timing of Social Support.' *Journal of Health and Social Behaviour 27*, 250–264.

James, W. (1902) *The Variety of Religious Experience.* New York: Modern Library.

Jaspers, K. (1959) *General Psychopathology.* (7th edition) (translated J. Hoenig and M. W. Hamilton, 1963). Manchester: Manchester University Press.

Jeeves, M.A. (1997) *Human Nature at the Millennium: Reflections on the Integration of Psychology and Christianity.* Leicester: Apollos.

Jenkins, R.A. and Pargament, K.I. (1995) 'Religion and Spirituality as Resources for Coping with Cancer.' *Journal of Psychosocial Oncology 13*, 51–74.

Jerotic, V. (1997) 'The Role of Religion in Rehabilitation of Psychiatric Patients.' *Psihijat.dan 29*, 3–4, 279–285.

Jung, C. (1933) *Modern Man in Search of a Soul.* San Diego: Harcourt Brace.

Kahoe, R.D. (1974) 'Personality and Achievement Correlates on Intrinsic and Extrinsic Religious Orientations.' *Journal of Personality and Social Psychology 29*, 812–818.

Karp, D. (1996) *Speaking of Sadness: Depression, Disconnection, and the Meanings of Illness.* New York: Oxford University Press.

Kendell, R.E. and Zealley, A.K. (eds) (1993) *Companion to Psychiatric Studies.* Edinburgh: Churchill Livingstone.

King, M.B. and Dein, S. (1998) 'The Spiritual Variable in Psychiatric Research.' *Psychological Medicine 28*, 6, 1259–1262.

Kirkpatrick, H., Landeen, J., Byrne, C., Woodside, H., Pawlick, J., and Bernardo, A. (1995) 'Hope and Schizophrenia: Clinicians Identify Hope-Instilling Strategies.' *Journal of Psychosocial Nursing and Mental Health Service 33*, 6, 15–19.

Kirkpatrick, L.A. and Hood, R.W. (1990) 'Intrinsic-Extrinsic Religious Orientation: The Boon or Bane of Contemporary Psychology of Religion.' *Journal for the Scientific Study of Religion 29*, 4, 442–462.

Kirkpatrick, L.A., Hood, R.W. and Hartz, G. (1991) 'Fundamentalist Religion Conceptualized in terms of Rokeach's Theory of the Open and Closed mind: New Perspectives on Some Old Ideas.' *Research in the Social Scientific Study of Religion 3*, 157–179.

Kitwood, T. (1997a) *Dementia Reconsidered: The Person Comes First.* Buckingham: Open University Press.

Kitwood, T. (1997b) 'Personhood, Dementia and Dementia Care.' In S. Hunter (ed) *Dementia: Challenges and New Directions.* London: Jessica Kingsley Publishers.

Kleinman, A. (1988) *The Illness Narratives: Suffering, Healing and the Human Condition.* New York: Basic Books.

Kleinman, A. and Good, B. (eds) (1985) *Culture and Depression: Studies in the Anthroplogy and Cross-Cultural Psychiatry of Affect and Disorder.* Los Angeles: University of California Press.

Koch, T. (1996) 'Implementation of a Hermeneutic Inquiry in Nursing: Philosophy, Rigour and Representation.' *Journal of Advanced Nursing 24*, 1, 174–184.

Koch, T. (1998a) 'Reconceptualizing Rigour: The Case for Reflexivity.' *Journal of Advanced Nursing 28*, 4, 882–890.

Koch, T. (1998b) 'Story Telling: Is It Really Research?' *Journal of Advanced Nursing 28*, 6, 118–119.

Koch, T. (1999) 'An Interpretive Research Process: Revisiting Phenomenological and Hermeneutical Approaches.' *Nurse Researcher 6*, 3, 20–34.

Koenig, H.G. (1997) *Is Religion Good for Your Health? The Effects of Religion on Physical and Mental Health.* New York: Haworth Press.

Koenig, H.G. (ed) (1998) *Handbook of Religion and Mental Health.* San Diego: Academic Press.

Koski-Jaennes, A. and Turner, N. (1999) 'Factors Influencing Recovery from Different Addictions.' *Addiction Research 7*, 6, 469–492.

Kroll, J. (1995) 'Religion and Psychiatry.' *Current Opinion in Psychiatry 8*, 335–339.

Kroll, J. and Sheehan, W. (1989) 'Psychiatric Patient's Belief in General Health Factors and Sin as Causes of Illness.' *American Journal of Psychiatry 147*, 112 ff.

Kuhn, T.S. (1970) *The Structure of Scientific Revolutions.* Chicago: The University of Chicago Press.

Kuttierath, S.K. (1998) 'Spirituality in the Secular Sense.' *European Journal of Palliative Care 5*, 5, 165–167.

Landis, B.J. (1996) 'Uncertainty, Spiritual Well-Being, and Psychosocial Adjustment to Chronic Illness.' *Issues in Mental Health Nursing 17*, 217–231.

Larson, D.B. and Larson, S.S. (1994) *The Forgotten Factor in Physical and Mental Health: What Does the Research Show?* National Institute for Healthcare Research.

Larson D.B., Pattison, E.M., Blazer, D.G., Omran, A.R. and Kaplan, B.H. (1986) 'A Systematic Analysis of Research on Religious Variables in Four Major Psychiatric Journals 1978–1982.' *American Journal of Psychiatry 143*, 329–334.

Larson, D.B., Sherrill, K.A., Lyons, J.S., Craigie, F.C., Thielman, S.B., Greenwood, M. A. and Larson, S.S. (1992) 'Associations between Dimensions of Religious Commitment and Mental Health Reported in the American Journal of Mental Health and Archives of General Psychiatry: 1978–1989.' *American Journal of Psychiatry 149*, 4, 557–559.

Larson, D.B., Swyers, J.P. and McCullough, M. (1997) *Scientific Research on Spirituality and Health: A Consensus Report.* National Institute for Healthcare Research.

Lartey, E.Y. (1997) *In Living Colour: An Intercultural Approach to Pastoral Care and Counselling.* London: Cassell.

Lea, G. (1982) 'Religion, Mental Health and Clinical Issues.' *Journal of Religion and Health 21*, 4, 336–351.

Levin, J.S. (1996a) 'How Religion Influences Morbidity and Health: Reflections on Natural History, Salutogenesis, and Host Resistance.' *Social Science Medicine 43*, 5, 849–64.

Levin, J.S. (1996b) 'How Prayer Heals: A Theoretical Model.' *Alternative Therapies Health and Medicine 2*, 1, 66–73.

Lewis, S.E. (1995) 'A Search for Meaning: Making Sense of Depression.' *Journal of Mental Health 4*, 369–382.

Lincoln, Y.S. and Guba, E.G. (1985) *Naturalistic Enquiry.* London: Sage Publications.

Lindgren, K.N. and Coursey, R.D. (1995) 'Spirituality and Serious Mental Illness: A Two-Part Study.' *Psychosocial Rehabilitation Journal 18*, 3, 93–111.

Lindsey, E. (1996) 'Health within Illness: Experiences of Chronically Ill/Disabled People.' *Journal of Advanced Nursing 24*, 3, 465–472.

Loewenthal, K.M. (1995) *Mental Health and Religion.* London: Chapman & Hall.

Long, A. (1997) 'Nursing: A Spiritual Perspective.' *Nursing Ethics 4*, 6, 496–510.

Lukoff, D., Turner, R. and Lu, F. (1992) 'Transpersonal Psychology Research Review: Psychoreligious Dimensions of Healing.' *The Journal of Transpersonal Psychology 24*, 1, 41–60.

Lukoff, D., Turner, R. and Lu, F. (1993) 'Transpersonal Psychology Research Review: Psychospiritual Dimensions of Healing.' *The Journal of Transpersonal Psychology 25*, 1, 11–28.

McBride, J.L., Arthur, G., Brooks, R. and Pilkington, L. (1998) 'The Relationship between a Patient's Spirituality and Health Experience.' *Family Medicine 30*, 2, 122–6.

McCain, N.L. and Swanson, B. (1996) 'Psychoneuroimmunology: An Emerging Framework for Nursing Research.' *Journal of Advanced Nursing 23*, 657–664.

McKie, A. and Swinton, J. (2000) 'Community, Culture and Character: The Place of the Virtues in Psychiatric Nursing Practice.' *Journal of Psychiatric and Mental Health Nursing 7*, 1, 35–42.

Macmurray, J. (1961) *Persons in Relation*. London: Faber and Faber.

McSherry, W. (1998) 'Nurses' Perceptions of Spirituality and Spiritual Care.' *Nursing Standard 13*, 4, 36–40.

McSherry, W. and Draper, P. (1998) 'The Debates Emerging from the Literature Surrounding the Concept of Spirituality as Applied to Nursing.' *Journal of Advanced Nursing 27*, 683–691.

Madjar, I. and Walton, J.A. (1999) *Nursing and the Experience of Illness: Phenomenology in Practice*. London: Routledge.

Maltby, J., Lewis, C.A. and Day, L. (1999) 'Religious Orientation and Psychological Well-Being: The Role of the Frequency of Personal Prayer.' *British Journal of Health Psychology 4*, 4, 363–378.

Mandel, A.J. (1980) 'Towards a Psychobiology of Transcendence: God in the Brain.' In R.J. Davidson, and J.M. Davidson *The Psychobiology of Consciousness*. New York: Plenum.

Martin, J.E. and Carlson, R. (1988) 'Spiritual Dimensions of Health Psychology.' In R. Millar and J.E. Martin (eds) (1988) *Behaviour Therapy and Religion: Integrating Spiritual Behavioural Approaches to Change*. London: Sage Publications.

Martsolf, D.S. and Mickley, J.R.(1998) 'The Concept of Spirituality in Nursing Theories: Differing World-Views and Extent Focus.' *Journal of Advanced Nursing 27*, 294–303.

Maslow, A. (1968) *Toward a Psychology of Being* (2nd edition). New York: Van Nostrand.

Maslow, A. (1970) *Motivation and Personality*. London: Harper & Row Publishers.

Maslow, A. (1985) *The Farther Reaches of Human Nature*. New York: Penguin.

Mason T. and Mercer D. (1996) 'Nursing: Visions of Social Control.' *Australian and New Zealand Journal of Mental Health Nursing 5*, 4, 153–62.

Maton, K. (1989) 'The Stress Buffering Role of Spiritual Support: Cross Sectional and Prospective Investigations.' *Journal of the Scientific Study of Religion 28*, 3, 310–323.

Matthews, D. (1999) *The Faith Factor: Scientific Proof of the Power of Prayer.* London: Penguin.

Matthews, D.A., McCullough, M.E., Larson, D.B., Koenig, H.G., Swyers, J.P. and Milano, M.G. 'Religious Commitment and Health Status: A Review of the Research and Implications for Family Medicine.' *Archives of Family Medicine 7*, 118–24.

Maugan, T.A. (1996) 'The SPIRITual history.' *Archives of Family Medicine 5*, 1, 11–16.

May, G.G. (1982) *Will and Spirit.* San Francisco: Harper.

Mental Health Foundation (1998) *The Courage to Bear Our Souls.* London: Mental Health Foundation.

Mickley, J.R., Carson, V. and Soecken, K.L. (1995) 'Religion and Adult Mental Health: The State of the Science in Nursing.' *Issues in Mental Health Nursing 16*, 345–360.

Miller, J.F. (1985) 'Assessment of Loneliness and Spiritual Well-Being in Chronically Ill and Healthy Adults.' *Journal of Professional Nursing 1*, 79–85.

Miller, J.S. (1991) 'Mental Illness and Spiritual Crisis: Implications for Psychiatric Rehabilitation.' *Psychosocial Rehabilitation Journal 14*, 2, 29–47.

Miller, W.R. (1990) 'Spirituality: The Silent Dimension in Addiction Research.' *Drug and Alcohol Review 9*, 259–266.

Miller, W.R. (1998) 'Researching the Spiritual Dimensions of Alcohol and Other Drug Problems.' *Addiction 93*, 7, 979–990.

Moberg, D.O. (1984) 'Subjective Measures of Spiritual Well-Being.' *Review of Religious Research 25*, 351–364.

Moltmann, J. (1985) *God in Creation: An Ecological Doctrine of Creation.* London: SCM Press Ltd.

Moore, T. (1992) *Care of the Soul: A Guide for Cultivating Depth and Sacredness in Everyday Life.* New York: HarperCollins.

Moore, T. (1993) 'Care of the Soul: The Benefits – and Costs – of a More Spiritual Life.' *Psychology Today 26*, 3, 28 ff.

Morel, C. (1996) 'Radicalizing Recovery: Addiction, Spirituality and Politics.' *Social Work 41*, 3, 306–312.

Morris, L. and Elizabeth, H. (1996) 'A Spiritual Well-Being Model: Use with Older Women who Experience Depression.' *Issues in Mental Health Nursing 17*, 5, 439–456.

Moustakas, C. (1994) *Phenomenological Research Methods.* London: Sage Publications.

Muir Gray J.A. (1997) *Evidence-based Healthcare: How to Make Health Policy and Management Decisions.* London: Churchill Livingstone.

Narayanansamy, A. (1993) 'Nurses' Awareness and Educational Preparation in Meeting their Patients' Spiritual Needs.' *Nurse Education Today 13,* 196–201.

National Association of Health Authorities and Trusts (1995) *Spiritual Care in the NHS: A Guide for Purchasers and Providers.* NAHAT.

Neeleman J. and King, M.B. (1993) 'Psychiatrists' Religious Attitudes in Relation to Their Clinical Practice: A Survey of 231 Psychiatrists.' *Acta Psychiatrica Scandinavica 88,* 420–424.

Neeleman, J and Lewis, G. (1994) 'Relgious identity and comfort beliefs in three groups of psychiatric patients and a group of medical controls.' *International Journal of Social Pstchiatry 40,* 124-34.

Neeleman, J. and Persaud, R. (1995) 'Why Do Psychiatrists Neglect Religion?' *British Journal of Medical Psychology 68,* 169–178.

Newbigin, L. (1989) *The Gospel in a Pluralist Society.* London: SPCK

Nino, A.G. (1997) 'Assessment of Spiritual Quests in Clinical Practice.' *International Journal of Psychotherapy 2,* 2, 193–212.

Nolan, P. and Crawford, P. (1997) 'Towards a Rhetoric of Spirituality in Mental Health Care.' *Journal of Advanced Nursing 26,* 2, 289–94.

O'Brien, M.E. (1982) 'Religious Faith and Adjustment to Long-Term Hemodialysis.' *Journal of Religion and Health 21,* 68–80.

O'Laoire, S. (1997) 'An Experimental Study of the Effects of Distant, Intercessory Prayer on Self-Esteem, Anxiety, and Depression.' *Alternative Therapies in Health and Medicine 3,* 6, 38–53.

Oldnall, A. (1995) 'On the Absence of Spirituality in Nursing Theories and Models.' *Journal of Advanced Nursing 21,* 3, 417–418.

Oldnall, A. (1996) 'A Critical Analysis of Nursing: Meeting the Spiritual Needs of Patients.' *Journal of Advanced Nursing 23,* 138–144.

Paloutzian, R.F. (1996) *Invitation to the Psychology of Religion.* (2nd edition) London: Allyn and Bacon.

Pargament, K.I. (1997) *The Psychology of Religion and Coping: Theory, Research, Practice.* New York: Guildford Press.

Pargament, K., Grevengoed, N., Hathaway, W., Kennell, J., Newman, J. and Jones, W. (1988) 'Religion and Problem Solving: Three Styles of Coping.' *Journal for the Scientific Study of Religion 27,* 90–104.

Pascoe, E. (1996) 'The Value to Nursing Research of Gadamer's Hermeneutic Philosophy.' *Journal of Advanced Nursing 24,* 6, 1309–1314.

Patterson, E.F. (1998) 'The Philosophy and Physics of Holistic Health Care: Spiritual Healing as a Workable Interpretation.' *Journal of Advanced Nursing 27*, 287–293.

Peplau, H.E. (1952) *Interpersonal Relations in Nursing.* New York: G.P. Putnam and Sons.

Pesut, D.J. (1991) 'The Art, Science and Techniques of Reframing in Psychiatric Mental Health Nursing.' *Issues in Mental Health Nursing 12*, 1, 9 ff.

Peterson, L. and Roy, A. (1985) 'Religiosity, Anxiety, and Meaning and Purpose: Religious Consequences for Psychological Well-being.' *Review of Religious Research 27*, (1), 49-62.

Pilch, J.J. (2000) *Healing in the New Testament: Insights from Medical and Mediterranean Anthropology.* Minneapolis: Fortress Press.

Piles, C.L. (1990) 'Providing Spiritual Care.' *Nurse Education 15*, 36–41.

Pollner, M. (1989) 'Divine Relations, Social Relations, and Well-Being.' *Journal of Health and Social Behaviour 30*, 92–104.

Post, S.G. (1995) *The Moral Challenge of Alzheimer Disease.* London: Johns Hopkins University Press.

Pullen, L. Tuck, I. and Mix, K. (1996) 'Mental Health Nurses' Spiritual Perspectives.' *Journal of Holistic Nursing 14*, 2, 85–97.

Reed, P.G. (1986) 'Religiousness among Terminally Ill and Healthy Adults.' *Research in Nursing and Health 10*, 35–41.

Reed, P.G. (1991) 'Self-Transcendence and Mental Health in Oldest Old Adults.' *Nursing Research 40*, 1, 5–11.

Reed, P.G. (1992) 'An Emerging Paradigm for the Investigation of Spirituality in Nursing.' *Research in Nursing and Health 15*, 349–357.

Reedier, F. (1988) 'Hermeneutics.' In B. Sartor (ed) *Paths of Knowledge: Innovative Research Methods for Nursing.* New York: National League for Nursing Press.

Rees, B.L. (1995) 'Effects of Relaxation with Guided Imagery on Anxiety, Depression, and Self-Esteem in Primiparas.' *Journal of Holistic Nursing 13*, 3, 255–267.

Restak, R.M. (1989) 'The Brain, Depression and the Immune System.' *Journal of Clinical Psychiatry 50*, 5, 23–26.

Richards, P.S. and Bergin, A.E. (1997) *A Spiritual Strategy for Counselling and Psychotherapy.* Washington: American Psychological Association.

Roberts, G. (1991) 'Delusional Belief and Meaning in Life: A Preferred Reality.' *British Journal of Psychiatry 159*, 19–28

Roberts, L., Ahmed, I. and Hall, S. (2000) 'Intercessory Prayer for the Alleviation of Ill Health.' *The Cochrane Database of Systematic Reviews 1.*

Robertson, S. (1999) 'Listening to Them and Reading Me: A Hermeneutic Approach to Understanding the Experience of Illness.' *Journal of Advanced Nursing 29*, 2, 290–297.

Robinson, J.S.T. (1957) *The Body*. London: SCM Press Ltd.

Roe, B. (1993) 'Undertaking a Critical Review of the Literature.' *Nurse Researcher 1*, 1, 31–42.

Rokeach, M. (1960) *The Open and Closed Mind*. New York: Basic Books.

Romme, M. and Escher, S. (1993) *Accepting Voices*. London: MIND Publications.

Roper, N., Logan, W.W. and Tierney, A.J. (1996) *The Elements of Nursing* (4th edition). Edinburgh: Churchill Livingstone.

Rosenham, D.L. and Seligman, M.E.P. (1995) *Abnormal Psychology*. New York: W.W. Norton.

Ross, C. (1990) 'Religion and Psychological Distress.' *Journal for the Scientific Study of Religion 29*, 2, 235–245.

Ross, L. (1994) 'Spiritual Aspects of Nursing.' *Journal of Advanced Nursing 19*, 439–447.

Ross, L. (1994) 'Spiritual Care: The Nurses' Role.' *Nursing Standard 8*, 29, 33–37.

Ross, L. (1998) 'The Nurse's Role in Spiritual Care.' In M. Cobb and V. Robshaw *The Spiritual Challenge of Health Care*. Edinburgh: Churchill Livingstone.

Ryan, S. (1996) 'Living with Rheumatoid Arthritis: A Phenomenological Exploration.' *Nursing Standard 10*, 41, 45–48.

Sandelowski, M. (1986) 'The Problem of Rigour in Qualitative Research.' *Advances in Nursing Science 8*, 3, 27–37.

Scottish Office (1994) *Meeting the Spiritual Needs of Patients and Staff*. London: NHS in Scotland Management Executive.

Seidman, I.E. (1991) *Interviewing as Qualitative Research: A Guide for Researchers in Education and the Social Sciences*. New York: Teachers College Press.

Shafranske, E.P. (ed) (1996) *Religion and the Clinical Practice of Psychology*. Washington: American Psychological Association.

Shams, M. and Jackson, P.R. (1993) 'Religiosity as a Predictor of Well-Being and Moderator of the Psychological Impact of Unemployment.' *British Journal of Medical Psychology 66*, 342.

Shelly, J.A., John, S.D. *et al*. (1983) *Spiritual Dimensions of Mental Health*. Illinois: InterVarsity Press.

Sherrill, K.A. and Larson, D.B. (1994) 'The Anti-Tenure Factor in Religious Research in Clinical Epidemiology and Aging.' In J.S.Levin (ed) *Relgion in Aging and Health*. California: Sage.

Shuler, P.A., Gelberg, L. and Brown, M. (1994) 'The Effects of Spiritual/Religious Practices on Psychological Well-Being among Inner City Homeless Women.' *Nurse Practitioner Forum 5*, 2, 106–13.

Sicher, F., Targ, E., Moore, D. and Smith, H.S. (1998) 'A Randomized Double-Blind Study of the Effect of Distant Healing in a Population with Advanced AIDS. Report of a small scale study.' *Western Journal of Medicine 169*, 6, 356–363.

Sims, A.C.P. (1992) 'Symptoms and Beliefs.' *Journal of the Royal Society of Health 112*, 42–46.

Sims, A.C.P. (1994) '"Psyche"-Spirit as Well as Mind.' *British Journal of Psychiatry 165*, 441–446.

Sims, A.C.P. (1997) 'Commentary on "Spiritual Experience and Psychopathology".' *Philosophy, Psychiatry and Psychology 4*, 1, 79–81.

Sims, A.C.P. (1999) 'The Cure of Souls: Psychiatric Dilemmas.' *International Review of Psychiatry 11*, 2/3, 97 ff.

Smith, B.A. (1996) 'The Problem Drinker's Lived Experience of Suffering: A Hermeneutic Phenomenological Study.' Unpublished Msc Nursing Thesis, University of Aberdeen.

Smith, B.A. (1998) 'The Problem Drinker's Lived Experience of Suffering: An Exploration Using Hermeneutic Phenomenology.' *Journal of Advanced Nursing 27*, 213–222.

Smucker, C. (1996) 'A Phenomenological Description of the Experience of Spiritual Distress.' *Nursing Diagnosis 7*, 2, 81 ff.

Sodestrom, K.E. and Martinson, I.M. (1987) 'Patient's Spiritual Coping Strategies: A Study of Nurse and Patient Perspectives.' *Oncology Nursing Forum 14*, 41–46.

Soeken, K.L. and Carson, V.J. (1987) 'Responding to the Spiritual Needs of the Chronically Ill.' *Nursing Clinics of North America 22*, 3, 603–11.

Spencer, J., Davidson, H., and White, V. (1997) 'Helping Clients Develop Hopes for the Future.' *The American Journal of Occupational Therapy 51*, 3, 191–198.

Spilka, B., Shaver, P. and Kirkpatrick, L.A. (1985) 'A General Attribution Theory for the Psychology of Religion.' *Journal for the Scientific Study of Religion 24*, 1, 1–118.

Stark, R. (1971) 'Psychopathology and Religious Commitment.' *Review of Religious Research 12*, 3, 165–176.

Steketee, G.S., Quay, K., and White, K. (1991) 'Religion and Guilt in OCD Patients.' *Journal of Anxiety Disorders 5*, 4, 359–367.

Stephen, D.J. (1986) 'The Patient as Text: A Model of Clinical Hermeneutics.' *Theoretical Medicine 7*, 195–210.

Stoll, R.I. (1979) 'Guidelines for Spiritual Assessment.' *American Journal of Nursing 79*, 9, 1574–7.

Stoter, D.J. (1995) *Spiritual Aspects of Health Care.* London: Mosby.

Strauss, J.S. (1992) 'The Person-Key to Understanding Mental Illness: Towards a New Dynamic Psychiatry, III.' *British Journal of Psychiatry 161* (suppl. 18), 19–26.

Strauss, J.S. (1994) 'The Person with Schizophrenia as a Person II: Approaches to the Subjective and Complex.' *British Journal of Psychiatry 164*, (suppl. 23), 103–107.

Strunk, O. (1965) *Mature Religion: A Psychological Study.* New York: Abingdon Press.

Stutzman, J. and Schrock-Shenk, C. (1995) *Mediation and Facilitation Training Manual.* Akron: Mennonite Conciliation Service.

Styles, M.K. (1994) 'The Shining Stranger: Application of the Phenomenological Method in the Investigation of the Nurse-Family Spiritual Relationship.' *Cancer Nursing 17*, 1, 18–26.

Suess, L. and Halpern, M.S. (1989) 'Obsessive-Compulsive Disorder: The Religious Perspective.' In J. Rapport (ed) *Obsessive-Compulsive Disorder in Children and Adolescents.* Washingdon DC: American Psychiatric Press, Inc.

Sullivan, W.P. (1993) '"It helps me to be a whole person": The Role of Spirituality amongst the Mentally Challenged.' *Psychosocial Rehabilitation Journal 16*, 3, 125–134.

Swinton, J. (1999a) 'Reclaiming the Soul: A Spiritual Perspective on Forensic Nursing.' In A. Kettles and D. Robinson (eds) *Forensic Nursing and the Multidisciplinary Care of the Mentally Disordered Offender.* London: Jessica Kingsley Publishers.

Swinton, J. (1999b) *Building a Church for Strangers: Theology, Church and Learning Disabilities.* Edinburgh: Contact Pastoral Trust.

Swinton, J. (2000a) *From Bedlam to Shalom: Towards a Practical Theology of Human Nature, Interpersonal Relationships and Mental Health Care.* New York: Peter Lang Press.

Swinton, J. (2000b) *Resurrecting the Person: Friendship and the Care of Those Suffering with Mental Health Problems.* Nashville: Abingdon Press.

Swinton, J. and Kettles, A.M. (1997) 'Resurrecting the Person: Redefining Mental Illness – a Spiritual Perspective.' *Psychiatric Care 4*, 3, 1–4.

Szasz, T. (1973) *The Myth of Mental Illness.* London: Penguin.

Szasz, T. (1979) *Schizophrenia: The Sacred Symbol of Psychiatry.* London: Oxford University Press.

Taggart, S.R. (1994) *Living as If: Belief Systems in Mental Health Practice.* San Francisco: Jossey-Bass Publishers.

Targ, E., Sicher, F., Moore, D. and Smith, H. (1998) 'A Randomized Double-Blind Study of the Effect of Distant Healing in an Advanced AIDS Population.' *Psychosomatic Medicine 60*, 1, 120 ff.

Taylor, E.J., Amenta, M. and Highfield, M. (1994) 'Attitudes and Beliefs Regarding Spiritual Care: A Survey of Cancer Nurses.' *Cancer Nursing 17*, 6, 479–487.

Taylor, E.J., Amenta, M. and Highfield, M. (1995) 'Spiritual Care Practices of Oncology Nurses.' *Oncology Nursing Forum 22*, 1, 31–39.

Thompson, T. and Mathias, P. (1994) *Lyttle's Mental Health and Disorder*. London: Ballière Tindall Ltd.

Thomson, J. (1990) 'Hermeneutic Inquiry.' In L. Moody *Advancing Nursing Through Research* (Vol 2). Newbury Park: Sage Publications.

Tongprateep, T. (2000) 'The Essential Elements of Spirituality among Rural Thai Elders.' *Journal of Advanced Nursing 31*, 1, 197–203.

Toone, B.K., Murray, R., Clare, A., Creed, F. and Smith, A. (1979) 'Psychiatrists' Models of Mental Illness and their Personal Backgrounds.' *Psychological Medicine 9*, 165–178.

Trent, D. (1997) 'A Cocept of Mental Health.' In M. Money and L. Buckley (eds) *Positive Mental Health and its Promotion*. Liverpool: John Moores University.

Tuck, I., Pullen, L. and Lynn, C. (1997) 'Spiritual Interventions Provided by Mental Health Nurses.' *Western Journal of Nursing Research 19*, 3, 351–363.

Tudor, K. (1996) *Mental Health Promotion: Paradigms and Practices*. London: Routledge.

Turbott, J. (1996) 'Religion, Spirituality and Psychiatry: Conceptual, Cultural and Personal Challenges.' *Australian and New Zealand Journal of Psychiatry 30*, 6, 720–727.

Turner, R.P., Lukoff, D., Barnhouse, R.T. and Lu, F.G. (1995) 'Religious or Spiritual Problem: A Culturally Sensitive Diagnostic Category in the DSM-IV.' *Journal of Nervous and Mental Disease 183*, 7, 435–444.

Twibell, R.S., Wieseke, A.W., Marine, M. and Schoger, J. (1996) 'Spiritual Coping Needs of Critically Ill Patients: Validation of Nursing Diagnoses.' *Dimensions of Critical Care Nursing 15*, 5, 245–253.

UW–Madison School of Nursing (2000) MARTIN v.2. software site (1999) [online] http//: www./~schuster/martin.htm

Van der Bruggen, H. (1999) 'A Leg to Stand On: An Existential-Phenomenological Analysis.' *International Journal of Nursing Practice 5*, 4, 174–183.

Van der Zalm, J.E. (2000) 'Hermeneutic-Phenomenology: Providing Living Knowledge for Nursing Practice.' *Journal of Advanced Nursing 31*, 1, 211–218.

Van Kaam, A. (1976) *The Dynamics of Spiritual Self Direction*. New Jersey: Denville.

Van Manen, M. (1990) *Researching Lived Experience: Human Science for an Action Sensitive Pedagogy.* New York: State University of New York Press.

VandeCreek, L. (ed) (1998) *Scientific and Pastoral Perspectives on Intercessory Prayer: An Exchange Between Larry Dossey M.D. and Health Care Chaplains.* New York: Haworth Press.

VandeCreek, L., Bender, H., and Jordan, M.R. (1994) *Research in Pastoral Care and Counselling.* Journal of Pastoral Care Publications, Inc.

Ventis, W.L. (1995) 'The Relationships Between Religion and Mental Health.' *Journal of Social Issues 51,* 2, 33–48.

Von Post, I. (1999) 'A Hermeneutic Textual Analysis of Suffering and Caring in the Peri-Operative Context.' *Journal of Advanced Nursing 30,* 4, 983–989.

Walker, L.G. and Eremin, O. (1995) 'Psychoneuroimmunology: A New Fad or the Fifth Cancer Treatment Modality.' *The American Journal of Surgery 170,* 2–4.

Walker, S.R., Tonigan, J.S., Miller, W.R., Corner, S. and Hahlich, L. (1997) *Alternative Therapies in Health and Medicine 3,* 6, 79–86.

Watson, J. (1988) *Nursing: Human Science and Human Care, a Theory of Nursing.* New York: National League for Nursing.

Watters, W. *et al.* (1992) *Deadly Doctrine: Health, Illness and Christian God Talk.* Buffalo, New York: Prometheus Books.

Weaver, A.J., Flannelly, L.T., Flannelly, K.J., Koenig, H.G. and Larson, D.B. (1998) 'An Analysis of Research on Religious and Spiritual Variables in Three Major Mental Health Nursing Journals, 1991–1995.' *Issues in Mental Health Nursing 19,* 2632–2676.

Weinsheimer, J. (1985) *Gadamer's Hermeneutics: A Reading of Truth and Method.* New Haven: Yale University Press.

Wiebe, K.F. and Fleck, J.R. (1980) 'Personality Correlates of Intrinsic, Extrinsic and Non-Religious Orientations.' *Journal of Psychology 105,* 111–117.

Wig, N.N. (1995) Plenary Lecture delivered at the Mary Hemingway Rees Memorial Lecture. World Federation of Mental Health, Trinity College, Dublin.

Wig, N.N. (1999) 'Mental health and spiritual values.' *International Review of Psychiatry 11,* 2/3, 92 ff.

Williams, R., and Faulconer, J.E. (1994) 'Religion and Mental Health: A Hermeneutical Reconsideration.' *Review of Religious Research 35,* 4, 335–349.

Wirth, D.P. and Cram, J.R. (1994) 'The Psychophysiology of Nontraditional Prayer.' *International Journal of Psychosomatics 41,* 1–4, 68–75.

Zerwekh, J. (1993) 'Transcending Life: The Practice Wisdom of Nursing Hospice Experts.' *The American Journal of Hospice and Palliative Care* September/October 26–31.

Subject Index

Author Index